WORLD
LIBRARIANSHIP

Vol. 1   Classified Library of Congress Subject Headings, Volume 1—Classified List, *edited by James G. Williams, Martha L. Manheimer, and Jay E. Daily* (out of print; see Vol. 39, Part A)

Vol. 2   Classified Library of Congress Subject Headings, Volume 2—Alphabetic List, *edited by James G. Williams, Martha L. Manheimer, and Jay E. Daily* (out of print; see Vol. 39, Part B)

Vol. 3   Organizing Nonprint Materials, *by Jay E. Daily*

Vol. 4   Computer-Based Chemical Information, *edited by Edward McC. Arnett and Allen Kent*

Vol. 5   Style Manual: A Guide for the Preparation of Reports and Dissertations, *by Martha L. Manheimer*

Vol. 6   The Anatomy of Censorship, *by Jay E. Daily*

Vol. 7   Information Science: Search for Identity, *edited by Anthony Debons* (out of print)

Vol. 8   Resource Sharing in Libraries: Why • How • When • Next Action Steps, *edited by Allen Kent* (out of print)

Vol. 9   Reading the Russian Language: A Guide for Librarians and Other Professionals, *by Rosalind Kent*

Vol. 10   Statewide Computing Systems: Coordinating Academic Computer Planning, *edited by Charles Mosmann* (out of print)

Vol. 11   Using the Chemical Literature: A Practical Guide, *by Henry M. Woodburn*

Vol. 12   Cataloging and Classification: A Workbook, *by Martha L. Manheimer* (out of print; see Vol. 30)

Vol. 13   Multi-media Indexes, Lists, and Review Sources: A Bibliographic Guide, *by Thomas L. Hart, Mary Alice Hunt, and Blanche Woolls*

Vol. 14   Document Retrieval Systems: Factors Affecting Search Time, *by K. Leon Montgomery*

Vol. 15   Library Automation Systems, *by Stephen R. Salmon*

Vol. 16   Black Literature Resources: Analysis and Organization, *by Doris H. Clack*

Vol. 17   Copyright—Information Technology—Public Policy: Part I—Copyright—Public Policies; Part II—Public Policies—Information Technology, *by Nicholas Henry* (out of print)

Vol. 18   Crisis in Copyright, *by William Z. Nasri*

Vol. 19   Mental Health Information Systems: Design and Implementation, *by David J. Kupfer, Michael S. Levine, and John A. Nelson*

Vol. 20   Handbook of Library Regulations, *by Marcy Murphy and Claude J. Johns, Jr.* (out of print)

Vol. 21   Library Resource Sharing, *by Allen Kent and Thomas J. Galvin*

Vol. 22   Computers in Newspaper Publishing: User-Oriented Systems, *by Dineh Moghdam*

Vol. 23   The On-Line Revolution in Libraries, *edited by Allen Kent and Thomas J. Galvin*

Vol. 24   The Library as a Learning Service Center, *by Patrick R. Penland and Aleyamma Mathai*

Vol. 25   Using the Mathematical Literature: A Practical Guide, *by Barbara Kirsch Schaefer*

Vol. 26   Use of Library Materials: The University of Pittsburgh Study, *by Allen Kent et al.*

Vol. 27   The Structure and Governance of Library Networks, *edited by Allen Kent and Thomas J. Galvin*

Vol. 28   The Development of Library Collections of Sound Recordings, *by Frank W. Hoffmann*

Vol. 29   Furnishing the Library Interior, *by William S. Pierce*

Vol. 30   Cataloging and Classification: A Workbook Second Edition, Revised and Expanded, *by Martha L. Manheimer*

Vol. 31 Handbook of Computer-Aided Composition, *by Arthur H. Phillips*

Vol. 32 OCLC: Its Governance, Function, Financing, and Technology, *by Albert F. Maruskin*

Vol. 33 Scientific and Technical Information Resources, *by Krishna Subramanyam*

Vol. 34 An Author Index to Library of Congress Classification, Class P, Subclasses PN, PR, PS, PZ, General Literature, English and American Literature, Fiction in English, and Juvenile Belles Lettres, *by Alan M. Greenberg*

Vol. 35 Using the Biological Literature: A Practical Guide, *by Elisabeth B. Davis*

Vol. 36 An Introduction to Automated Literature Searching, *by Elizabeth P. Hartner*

Vol. 37 The Retrieval of Information in the Humanities and the Social Sciences: Problems as Aids to Learning, *edited by Thomas P. Slavens*

Vol. 38 The Information Professional: Survey of an Emerging Field, *by Anthony Debons, Donald W. King, Una Mansfield, and Donald L. Shirey*

Vol. 39 Classified Library of Congress Subject Headings, Second Edition: Part A—Classified List; Part B—Alphabetic List, *edited by James G. Williams, Martha L. Manheimer, and Jay E. Daily*

Vol. 40 Information Technology: Critical Choices for Library Decision-Makers, *edited by Allen Kent and Thomas J. Galvin*

Vol. 41 Structure and Subject Interaction: Toward a Sociology of Knowledge in the Social Sciences, *by Stephen Bulick*

Vol. 42 World Librarianship: A Comparative Study, *by Richard Krzys and Gaston Litton*

Additional Volumes in Preparation

WORLD LIBRARIANSHIP

A COMPARATIVE STUDY

RICHARD KRZYS

Director, International Library Information Center
University of Pittsburgh
Pittsburgh, Pennsylvania

GASTON LITTON

Consultant to the Colombian Government
in Archives and Libraries
Bogota, Colombia

with the assistance of
Ann Hewitt
Director, Long Branch Public Library
Long Branch, New Jersey

MARCEL DEKKER, INC.   New York and Basel

Library of Congress Cataloging in Publication Data

Krzys, Richard.
  World librarianship.

  (Books in library and information science ; v. 42)
  Bibliography: p.
  Includes index.
  1. Comparative librarianship. 2. International
librarianship. I. Litton, Gaston, [date].
II. Hewitt, Ann, [date]. III. Title. IV. Series.
Z672.2.K79 1983 020'.9 82-22213
ISBN 0-8247-1731-7

MARCEL DEKKER, INC.
270 Madison Avenue, New York, New York 10016

Current printing (last digit):
10 9 8 7 6 5 4 3 2 1

PRINTED IN THE UNITED STATES OF AMERICA

Dedicated to the memory of Dr. Louis Shores and to Mrs. Gerry Shores who throughout their careers were ambassadors-at-large of world librarianship.

It is by comparison that
judgments are made possible.

Leopold Stokowski

Foreword

The enormously high speed of change in all areas of human activity, the main characteristic of our time, has had its impact on the development of librarianship by giving rise to many new elements. The most significant are the gradual acceptance of librarianship as a profession and the inevitable integration of library science as a full and equal branch of the social sciences.

Many factors have helped to accelerate these processes: the pressure of growing demands of library users, extensive progress in automation, the inspiring rivalry of a new cognate discipline—information science—the increase in international contacts, and the infusion of new research methods, borrowed and adopted from other fields of knowledge.

The present state of development of both the sciences and humanities is characterized by integration of knowledge and interdisciplinary cooperation among their researchers. These most fruitful processes have strongly influenced the field of library theory. Also due to these processes, library science has been enriched by new fields of research, among which is comparative study in librarianship.

As indicated by Drs. Richard Krzys and Gaston Litton, the principal researchers of this study, increasing of information in our profession through contacts among practitioners of various nations of the world has played the role of a catalyst by adding an international dimension to the profession and helping to raise comparative study in our profession from the level of "semiconscious" use to the level of serious scientific research that the authors have designated as world study in librarianship.

This book, yet another link in that chain of development, introduces the concept of world study in librarianship and places it over the field of international and comparative study in librarianship. Chapter 1 discusses some theoretical aspects of the new field and while introducing it, traces its development. Chapter 2 discusses the general research methodology of the field, and Chapter 3 explains the specific research design underlying this study. Then the bulk of the work presents a comparative study of the profession, including its history and interpretation as well as a juxtaposition and comparison of variants of professional practice throughout the world. The final part introduces two original concepts; they are *metalibrarianship*, a term by which Krzys and Litton identify the philosophy and theory of world librarianship, and, finally, the concept of *global librarianship*, which the principal authors define as "that phase of library development to be characterized by decision making for the purpose of satisfying humanity's information needs rather than purely regional or national needs." The authors even go beyond that topic at the close of their book. But rather than reveal that intriguing idea here, I shall leave it for the reader to discover.

It may well happen that the concepts introduced or reinterpreted here by the main authors will meet with a controversial response from readers. Such is the present level of development of library science that we are still "searching for the truth," attempting to formulate definitions, and reach common understanding of basic concepts, processes which are indispensable—in fact, most important —in the molding of any complex human knowledge into a separate discipline.

Only experienced researchers and mature students will fully appreciate what the editors and their research associates have accomplished here. In making a first attempt at total anaylsis of our profession, they have achieved the research equivalent of Magellan's circumnavigating the globe. Fortunately, our collaborators have emerged with a happier fate than befell the sixteenth century Portuguese navigator and his crew!

Librarians and library educators have long hoped for a monograph that would survey our profession throughout the world, but some have considered even entertaining that hope as "to dream the impossible dream." Krzys and Litton have brought us a step closer to realizing that dream by designing *World Librarianship* as a comparative study of librarianship on the five continents written by resident researchers. Also, they have developed content for a new course in the library school curriculum—World Librarianship—and simultaneously created a new body of knowledge within library science. In doing so, Krzys and Litton have supplied the library educator's "missing link," bridging the gap between the study of librarianship per se and the research course of international and comparative study of the profession. In this regard *World Librarianship* contributes to the substantive and theoretical bases of library science as a whole.

In conclusion, the value of this book seems to be even greater. We live in a time when significant efforts are made by different countries, nations, and peoples toward better understanding of each other, in the knowledge that mutual understanding is the most important condition for maintaining peace in the world. As technology acts as a cultural eraser, librarianship serves an increasingly important role, bringing together the records of the best achievements of humanity and the individual human being, thus helping to establish better understanding among people. In this respect our profession may be considered one of the "peace-keeping tools." And, surely, world study in librarianship as a field will prove to be one of the most important parts of that tool.

Because I found *World Librarianship* a fascinating book and consider it indispensable for understanding the state of the art of our profession, I urge that it be read by my colleagues, individuals involved in library planning, and serious students of our profession throughout the world. I hope that this book will help them in their attempt not only to formulate common concepts of library science, but also to achieve better knowledge of each other, and through it to be increasingly successful in attaining the common and peaceful goals to which our profession is dedicated.

Natalia Tyulina
Moscow, USSR

Preface

Shortly following the close of World War II in 1945, librarianship progressively became an international profession as evidenced by the ever-increasing cross-national contacts among its practitioners. Today, as this process continues, librarians throughout the world are involved in multinational cooperation to achieve effective information networks, shared cataloging, and eventual universal bibliographic control. Judging from these trends, we predict a converging of the varying library practices throughout the world into a global librarianship within the next century. Despite these activities and tendencies, with the exception of the present work, no introductory textbook in librarianship is predicated throughout on the assumption that librarianship today is a world phenomenon.

It is in this spirit of ecumenism that we offer *World Librarianship* as a comparative study of librarianship on the five continents. Designed with the purpose of serving as an introductory and comparative textbook, this book offers the student, practitioner, or interested layman a comprehensive overview of the world aspects of our profession—its constituent elements, for example a description of its diverse philosophies and services. The goal of this book is to expand the readers' perception of librarianship from an activity practiced within the confines of a library to a profession serving people throughout the world.

"How," the reader may logically ask, "can two researchers presume to be sufficiently acquainted with so vast a subject as to be able to describe and interpret its worldwide significance?" Accepting the premise that no one or even two individuals could possibly possess such comprehensive knowledge, we invited highly respected researchers from around the world to write area studies describing the current status of the profession in the various regions of the world. Although not presented in this book, the area studies provided Krzys and Litton the data for their comparative study. As the reader will note, most of the specialists represented in this book live in the geographical area whose librarianship they describe. To assure the necessary degree of comparability throughout, each chapter was produced in conformity with a common outline devised by Drs. Richard Krzys and Gaston Litton. Our purpose in writing *World Librarianship* will perhaps be clearer through relating an anecdote about a great researcher of this century.

Albert Einstein, accompanied by his wife, visited Mount Palomar where the observatory's director proudly showed the couple through the huge installation. "What do you intend to do with this giant telescope?," asked Mrs. Einstein. Disarmed by the simple directness of her question, the director paused for a thoughtful moment and improvised, "We're trying to figure out the size of the universe." "That's all?," questioned Mrs. Einstein incredulously. "My Albert does that on the back of an envelope."

We, too, may be said to be trying to determine the size of a universe—the universe of graphic records and those who work with them. To measure it we use a composite research methodology, combining elements of the area study, descriptive survey, and the comparative study. Incidentally, it was also on the back of an envelope where the dimensions of this work were first sketched, but that event figures slightly later in our story.

Since 1954, when the term "comparative librarianship" first appeared in print, writers in the broader field of world study in librarianship have generally produced area studies that have been more impressionistic than analytical; and few genuine comparative studies are to be found in the literature of librarianship. Having discovered that students of our profession for the most part are unable to produce comparative studies of genuine research value, we attribute this situation partly to inadequate training in research methodology and partly to a deficiency in our professional literature, which until the appearance of this book, had not provided an analysis of world library development. This textbook is the first attempt to supply that basic need.

The practical background for this book was gathered by Krzys and Litton through international experience. Krzys began his doctoral study in library science under the august guidance of Dr. Jesse Shera, Dean of the School of Library Science of Case Western Reserve University. As a Fulbright scholar, Krzys was able in 1960 to broaden his perspective of librarianship though international study in Colombia, South America. There he met Dr. Gaston Litton, an American librarian and library educator with approximately four decades of international experience throughout Latin America, where he has been devoted to various phases of library development.

Inspiration for this book can be traced to 1965, when Dr. Louis Shores, then Dean of the School of Library Science at Florida State University, invited Dr. Richard Krzys to join his faculty. While on a student-faculty outing, Dr. Shores in a characteristically ebullient mood suggested that Krzys teach a new subject then called "Comparative Librarianship." Pulling an envelope from his pocket, Dean Shores sketched with almost Grecian simplicity, in the small space available, an outline he proposed that his new instructor follow in development of the course. Basically, it was an area study approach, proceeding geographically continent by continent.

As a tribute to Dean Shores's insight and erudition, it should be stated for the records that his few seconds of sketching that day provided the research parameters for this study which have taken an international team of researchers several years to carry out. In retrospect, we can observe that based on our teaching experience Dr. Shores's proposed geographical approach to world librarianship has proved to be both eminently practical and pedagogically sound. Its practicality has been demonstrated on countless occasions when beginning students of world librarianship state, usually during their first session of the course, that they are "especially interested in studying librarianship in Africa, Asia, or Latin America;" its pedagogical soundness rests on the study procedure's progressing from the familiar to the unfamiliar, in other words progressing from the geographical frame of reference in Chapters 4 and 5 to concepts involving in Chapters 6 and 7, for example "librarianship in developing nations," "countries of the third world," or "the correlations between population density and the number of libraries in given countries." As the students proceed from the familiar and simple geographical concept to the unfamiliar and more complex multidimensional concept, the instructor is convinced empirically of the inherent pedagogical soundness of Dr. Shores's proposed geographical approach to world study in librarianship.

We believe that world study in librarianship, of which international and comparative study are components, has a definite scope and content. For the introductory course in the field, which we call World Librarianship, we specify as essential a rudimentary knowledge of librarianship, its diverse philosophies and services in all parts of the world, presented in an introductory textbook in the form of a comparative study. Combining these two elements—rudiments and comparisons—we have in collaboration with our distinguished research associates written an introductory textbook analyzing the worldwide aspects of our profession; this work may thus properly be called *World Librarianship*. Advanced courses in this field should be methodologically oriented for the purpose of producing true research studies. Beyond these offerings, specialized courses should be devoted to area study, for example African librarianship, or to aspects, like comparative library education.

World Librarianship, the first attempt to produce a total analysis of librarianship, will doubtless provoke discussion and controversy, if we may judge from the occasional disagreements expressed by various persons during the conception and gestation of this work. Any resultant dialog which may appear in the professional literature following the publication of *World Librarianship*, should benefit the present writers in their preparation of any revision and subsequent editions of this work which may be requested.

Usually, a preface closes with acknowledgments. So extensive is the list of the individuals who have contributed to this book that we include them in a separate Acknowledgments section. Without their assistance *World Librarianship* would probably still be some doodlings on the back of an envelope.

Richard Krzys

Gaston Litton

Acknowledgments

The publication of *World Librarianship* represents for its principal researchers, Drs. Richard Krzys and Gaston Litton, an odyssey through the profession's most fascinating concepts. Now that our voyage is completed, our reluctance to disembark allows us time to thank our associates for the research "first" for circumnavigating world librarianship.

We owe the inspiration for this study to the late American educator and encyclopedist, Dr. Louis Shores. Although our research methodology is theoretically different from that espoused by Shores for the investigation of problems in world librarianship, we have devoted ten years of labor to this study with the hope that our result might be worthy of the book's inspirer.

A debt of gratitude is owed to our research associates for their original area studies that provided the data for our comparative study that follows. They, and the areas that they described, are as follows:

Mohammed Aman, Middle East
Hedwig Anuar, Asia
Harry Kibirige, Africa
Jean-Pierre Clavel, Western Europe
B. P. Kanevsky, Soviet Union

M. B. Nabatova, Eastern Europe
H. C. Campbell, United States and Canada
D. H. Borchardt, Australia, New Zealand, and Oceania

Also, we have profitted from the comments of reviewers, including:

Mr. Paul Bixler
Dr. Katherine Cveljo
Dr. Richard Gardner
Mr. Donald Hasrauth
Dr. Norman Horrocks
Dr. Harold Lancour

Mr. John David Marshall
Dr. Samuel Rothstein
Mrs. Marietta Daniels Shepard
Mr. Glen Sitzman
Dr. Abbas Tashkandy

Students and researchers from around the world have made useful comments as the numerous drafts of the manuscript were tested in the classes of Richard Krzys in the School of Library and Information Science at the University of Pittsburgh.

No one at the school was more interested in the progress of the manuscript than Mr. Grant Lee and Mrs. Gertrude Mazefsky. Fortunately we have benefitted from the assistance of two excellent typists, Mrs. Susan Gray and Mrs. Alyce Patterson.

Thanks are also due to Mr. Marcel Dekker, President of Marcel Dekker, Inc., and Professor Allen Kent, Editor of the Series in Library and Information Science, for their interest in publishing the manuscript.

Richard Krzys is especially grateful to Dr. Wesley Posvar, Chancellor of the University of Pittsburgh, for granting him the sabbatical leave that provided time for the completion of this book.

We thank Dr. Jashu Patel and Mr. Naimuddin Qureshi for their bibliographic assistance in the early stages of the research. We are also grateful to the individuals and organizations who supplied us with appropriate illustrations; they are acknowledged under each illustration.

To all the individuals named above, and to anyone who assisted us but whose name we have inadvertently omitted, we give our sincere thanks.

Contents

Foreword   *Natalia Tyulina*   v
Preface   vii
Acknowledgments   xi

PHILOSOPHY AND THEORY

1 World Study in Librarianship   3
   Richard Krzys and Gaston Litton

2 Research Methodology: A General Discussion   27
   Richard Krzys

3 The Research Methodology Underlying this Study   45
   Richard Krzys and Gaston Litton

THE STUDY

4 The Historical Bases of World Librarianship   57
   Richard Krzys, Gaston Litton, and Area Research Associates

5 Analysis: Worldwide Perspective on the Profession   105
   Richard Krzys, Gaston Litton, and Area Research Associates

6 Juxtaposition: Consideration of the Profession's Variants   167
   Richard Krzys and Gaston Litton

7 Comparison: Metalibrarianship—The Philosophy and Theory
   of World Librarianship   179
   Richard Krzys and Gaston Litton

CONCLUSIONS

8 Our Professional Destiny: A Global Librarianship   201
   Richard Krzys and Gaston Litton

Appendix   The International Library Information Center of
the University of Pittsburgh   205
Bibliography   211
Index   221
About the Area Research Associates   237

WORLD
LIBRARIANSHIP

PHILOSOPHY AND THEORY

1

World Study in Librarianship

Richard Krzys and Gaston Litton

Librarianship during the twentieth century has experienced a growth which truly can be called phenomenal. Aiding humanity in its search for truth, which remains the basic function of librarians, has expanded from interpretation of graphic records in one isolated library to greatly expanded and highly integrated information networks, involving first municipal, then national, and now international participants. This expansion of librarianship has been paralleled by a corresponding deepening, diversification, and growth in the theory of library science, and the discipline has been enlarged during the present century by various new branches which have burgeoned from the main trunk of librarianship. Currently prominent among them is an offshoot which we identify as world study in librarianship.

DEFINITIONS AND PURPOSES

To gain a clearer understanding of the nature of world study in librarianship requires comprehending definitions of its basic terminology. We define world librarianship as the abstraction referring to the status of the profession in all parts of the world during a specified period of time. That period may be the present or a retrospective era. As we examine that abstraction through investigating its aspects for the purpose of formulating a *metalibrarianship*, the philosophy and theory underlying the practice of librarianship throughout the world, we are engaged in world *study* in librarianship. Our description will attempt to

3

delineate various geographical areas of librarianship and outline the form that each aspect has taken within those areas. Our analytic statements will attempt to interpret these forms and identify variables that may interact with the aspects. We use the word "attempt" advisedly because ours represents the first endeavor to describe and analyze our profession throughout the world. It is our hope that the present work will stimulate our readers to further study and research of the topics presented here.

As the next step of the process initiated here, researchers may want to investigate further some of the relationships suggested within this book; for example, the hypothesis linking legislation and bibliographic control, to be discussed in a later chapter, may be investigated through appropriate research methodology, such as comparative method, or quantitative methods when statistical correlations are deemed desirable.

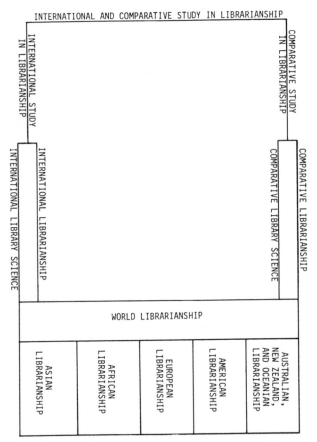

Figure 1.1.   Relationship of world study in librarianship to its cognate fields.

What is the distinction between traditional library science research and world study in librarianship? Admittedly, world study of our profession is a branch of library science research; however, world study in librarianship has as its end the formulation of theoretical knowledge that underlies librarianship and transcends present-day library science by exploring the possibility of developing entirely new areas of the discipline, the lack of which presently limits our effectiveness as practitioners in our service to mankind; however, we can make further distinctions between the two fields.

Traditional library science research may investigate, for example, the reference service at a particular agency in order to analyze the service at that agency; whereas, an investigation of reference service for the purposes of formulating hypotheses, theories, and laws that will explain, predict, and control the phenomenon of reference throughout the world falls within the discipline of world study in librarianship. We may conclude then that library science research per se concerns understanding a particular aspect of librarianship within a specified agency or a circumscribed situation; world study in librarianship addresses certain aspects of librarianship or all of librarianship in their diverse forms and broadest context, that is, the various forms that an aspect, or the entire profession, may assume throughout the world. The relationship among world study in librarianship and its cognate fields may be visualized in Figure 1.1.

ORIGIN OF WORLD STUDY IN LIBRARIANSHIP

How and when did world study in librarianship develop? The explanation which one accepts depends upon one's view of the development of librarianship. On the one hand, if the reader believes that the profession began at a particular time, when its practitioners performed certain unique bibliothecal functions, he most likely fixes the beginning of world study in librarianship with the appearance of the first work in the field to include the international element or to employ comparative research methodology. However, if the reader views librarianship as a professional activity with a long evolutionary development, he is likely to accept a similar explanation for the development of each of the field's subdivisions.

Because we espouse the evolutionary development of librarianship, we submit that, considered epistemologically, world study in librarianship has evolved through six distinct phases and will experience at least three additional phases. They are (1) the application of the comparative principle to librarianship, (2) the borrowing of library practices or concepts, (3) the appearance of a comparative attitude in a treatise on librarianship, (4) the publication of a monograph comparing aspects of librarianship, (5) the search for an identity, (6) the publication of a manual outlining the research methodology of international and comparative study in librarianship, (7) the appearance of a magnum opus in the field,

(8) the full development of world study in librarianship, (9) followed by the dissolution of the discipline into various logical areas. Our explanation of this development involves an understanding of the nature of librarians as well as distinguishing clearly between the application of the comparative principle to librarianship (i.e., comparative librarianship) on the one hand, and, on the other, the expansion and refinement of this principle into a formalized discipline with its distinct research methodology (i.e., comparative library science).

Of all the characteristics attributed to librarians, the desire to improve their professional practice must be ranked among the foremost. If one accepts in principle a basic immutability of human nature, hypothesizing that librarians from centuries immemorial have shared this quest for perfectibility becomes as easy to do as it is difficult to document instances to substantiate that thesis. Indeed, it may be true that generally the comparative principle is inherent in professionalism. If so, the principle of comparative study in librarianship may have been born at that uncertain date when librarians began their gradual transition from the status of an occupation to that of a fully developed profession. We submit that whenever individuals have borrowed principles of librarianship or compared their librarianship with some counterpart, analyzed these practices, and applied or adapted them to their own needs, the principle underlying comparative study in librarianship has been operative. Consequently, throughout history as librarians have aspired towards professionalism, they have knowingly or unknowingly engaged in the practical activity of comparative librarianship long before the actual formalizing of the research discipline which we call comparative library science. It is our thesis, furthermore, that ordinary librarians have done so occasionally, and that the great ones have done so often.

AN OUTLINE HISTORY OF WORLD STUDY IN LIBRARIANSHIP

To gain a better understanding of the evolutionary nature of world study in librarianship, we invite the reader to consider our outline which summarizes the history of the field as of this writing in six phases, as follows:

Phase 1:   The application of the comparative principle to librarianship
Phase 2:   The borrowing of library practices or concepts
Phase 3:   The appearance of a comparative attitude in a treatise on librarianship
Phase 4:   Publication of a monograph comparing aspects of librarianship
Phase 5:   The search for an identity
Phase 6:   Publication of a manual outlining the research methodology of international and comparative study in librarianship

Phase 1: Application of the Comparative Principle to Librarianship

Just as we cannot be certain where libraries and librarianship originated, we are equally uncertain concerning the earliest application of the comparative principle to librarianship. On the origins of libraries, Elmer Johnson has stated:

It is difficult to say whether the first library in the Western World was located in Egypt or in Mesopotamia, but it is certain that in the civilizations emerging in those areas in the fourth and third Millennia before Christ, writing produced "books," and these were preserved in sufficient numbers to form a library.[1]

The beginnings of the application of the comparative principle to librarianship may have originated in the cradle of civilization, to which Johnson has referred, or possibly among the ancient Chinese, who had libraries for storing official documents as far back as the third millennium B.C.[2]

If future archeological discoveries, or an analog of the Dead Sea Scrolls, for example, enable us to resolve once and for all the ever-intriguing question of where libraries and librarianship began—Mesopotamia, China, or Egypt—then we can proceed at once and confidently to the solving of the related question of the origin of world study in librarianship. Meanwhile, we can only conjecture that the earliest application of the comparative principle to librarianship probably originated shortly after the beginnings of libraries in ancient Mesopotamia, China, or Egypt.

From early antiquity, librarians, by their very function and nature, have exhibited a strong inclination towards engaging in diverse comparative activities. In Ashurbanipal's library in the ancient Assyrian capital of Nineveh, in the public library of the Athens of Pericles and Herodotus, and in the now almost legendary Alexandrian library, when publishing was one facet of the librarian's function, the keepers and makers of books constantly compared variants of manuscripts in order to produce a text as faithful as possible to the author's intent.

Once this comparative attitude had revealed itself in one aspect of librarianship, applying this same principle to diverse aspects of librarianship, even internationally, was a logical, although perhaps not an easy thing do do. Thus, the transfer of the comparative approach from textual scholarship to an overall improvement of the complete professional activity would appear to have occurred at a very early date in library history. Eventually, this comparative attitude permeated all of librarianship, a phenomenon which accounts for the strength of the foundations of our profession existing since classical antiquity.

Although the remoteness of time and the inevitable fragmentation of sources prevent us from documenting examples of the application of the comparative principle by librarians during the Sumerian-Babylonian-Assyrian, ancient Chinese, or Egyptian periods, we are far more fortunate when we come to classical Greece because from this period forward there are inferences from library history, statements from classical authors, and evidence from archeological excavations that indicate numerous instances of the application of the comparative principle to librarianship.

If we seek tangible evidence that the comparative principle guided the librarianship of ancient Greece, we must examine its literature. The Greek scholar Artemon of Cassandreia (300 B.C.), for example, wrote two works relevant to our search, entitled *On Collecting Books* (περὶ βιβλίων συναγωγῆς) and *On the*

Use of Books (περὶ βιβλίων χρήσεως), which, unfortunately, are both lost, probably irretrievably.[3] Their titles are so intriguing that we would gladly exchange all extant writings of lesser authors of classical Greece for a glimpse of the texts of these two lost treatises of librarianship of the Ancient World.

An examination of references to the public library, which was reputedly established in Athens by the tyrant Peisistratus (605-527 B.C.), affords not only a better understanding of the motive for the establishment of this institution—the provision of authoritative texts of the Greek classics—but also provides an insight into the general diffusion of libraries in that part of the world, which facilitated the transmission of professional concepts from Greek to Persian librarians of the time.

A passage from the Greek author Tzetzes comments on the nature of the textual scholarship motivated by Peisistratus, as follows:

> Aside from translating the foreign books, he had the Greek book edited, as I said before, those of tragedy by Alexander of Aetolia, comedy by Lycophren, the other poets by Zenodotus of Ephesus and in particular the books, Homer which, at the instance of Peisistratus, were put together by four wise men, Epiconcylus, Onomacritus of Athens, Sepyrus of Heraclea and Orpheus of Croton, two hundred or more years before Ptolemy Philadelphus and the edition of Zenodotus. So, at the time of Peisistratus, the Homeric writings which circulated in separate pieces, were put together by these four wise men and became books.[4]

Central to this "putting together" of books was textual comparison, that is, the comparison of variants of a manuscript to determine the authentic text. Thus, we see, that comparison—the essential process of comparative study in librarianship—was operative within the early libraries of Antiquity.

Phase 2: The Borrowing of Library Practices or Concepts

Cultural borrowing of principles or practices of librarianship was an early manifestation of comparative librarianship, and the pattern for this borrowing during antiquity paralleled the cultural diffusion of that period; the practices of dominant cultures served as models for subservient cultures. This practice was evident in the spread of libraries throughout the ancient world, and particularly from Greece to Persia to Greece and then to Alexandria, in the following passage of *Etymologiarum Sive Originum*, by the Spanish bishop Isidore of Seville (ca. 560-636).

> Peisistratus is credited first among the Greeks with the establishment of a library which, after the Athenians had increased the collection, was carried off to Persia by Xerxes, after the burning of Athens, and long afterwards was it returned to Greece by Seleucus Nicanor. Hence, the interest in getting books of the various nations and of translating them into Greek through interpreters,

which was accomplished together with other kings and cities. In this connection Alexander the Great and his successors took an interest in building libraries full of books; especially Ptolemy, whose surname was Philadelphus, most deeply versed in all literature, who was emulating Peisistratus in his interest in libraries. Not only the scriptures of the pagans but also the holy books were collected in his library. For seventy-thousand books were to be found at Alexandria in his time.[5]

Although we have been unable to locate particular examples which document the use of the comparative principle by librarians during the ancient Egyptian or Sumerian-Babylonian-Assyrian period, that such instances probably occurred during antiquity may be inferred from the writings of library historians. Alfred Hessel, for example, detected some tenuous lines of connection between Ashurbanipal's library at Nineveh and the Alexandrian library.* Hessel stated:

> There were undeniably remarkable resemblances between the libraries of Nineveh and Alexandria. Both were institutions of a universal character brought into being by reigning princes. It is also proper to point out that in more than one respect the inner organization of the Hellenistic library calls to mind the Assyrian library, and that there are even more similarities in the treatment of the individual literary work in both places despite the difference in writing material (clay tablets at Nineveh, papyrus rolls at Alexandria). Nevertheless it seems to me at present still too risky to insist upon establishing a direct connection of Alexandria with Nineveh. Between them lie four centuries; between them lies the reign of the Medo-Persian kings, who, so far as is known, paid no attention to library matters. It must be left to the future to disclose lines of connection which at present are obscure.[6]

Surely one of the earliest documented instances of a librarian having engaged in the borrowing of library practices is that of the ancient Greek scholar Demetrius of Phalerum (born ca. 350 B.C.). Invited by Ptolemy Soter, this Peripatetic modeled the Alexandrian library on examples of institutions he had observed earlier in Athens. That library and its rival at Pergamum are both outstanding examples of cultural borrowing because their physical layouts were known and copied throughout the ancient world. Excavations made during the nineteenth century at Pergamum reveal the following pattern for the libraries of ancient Greece:

> Near the temple of Athena Polias an open court with a two-storied portico with four adjoining rooms was uncovered. In the largest was found the great statues of Athena and also pedestal inscriptions referring to well-known

---

*For an extended discussion of the Assyrian rather than the Greek influence on the Alexandrian Library, the reader is directed to H. J. de Vleeschauwer and H. Curtis Wright, "Origins of the Mouseion of Alexandria," in *Toward a Theory of Librarianship: Papers in Honor of Jesse Hauk Shera*, Conrad H. Rawski, ed. (Metuchen, N.J.: The Scarecrow Press, 1973), pp. 87-113.

writers of Asia Minor, among them one in verse by Homer. Here we have the typical layout of the ancient library: the stoa serving as a study, the entrance hall adorned with statues, and the remaining chambers given over to book storage—the whole closely adjoining a temple.[7]

If the Greeks engaged widely in cultural borrowing and the principle of comparative librarianship, the Romans—by all standards the greatest borrowers of antiquity—were doubtless even more involved in this give-and-take in the formation and management of their libraries. Certainly, the physical arrangement of Roman libraries, bearing a close resemblance to the Pergamum library, suggests the existence of yet another link in the chain of comparative librarianship. Bernt Götze indicated the arrangement of Roman libraries and their resemblance to Pergamum as follows:

> . . . a book-room without a portico but having instead a facade with ornamental columns and an outside staircase. Vitruvius urged that the rooms face the East to take advantage of the morning light, but in practice his requirements were not always fulfilled. In order specially to protect the papyrus rolls from dampness an outer wall was frequently built around the inner wall, so that a narrow passage ran between the two. For the rest, so far as stonework, architectural style, and artistic decoration are concerned, libraries resembled the other monumental structures of the age. Very likely there was always a statue of some diety which was placed in a recess of the great hall. Accompanying it were busts and medallions of scholars and writers "whose immortals speak in these very places" (*immortales animae in locis iisdem loquunter*). A good deal of ornamentation was in evidence, but in order to spare the eyes, gold was avoided and a greenish marble selected for the floors. The book rolls, with tickets bearing their titles outward, lay in pigeon-holes of the wooden presses. These were often symmetrically arranged and sunk into niches in the walls. When necessary there were several such rows, one above the other. The top rows were then reached by means of galleries, which rested on columns. We can say nothing exact about leading practices in the arrangement of the book stock, since only quite scanty fragments have been preserved. Some of the public libraries circulated their books. Their administration was frequently in the hands of priests, when as very commonly occurred, they were connected with a temple.[8]

Summarizing the earliest development of world study in librarianship, based on various types of evidence, we may conclude, albeit sketchily at this writing, that very rudimentary manifestations of the discipline existed during classical antiquity, revealing themselves in two forms: (1) application of the comparative principle to librarianship; (2) borrowing of examples of libraries and concepts of librarianship.

When we approach the period of medieval librarianship, we discover continued examples of the application of the comparative principle to the discipline and of borrowing of library concepts, but presently available knowledge does not indicate a more sophisticated maturation of comparative study in librarianship.

We can point to Flavius Magnus Aurelius Cassiodorus (ca. 480-583), whose *An Introduction to Divine and Human Reading* (*Institutiones Divinarum et Saecularium Litterarum*) was a manual for the conduct of scriptoria and libraries in the Middle Ages, but his writing merely recommended a continuation of the traditional textual scholarship as practiced by ancient librarians, and did not propose any innovative concepts. The monastic manual of Cassiodorus was extremely influential because it was widely distributed among medieval libraries. In addition to applying to librarianship the ancient but limited, comparative principle, Cassiodorus also may be said to have engaged in cultural borrowing in librarianship, since the Vivarium monastery which he founded in southern Italy was based on Eastern lines, that is, it emulated examples of the monastic libraries of Byzantium.[9] Further exploration of medieval librarianship provides additional examples of the already discussed phases of comparative study in librarianship.

To discover progress in the development of this subject we must proceed to the period of Renaissance librarianship. The Humanists of the fourteenth century reacted against the scholastic entrenchment which had occurred during the 1000-year span of the Middle Ages. Rejecting medieval learning, Petrarch and Boccaccio read extensively the texts of classical Greece and Rome, so it was quite natural that their cultural borrowing in librarianship would be based on ancient principles rather than on medieval models. It was also quite natural that Petrarch would become enamored of three concepts of librarianship resurrected from classical antiquity: (1) the development of private book collections, (2) the establishment of public libraries, and (3) the amassing of comprehensive collections similar to those of the Alexandrian and the Pergamum libraries.[10] But it was characteristic of the genius of Petrarch that he would reconcile these three seemingly disparate concepts when, in 1362, he gave his private book collection to the Basilica of Saint Mark in Venice, "for the comfort of the intelligent and noble people who may happen to take delight in such things."[11]

Commenting on Petrarch's generous and, for those times, most unusual act, Alfred Hessel stated: ". . . in so doing Petrarch expressed the wish that the Venetian government might provide for its care and growth in such a way that it would become the equal of ancient libraries."[12] Unfortunately, Petrarch's desires were not honored, but, even so, his intention ultimately benefited posterity. It remained for the scholarship of Niccolo Niccoli, literary minister of Cosimo de Medici, and the power and wealth of Cosimo de Medici himself, to make possible during the fifteenth century the implementation of a plan for a comprehensive public library. Again, in the words of Alfred Hessel, we learn that:

> Niccoli designated 1430 manuscripts which he left behind to the public "for the common use of all" (*in publico a commune utilità di comuno*), and

Cosimo provided for them in a worthy dwelling in the Monastery of Saint Mark, which he himself had erected. He also gave liberally to other religious institutions, but did not as a consequence forget the later Laurentian Library (Biblioteca Medicco-Laurenziana), which was fostered and enriched most of all by his grandson Lorenzo.[13]

Despite the scholarship of Petrarch, the acquisitiveness of Niccolo Niccoli, and the incredible wealth of the Medicis, full realization of that ancient concept of developing a comprehensive collection similar to the Alexandrian Library awaited the coming of another Renaissance achievement, the invention of printing, and the stimulation afforded by the new tendencies of research and librarianship, which developed during the later Renaissance and Enlightenment.

Phase 3: The Appearance of a Comparative Attitude in a Treatise on Librarianship

One of the principal consequences of the invention of printing was the relatively facile, rapid, and economic multiplication of books. During the interval between that miraculous invention in the fifteenth century and the beginning of the Enlightenment in the seventeenth century, books—a scarce commodity throughout the Middle Ages—became more plentiful, causing great expansion in the size of library collections. This growth of libraries occasioned a parallel expansion in librarianship, which obliged its practitioners to cope with the new and vastly important and vexatious problem of bibliographic control. Librarians, working on a plane of pragmatism and utility, unfortunately did not at once grasp the full implication of Sir Francis Bacon's reorganization of all human knowledge in his *Instauratio Magna*, for what it was, an attempted solution to the problem of the classification of all knowledge with strong implication for library classification; instead, they preferred schemes patterned after the five divisions of knowledge elaborated by the French booksellers (these divisions being: theology, jurisprudence, arts and sciences, *belles lettres*, and history).[14] Earlier, during the Renaissance, librarians had similarly failed to effect the interdisciplinary transfer of the methodology of comparative studies from the natural sciences to librarianship.

Undoubtedly, the research technique of comparative studies was indispensable to the formulation of a true comparative library science, and, although its underlying principle had been operative from early antiquity, as we have already indicated in our discussion of the early phases of librarianship, the natural scientists were first to sharpen the principle into a research tool and to channel its implications into a formalized discipline. Pierre Belon, the French naturalist, may be said to have started the trend when, in 1555, in his *The History of the Nature of Birds* (*l'Histoire de la Nature des Oyseaux*), he indicated the homologies of birds and humans.[15]

The consequences of the invention of printing and the growth of knowledge, which had resulted during the later Renaissance and Enlightenment, were understood by the French librarian Gabriel Naudé, who delineated their implications for librarians in his *Advice on Establishing a Library* (*Avis pour Dresser une Bibliothèque*). Published in 1627, this first comprehensive treatise on librarianship outlined the qualifications necessary to librarians, the means by which, and the reasons for which, libraries are established and maintained the world over. The example of Naudé's own life reflected unequivocally his personal conviction that librarianship should be a full-time occupation; and his book contained for the first time in print, to our knowledge, the comparative attitude in library literature, thus marking the second phase in the development of world study in librarianship, which we have elected to designate as the appearance of a comparative attitude in a treatise in librarianship.

That this attitude should appear in librarianship during the Enlightenment, and in the person of Gabriel Naudé as its exponent, was not accidental but was appropriate both to the times and to the man. The Enlightenment was an age, let it be remembered, in which all knowledge was scrutinized; logically, librarianship inevitably fell under that scrutiny. Furthermore, Naudé as a student of medicine and during his exhaustive examination of knowledge as a librarian, must surely have been aware of the research performed by Pierre Belon, by the year 1555, which originated the field of comparative anatomy. However, Naudé did not effect a direct transfer of Belon's methodology from one field to another, and rightly so, since comparative anatomy as a natural science was alien to library science, later to develop as a part of the social sciences. Nevertheless, Naudé was able to benefit librarianship by incorporating into his *Avis* the comparative attitude. When we consider Naudé's Enlightenment tendencies, his devotion to libraries, his penchant for traveling and studying abroad—he toured Italy, France, Sweden, England, and Germany—we then begin to understand why it is perfectly conceivable that Naudé should espouse the concept of comparative study in librarianship and contribute to its development through his popular treatise, *Avis*.

This work of Naudé demonstrates the effective synthesis of the elements useful, if not indispensable, to comparative study in librarianship—the scientific attitude, a preoccupation with the status and improvement of libraries, a recognition of the necessity for travel in order to appreciate visual differences, and as an easier means of dialogue between colleagues—which are necessary to a full comparison of phenomena.

In the address to his patron, Henri de Mesme, Naudé described his method for acquiring his knowledge of librarianship, clearly implying that the comparative attitude was an essential component of his modus operandi. The appropriate passage reads as follows:

And if I, Monseigneur, assume the boldness to present these notes and instructions, it is not that I so much value and esteem my own judgment as to inject it into an affair of so great difficulty, . . .

. . . or that I am so far tickled with self-love as to imagaine there is that in me which is so rarely to be encountered among others; but the warm desire that I have to do something which may be acceptable to you is the only reason that prompts me to *combine the opinions* [the authors' italics] common to many learned persons, versed in the knowledge of books, and *the several practices of the most famous librarians* [authors' italics] with what I could supply from my own limited study and experience, that I may set before you in these counsels the principles and practices which one must follow in order to succeed in this noble and generous enterprise.[16]

In his treatise, Naudé explicitly urged upon librarians the convenience of cultural borrowing, in a reference to earlier libraries, suggesting to the Abbé de Mesme the following course of action:

Therefore, Monseigneur, after I have made it my most humble request that you would attribute this tedious discourse rather to the candor and sincerity of my affection than to any presumption of being able to acquit myself in it more worthily than another, I shall tell you frankly that unless your designs be equal to the Vatican Library or the Ambrosian of Cardinal Borromeo, you already have herewith to set your mind at rest and to keep you happy and contented in possessing such a quantity of well-chosen books that though your library be not of the dimensions of those others it is yet more than sufficient not only to serve your own personal and the eager interest of your friends but to maintain likewise the reputation of being one of the most considerable and best provided libraries in France since you have in it all the most important volumes in the principal divisions of learning, and a very great number of others which may be useful for the special and unusual subjects that present themselves from time to time.[17]

In his justification for the establishment of a library, Naudé referred to exemplary collections of the past, and to their initiators; and he affirmed his belief that libraries had contributed to the common good and that they had enhanced the reputations of their initiators, citing the names of "the great kings of Egypt and of Pergamum, Xerxes, Augustus, Lucullus, Charlemagne, Alfonso of Aragon, Mattias Corvinus, and the great prince Francis the First,"[18] all of whom were patrons or initiators of libraries.

In addition to his advice to librarians that they should take counsel with their colleagues, reading also whatever might be available on libraries for the advice needed on what to do in their establishment, Naudé also urged them "to have all the catalogues transcribed, not only of the great and most famous libraries—whether ancient or modern, public or private, in this country or abroad—but also of the small private collections which for not being much known or frequented remain buried in a perpetual silence."[19] Among the various reasons which Naudé enumerated for collecting and studying library catalogs, he stated that it was done because *"nothing can be done in imitation of other libraries unless by means of their catalogues* which have been compiled . . . [the authors' italics] ."[20]

Throughout this treatise Naudé gave relevance to the research techniques of comparative library science.

What of the writings of the Abbé Jean Baptiste Cotton des Houssayes, John Dury, James Kirkwood, and, of course, Gottfried Wilhelm Leibniz? While it may be said that each of these intellects reflects the spirit of the comparative attitude, so superbly synthesized by Naudé, no original concepts relevant to the development of world study in librarianship are advanced in these writings and, to cite them, would only accumulate repetitive examples of the comparative attitude in library literature without reflecting any advancement in the development, properly speaking, of world study in librarianship.

Phase 4: Publication of a Monograph Comparing Aspects of Librarianship

A notable and consistent development of world study in librarianship becomes apparent when we examine the state of librarianship of the eighteenth and nineteenth centuries. The abundance of books amassed through systematic selection, following principles suggested by Naudé and Leibniz, required library planning of a far vaster scale than had previously been necessary. Joseph Van Praet reacted to the demands placed upon French libraries by the incredibly large accumulations of books confiscated during the Revolution, by contributing a master plan which called for a rational distribution of library resources of the nation in a network of libraries located in all sections of the country, with the Bibliothèque Nationale, in Paris, as its hub. In England, the Industrial Revolution also made similar heavy demands on libraries, and, fortunately for librarianship in that country, there were two librarians equal to the exigencies of the situation, in the persons of Sir Anthony Panizzi and Edward Edwards, both of whom avidly applied the concept of the comparative attitude to librarianship.

It may also be pertinent to this discussion to note that, shortly before Panizzi and Edwards made their comparative studies in librarianship, a new field of social science research was emerging. Comparative education had its beginnings in the work of Johann Gottfried Herder, who, in 1769, wrote *Journal Meiner Reise im Jahre 1769*, the first work on comparative pedagogy.[21]

Although the research methodology of comparative education in general bears a close resemblance to the investigations of Panizzi and Edwards, we cannot be certain at this writing that their work bore in any manner a resemblance to the research of Herder, or even to the better known work of Marc-Antoine Jullien de Paris, who in 1817 compiled the first systematic schedule permitting the comparison of school systems.[22]

Being an Italian immigrant in England, Panizzi was familiar by reason of his birth and prior residence with an extensive library tradition on the continent, and he intensified that awareness of difference in librarianship from one place to another, during his long service at the British Museum. In his capacity of assistant librarian and, later, as Keeper of Printed Books, Panizzi at times introduced or enforced various ideas at the British Museum which were continental in origin. The depository law, for example, had been effective in France since 1537,[23] but in England it was honored more in the breach than in compliance. Panizzi aggressively enforced this law, from his position as director of the British Museum, much to the initial ire and obstinate resistance of certain British booksellers.

Panizzi's comparative attitude in librarianship was revealed also when, shortly after being charged with the reorganization of the British Museum, he made an extensive tour of European libraries for the explicit purpose of observing and comparing the various methods of organization and operation in force in those different institutions. Panizzi's observations were so vast that, after his return, he facilitated the work of a parliamentary committee then studying the British Museum, by making available for the use of the members a large amount of comparative statistics about foreign libraries.[24] Being a lawyer by training, Panizzi was well aware of the principles and benefits of codification and, with these convictions in mind, he attacked the problem of cataloging the vast bibliographical resources of the British Museum, producing as a by-product the basic ninety-one rules for cataloging which, in time, came to be used extensively as a cataloging code throughout the Anglo-American world.

Panizzi applied similar acumen and comparative methodology to a study of the architectural problems of the British Museum. Impressed by the Crystal Palace recently built for the Great Exhibition in 1852, Panizzi applied its technique of iron construction in plans for the Reading Room of the Museum, utilizing thus his "intertechnological" borrowing to surpass his seemingly progressive colleagues who were then propounding the principle of cultural borrowing in librarianship.[25]

A truly progressive contemporary of Panizzi was Edward Edwards, a staunch supporter of the public library movement, and judging from his writing, an apostle of the comparative attitude in librarianship. Edwards supplied William Ewart, chairman of a parliamentary committee studying public libraries, with abundant data about public libraries which enabled proponents of the project to win support necessary to the passage of the Public Libraries Act of 1850. Later, in 1869, Edwards published his data in *Free Town Libraries, Their Formation, Management, and History, in Britain, France, Germany, and America*, which we wish to cite here as the first monograph in the field of comparative study in librarianship known to the authors.

On the other side of the Atlantic, as the American states were approaching their first centennial as an independent nation, the country's librarians were beginning to stir. In 1853 a group of them met in New York for the first national convention of librarians to be held in the United States, and, so far as is known to library historians, also the first such conference to be held in the world.

Charles Coffin Jewett, librarian of the Smithsonian Institution and president of the Convention of Librarians, stated at its first meeting on September 15,

1853: "We meet to provide for the diffusion of a knowledge of good books and for enlarging the means of public access to them. Our wishes are for the public, not for ourselves."[26] An editorial in *Norton's Library Gazette* of July 15, 1852, discussed the conference, and from George Burwell Utley we have the following comment:

> The proper way to accomplish the desired object, it was felt, would be to have some of the librarians of the larger institutions unite in calling such a meeting. Their names would be a guarantee for the interest in the gathering and "insure a large assembly." The topics for discussion, the editorial went on to say, would be almost "innumerable." Aside from papers on biblio-graphical subjects, there were a great many points in regard to the manage-ment of libraries, the purchase and arrangement of books, the formation and publication of catalogs, the delivery of books, their protection from mold, worms, and other inquiry, on almost all of which points there existed, it was said, a difference of opinion, or, at any rate, of practice. Indeed, said the writer, we have hardly ever known two librarians to agree upon these minor matters, so that *a little discussion could not fail to elicit various observations and suggestions by which all might be benefited.* [the authors' italics].[27]

In the true spirit of comparative study in librarianship, the members met on equal footing, or, as Howard W. Winger expressed it, ". . . this call for meeting ranked the librarian of a small library in a frontier town with those of estab-lished institutions in Boston, New York, Charleston, and Philadelphia."[28] Owing to the diversity of the topics discussed, the tenor of the conference, and the wide representation of its membership, it may be said that the comparative attitude played an important role at this first conference of librarians. In some respects, these meetings qualify for the designation as the first gatherings devoted to comparative librarianship.

That the comparative attitude played a significant role in three milestone events in library history, subsequent to the 1853 conference, has not been emphasized by library historians, but for our purposes this fact needs under-scoring. The 1876 Conference of Librarians, the publication of the *American Library Journal*, and the establishment of the School of Library Economy at Columbia College in 1887, all incorporated the cooperative attitude into their activity. Certainly, that attitude was very much in the air during the 1876 Con-ference of Librarians, which was not only national but also international. During the three-day conference, begun on October 4, 1876, 103 delegates from throughout the United States, Canada, and the United Kingdom, convened in Philadelphia to discuss cooperative indexing, cooperative cataloging, classifi-cation, relations with publishers and booksellers, copyright, as well as all aspects of "library economy" which the association wished to promote.

On September 30, 1876, four days prior to the 1876 Conference of the American Library Association, a new journal appeared which would become of considerable interest to librarians.[29] Called the *American Library Journal*, this publication had as its managing editor a then little-known librarian from Amherst, Massachusetts, whose name was eventually to become world-known, Melvil Dewey, and twenty-one leading librarians who collaborated as associate editors. The comparative attitude of the *American Library Journal* was well illustrated by an article by Justin Winsor on the subject of starting a library. In the 1869 annual report of the Boston Public Library, Winsor, then superintendent of that library, commented on his helping other librarians. By 1876 this activity had lost most of its appeal to Winsor because of the considerable amount of time it entailed, and, to relieve himself of this onerous burden, Winsor considered the newly projected library periodical an ideal medium for his message. Winsor's suggestions for the initiators of libraries were as follows:

1. Procure what is in print.
2. Send to any library which is an exemplar, and ask for its rules and reports.
3. Take time to study all these documents and, when you have a clear idea of what a library is and how it should be maintained, consider closely the fitness of this or that community, or to these conditions under which you are to work.
4. If you have not time, resign your trust to someone who has, and who has a correct appreciation of the old adage that those who help themselves are soonest helped by others.
5. After studying and problems are still unsolved, write to an old librarian, but do not be surprised at the diversity of opinion among experts.
6. Choose that which you naturally take to; run to it, and do not decide that the other is not perfectly satisfactory to him who chose that.
7. Whichever you have chosen, study to improve it.[30]

Juding from the vantage point of today's knowledge of comparative study in librarianship, Winsor's suggestions still have validity as guidelines for attitudes and research methodology in the field.

No proposals were made at the 1876 conference covering specifically the training of librarians, but the need for such training was repeatedly recognized. At the 1877 Conference of Librarians of All Nations, in London, further references were made to this need and one of the conference delegates, Dr. Andreas Crestadoro, librarian of the Public Free Libraries of Manchester, informed his listeners that: "By a recent royal decree in Italy it is ordered that in every National Library (of which there are five) a chair of Librarianship shall be established, to teach and train students in the bibliothecal science, so as to qualify them for appointment as librarians."[31]

Attending the 1877 Conference of Librarians in London were seventeen American librarians, including Justin Winsor, William F. Poole, Samuel Sweet Green, Charles Ammi Cutter, and Melvil Dewey. Neither Dewey nor any of the U.S. librarians participated at the conference in the discussion of the formal training of librarians, according to Sarah Vann, ". . . the subject was discussed on the Atlantic crossing by the delegates,"[32] and there was concurrence among them "that such facilities should be somewhere provided."[33] Dewey did advance his personal views on the urgent need for systematic training of librarians, however, in the May 1879 issue of *American Library Journal*, in an article entitled "Apprenticeship of Librarians." His ideas on this important subject matured, and by 1883, Dewey had received institutional support for the establishment of a training school for librarians at Columbia College and he set about immediately to request professional support at the Conference of the American Library Association in August of that same year. Before obtaining the desired professional endorsement and support, Dewey secured a variety of opinions concerning the best means for the training of librarians. The view of Charles Ammi Cutter, because of its comparative attitude, is important to our study. On this occasion and subject Cutter stated:

> Undoubtedly it is well that a librarian should have worked in a library; there are some things which he will never understand unless he has. But any one merely employed as assistant in a large library is likely to be assigned to one particular department, and to understand that only. And, even if his chief takes care that he shall have variety of work, he only learns the methods of one establishment; and as these are probably all determined upon before he goes there, he only learns them by rote, and, unless he is unusually philosophic never thinks of the reasons for them. *No one is thoroughly fit to have charge of a library who has not pursued some comparative study, and learned to reason about what he does.* [the authors' italics].[34]

As library history records, Dewey established his School of Library Economy at Columbia College in 1887. It is significant that the comparative attitude was notably evident in Dewey's ideas for a "Bibliothecal Museum," which was described as a collection of materials and forms in use in various libraries, assembled for the comparative study and analysis by the students and teachers of the new School of Library Economy.[35]

Librarianship towards the end of the nineteenth and beginning of the twentieth centuries, while it reveals extremely significant developments in library history, does not expand the concept of world study in librarianship. The public library movement and library education in the United States both profited from the comparative attitude operating in their library associations and professional literature. This intensified activity produced such a large quantity of discussion of library techniques and procedures that the period between 1850 and the 1930s may be termed a period of considerable intranational comparative librarianship in the United States, a fact which explains in part the vigor and diversity of the profession of librarianship within this country.

Public libraries and library education—the two outstanding developments of librarianship in the United States during the nineteenth century—were both subject to intensive studies in intranational comparative study in librarianship during the first quarter of the twentieth century. Although considerable progress had been registered in both areas, public libraries and library education received strong and sustained criticism in the professional journals of the United States.

To investigate the state of public libraries throughout the country, Alvin S. Johnson made a study of selected Carnegie libraries in 1915, at the invitation of the Carnegie Corporation. Johnson's study indicated that many of the Carnegie-financed libraries were not serving their public well, a fact which was attributed to the general lack of trained personnel. These recommendations resulted in a specific study of library schools by C. C. Williamson, who was commissioned in 1919 for this purpose by the Carnegie Corporation. Williamson's report of library schools throughout the United States concluded that, in general, undue emphasis was being placed on training in the clerical and routine aspects of librarianship at the expense of the general education of the future librarians. Williamson's report cited various needs of library education in the United States, among them the need for standards for library education and the urgency for additional opportunities to enable librarians to continue their preparation; these recommendations resulted in the creation of the Board of Education for Librarianship within the American Library Association, in 1924, and four years later, the University of Chicago opened its Graduate Library School which offered the first doctoral program in library science. These latter achievements were a visible recognition of the growing sophistication of library science, and of the need for serious investigation of many of its areas and aspects.

Phase 5: Search for an Identity

Since the 1930s world study in librarianship has been a field in search of an identity; consequently, various terms have been associated with it. Resulting from the establishment of the Graduate Library School at the University of Chicago was an intense research activity which penetrated to the very roots of the practice of librarianship. Not only the central areas of librarianship were being investigated, but considerable attention was also being directed at its cognate areas, such as Mass Communications and Institutional History. These and similar areas were subjected for the first time to philosophical and statistical scrutiny, which were revealing and provocative of diverse comment, experimentation, and study. Librarians in the United States during the 1930s discussed the pros and cons of librarianship as a science, and publications such as the *Library Quarterly* and Pierce Butler's *An Introduction to Library Science* expressed the view that librarianship, although not currently scientific, possessed a potential for becoming a science. In his statement concerning library science, published in 1933, Pierce Butler indicated its requirements, purposes, and desired results. These ideas may be said to constitute the germinal concepts of comparative library science.

It would seem then that certain qualities might safely be predicted of any new science. Librarianship, in particular will become scientific only as it conforms in essentials to the habitual methods of thought in the modern temper. Every line in its intellectual synthesis must start from objective phenomena. These will be scrutinized with all the rigor of scientific observation. Elements will be identified and their functions determined. Every possible device will be utilized for the isolation of activities and their quantitative measurements. The intangible will be traced by whatever secondary effects may be perceptible. So far as they are possible, explanations will be formulated in chains of immediate causes. For complexities in which causal control is impracticable quantitative relationships will be established by a statistical analysis of numerical samples. Hypotheses will be devised to account for observed variations and new methods invented to test their validity. Moreover there will be a continuous mutual exchange of ideas with outside fields of scientific study. *Results will be borrowed from the other sciences and the findings in librarianship will be lent in return.* [the authors' italics]. The field of the new enterprise will always be regarded as essentially but one aspect of the whole compound of human activity.

In the course of the new departure librarians will win a new outlook. They will transfer their attention from process to function. They will come to strive for accurate understanding just as ardently as they now do for practical efficiency. They will temper their ideals with realistic considerations and discover standards in the nature of their elements rather than assume these as *a priori* values. They will seek for knowledge in typical phenomena instead of in particular occurrences. They will study librarianship rather than single libraries. Their enthusiasm for vocational unanimity will give way to a recognition of real differences in operative levels, but their quest they will still regard as a cooperative enterprise of the whole profession.[36]

Butler ignited an intellectual fire among library educators, which eventually spread from one library school to another within the United States, eventually having repercussions within the rank and file of the profession itself. The process, as the expression goes, had gone "full circle"; the spark ignited a generation before by the Carnegie Corporation, when it financed libraries, supported diverse studies of library conditions and the evaluation of library schools, and confirmed the need for increased research to reevaluate librarianship in the United States—a profession which because of its founder's keen personal interest in libraries, the Carnegie Corporation has generously and continuously supported.

In March 1936, Dr. F. P. Keppel, president of the Carnegie Corporation, invited Wilhelm Munthe, then director of the University Library of Oslo, Norway, to visit the United States and evaluate the policies and activities of librarianship. What resulted was Munthe's now-famous appraisal entitled *American Librarianship from a European Angle*, by all standards a landmark study in the development of world study in librarianship. It is paradoxical to observe that, while advancing the frontiers of knowledge in the fledgling field of comparative library science, Munthe questioned the possibility of creating such a field. He stated: "It is quite likely that it will never be possible to build such a thing as a *comparative library science*; [the authors' italics] but it is nonetheless true that knowledge of foreign methods and experience has always stimulated growth at home."[37]

In spite of Munthe's doubts concerning the newly emerging field of comparative library science, his book is significant both for its incisiveness in interpreting a foreign library system to continental Europeans and for its coining the term "comparative library science," which to our knowledge made its first appearance in print in the aforementioned work.

Unfortunately, researchers in library science have not taken up the gauntlet held aloft by Munthe in his work. Although using methodology similar to Munthe's, many researchers have passed over the term "comparative library science," in favor of "comparative librarianship." Periodicals and indexing services have also perpetuated this choice of the latter term in their selection of subject headings.

The spirit of internationalism which Munthe had stirred up within librarianship through his comparative study was not to develop continuously because international cultural achievement was to come up against a formidable obstacle —World War II. While engaged in the destructive activity of a world war, the major powers of the world—Germany, France, Great Britain, Italy, the United States, China, the Soviet Union, and Japan—were unable to pursue the constructive activity of comparative librarianship. Not until after the cessation of hostilities in 1945, and the establishment of the United Nations, were the major powers to attempt once again cooperative endeavors. Among their efforts were cultural projects affecting various areas of endeavor including librarianship. It was this spirit of cooperation and internationalism that prompted a group of libraries and library educators to meet in 1954 at the University of Chicago. One of the participants, Chase Dane, described their meeting in a journal article of that same year, in which was to appear for the first time in print the term "comparative librarianship."[38]

Further evidence of the increased interest in world study in librarianship was provided by the creation in 1964 of the International Library Information Center (ILIC) at the University of Pittsburgh. ILIC was established as a research library to collect primary source material relating to librarianship outside the United States. (For a detailed description of ILIC, refer to the Appendix).

Phase 6: Publication of a Manual Outlining the Research Methodology of World Study in Librarianship

World study in librarianship was clarified and has greatly benefited from the publication, in 1970, of *A Handbook of Comparative Librarianship*, by S. Simsova and M. MacKee. This first textbook in the field is a multipurpose work being a manual of research methodology and a bibliography. One can marvel at the book's international sweep and praise the authors for giving students of the field a functional research tool, and, since hope springs eternal, await other studies which may extend and improve upon the work's basic plan.

Also worth mentioning here is Dr. Louis Shores' essay, "A Theoretical Framework for Comparative Librarianship."[39] Although an essay, this writing by Shores is broad in scope; in our opinion, its useful guidelines and exposure of fruitful areas for investigation make the reading of it highly recommendable.

Where does the profession stand today in the development of world study in librarianship? Our answer is brief: Six significant phases of development have been observed, but three phases remain to be realized: (1) the appearance of a magnum opus in the field, (2) the full development of world study in librarianship, (3) the dissolution of the discipline into its principal areas. Our denial of the existence of a major work in the field may be criticized by some researchers who may possibly consider our judgment to be restrictive, since at present there exist: Asheim's *Librarianship in the Developing Countries*, Avicenne's *Bibliographical Services Throughout the World, 1960-1964*, Campbell's *Metropolitan Public Library Planning Throughout the World*, Harrison's *Libraries in Scandinavia*, Horecky's *Libraries and Bibliographical Centres in the Soviet Union*, Jackson's *Aspects of Librarianship in Latin America*, Ruggles's and Swank's *Soviet Libraries and Librarianship*, and of course the aforementioned work by Munthe.

All are useful contributions to world study in librarianship, but, we feel, they constitute preliminary works. In summarizing the literature, it may be pointed out that Munthe's study is considered by some library comparativists to be somewhat comparable to Alexis de Tocqueville's *Democracy in America*. This statement may be true; however, we would add that there is lacking in the literature of world study in librarianship a work whose analytical incisiveness and breadth of scope merit its being considered a magnum opus, to stand on a par with Arnold Toynbee's *A Study of History*. One might conclude, then, that to some extent world study in librarianship has a de Tocqueville but that it lacks a Toynbee.

SUMMARY AND CONCLUSIONS

Beginning with the earliest examples of librarianship drawn from our incomplete, conjectural, and scanty knowledge of librarianship in ancient times, followed by illustrations of librarianship traced from medieval times to contemporary days, the inescapable conclusion to which we come is that librarians were engaged in comparative librarianship long before the actual formulating of the academic discipline of world study in librarianship. Disputing the possibility of developing a practice, before formulating its underlying theory, is about as logical as denying birds their ability of flight simply because they are unable to articulate the principles of aeronautics.

Has our knowledge of world study in librarianship attained its fullest development? Certainly not! We presently have no definitive—or even clear—statement of the research methodology of the field, and many of the significant areas and topics of librarianship throughout the world remain uninvestigated. Today, the state of world study in librarianship may be likened to that of a giant jigsaw puzzle illustrating the entire world but lacking many significant and interesting pieces necessary to the full image. Researchers are continually completing these pieces and eagerly adding them to the puzzle, but far too much of our overall concept still awaits discovery, analysis, and interpretation. Even less complete is our knowledge of the philosophy of librarianship and of the theory of library science as understood in different parts of the world because an overemphasis by library educators on area studies of librarianship has caused neglect of consideration of the more important theoretical fields of our profession. Consequently, we here advocate an additional direction for world study in librarianship —the investigation of library philosophy and theory, as it has been formulated throughout the world, rather than a further concentration on aspects of national librarianship.

What remains for researchers in world librarianship to accomplish? Many gaps are to be filled before our knowledge of professional practice throughout the world will be adequate even at the descriptive level. We must return to the path of Martin Schrettinger, the nineteenth century German librarian, who stated, "To dispel the chimaera of detailed technique is to lay the foundation of a genuine library science."[40] We must also recall Pierce Butler who echoed the German's view when he wrote, a century later, that when we turn our attention from process to function we will create a library science.[41]

Now that our field has the fundamentals of a functional terminology, and now that S. Simsova and M. MacKee have given the field a practical study guide and research tool, and various writers, including Louis Shores, D. J. Foskett, and John Harvey, among others, have strengthened its theoretical framework, it is time that the profession abandon the parlor game of comparative librarianship and address whatever problems of librarianship that require investigation throughout the world, using appropriate research methodology—in other words, not only comparative methodology—so long as the solution of these problems render knowledge that will explain, predict, and control library phenomena throughout the world.

In addition, we should reinstate Munthe's term "comparative library science" to denote the research methodology underlying comparative study, and undertake analytical research emphasizing the true social science nature of world study in librarianship instead of the perpetuation of mere description. Finally, we who teach should install world librarianship as an integral part of the core curriculum of library education and instill the comparative attitude in each student. When we have taken these positive steps, we shall be far along on the path toward the creation of a true library science.

NOTES

1. Elmer Johnson, *A History of Libraries in the Western World* (New York: Scarecrow Press, 1965), p. 21.
2. Hedwig Anuar, "Asian Librarianship: Its Background, Emergence, and Development," in Chapter III: The Historical Bases of World Librarianship, in *World Librarianship*, p. 84.
3. Jenö Platthy, *Sources on the Earliest Greek Libraries with the Testimonia* (Chicago: Argonaut, Inc., 1969), p. 80.
4. Ibid., p. 107.
5. Ibid., p. 104.
6. Alfred Hessel, *A History of Libraries Translated with Supplementary Material, by Reuben Peiss* (New Brunswick, N.J.: Scarecrow Press, 1955), p. 2.
7. Ibid., p. 5.
8. Bernt Götze, quoted in Note 6, p. 7.
9. Alfred Hessel, *A History of Libraries*, p. 13.
10. Ibid., p. 39.
11. Ibid.
12. Ibid.
13. Ibid., pp. 41-42.
14. Ibid., p. 64.
15. S. Simsova and M. MacKee, *A Handbook of Comparative Librarianship* (London: Clive Bingley, [1970]), p. 12.
16. Gabriel Naudé, *Advice on Establishing a Library* (Berkeley, Calif.: University of California Press, 1950), pp. 2-3.
17. Ibid., pp. 3-4.
18. Ibid., p. 7.
19. Ibid., p. 11.
20. Ibid., pp. 11-12.
21. J. Periam Danton, *The Dimensions of Comparative Librarianship* (Chicago: American Library Association, 1973), pp. 15-16.
22. George Z. F. Bereday, *Comparative Method in Education* (New York: Holt, Rinehart and Winston, Inc., [c1964]), p. 7.
23. Alfred Hessel, *A History of Libraries*, p. 47.
24. Howard W. Winger, "Aspects of Librarianship: A Trace Work of History," in *Seven Questions About the Profession of Librarianship*, Philip H. Ennis and Howard W. Winger, eds. (Chicago: University of Chicago Press, [c1962]), p. 29.
25. Alfred Hessel, *A History of Libraries*, p. 84.
26. George Burwell Utley, *The Librarians' Conference of 1853* (Chicago: American Library Association, 1951), p. 1.
27. Ibid., p. 11.

28. Alfred Hessel, *A History of Libraries*, p. 32.
29. Sarah, K. Vann, *Training for Librarianship Before 1923*: *Education for Librarianship Prior to the Publication of Williamson's Report on Training for Library Service* (Chicago: American Library Association, 1961), p. 13.
30. Justin Winsor, "A Word to Starters of Libraries," *American Library Journal* 1 (September 1876), p. 1.
31. Conference of Librarians, London, 1877, "Proceedings," p. 280.
32. Justin Winsor, "A Word to Starters of Libraries," p. 23.
33. Ibid.
34. Ibid., p. 26.
35. Ibid., p. 29.
36. Pierce Butler, *An Introduction to Library Science* (Chicago: American Library Association [c1933]), pp. 25-26.
37. Wilhelm Munthe, *American Librarianship from a European Angle* (Chicago: American Library Association, 1936), p. 2.
38. Chase Dane, "The Benefits of Comparative Librarianship," *The Australian Library Journal* 3 (July 1954), p. 89.
39. Louis Shores, "Comparative Librarianship: A Theoretical Approach," in *Comparative and International Librarianship*: *Essays on Themes and Problems*, Miles M. Jackson, ed. (Westport, Conn.: [c1970]), pp. 3-24.
40. Alfred Hessel, *A History of Libraries*, p. 80.
41. Wilhelm Munthe, *American Librarianship from a European Angle*, p. 115.

2
Research Methodology: A General Discussion

Richard Krzys

HISTORICAL OVERVIEW

Since earliest antiquity, librarians have attempted to formulate principles and refine techniques involved in providing ever-improving information services to their communities. Centuries after ancient scribes in Mesopotamia, Egypt, and China first sought improved bibliographic techniques, librarians have continued to attempt to compile more effective catalogs and have searched for methods of improving technical and reader services. Solutions to these and other age-old problems of librarianship have been derived from five sources: (1) authority, (2) personal experience, (3) deductive reasoning, (4) inductive reasoning, and (5) scientific method.[1]

Research in world study in librarianship may be divided into three categories: (1) area studies, (2) case studies, and (3) total analyses. Research in international study takes the form of case studies; for example, an investigation into library cooperation between Canada and the United States or a study of exchange of library personnel between the Soviet Union and the United States. Research in comparative study may be divided into the same three categories. Although purists will maintain that area studies (e.g., a study of librarianship in Denmark or an interpretation of librarianship in Asia) are not comparative,

This chapter is a modification of an article which the author wrote for the Encyclopedia of Library and information Science (ELIS). The present version represents a maturation of the concepts introduced originally in ELIS.

they are necessary preludes to comparative study. Comparative study juxtaposes and analyses two or more area or case studies; the juxtaposition of librarianship in Denmark with its counterpart in Finland, when coupled with analysis, will produce a comparative study of librarianship in Denmark and Finland. A similar juxtaposition and analysis involving librarianship of Asia and its counterpart in Africa will result in a comparative study of librarianship in Asia and Africa. Case studies may revolve around aspects, topics, or themes of librarianship; a researcher may compare an aspect of librarianship in two geographical areas producing, for example, a comparative study of education for librarianship in India and Pakistan. A topical study may involve comparisons of the profiles of Uruguayan and Brazilian librarians, and a third type of comparative study, the thematic study, may produce a study of the pursuit of professionalism among librarians in Japan and Iran. Although comparative studies are usually thought of as being cross-national or cross-cultural in character, they need not be exclusively within these categories, since a comparison of state library associations in the North and South of the United States would also be considered a comparative study.

As difficult as such projects are, they do not approach the scope and complexity of total analysis, comparative study which attempts to analyze the overall impact which a discipline or profession has had upon global society. In commenting on such a study in education, George Z. F. Bereday referred to it as "the culminating point of the discipline. This is an area fitting for a *magnum opus* of a researcher's career."[2]

The writer of this article believes that in a space-age context researchers in comparative study in librarianship may very well have to extend the scope of their study; as man conquers outer space he may eventually reach other galaxies and make soft landings on their planets. When librarians accompany the astronauts who embark to establish space stations, librarianship will have taken on a new dimension requiring a parallel expansion in the field's comparative study. If extraterrestrial intelligence is encountered in the vast beyond, researchers in comparative study will be treated to their most fascinating adventure as we compare our approaches—that is, those devised on Earth—with those encountered on planets of other galaxies; or, comparative researchers in librarianship may find themselves without a research topic if the beings encountered have reached so advanced a state of development that they have transcended librarianship itself.

SCIENTIFIC METHOD

Fundamental to research in world study in librarianship is the scientific method, an investigative procedure used to solve problems through the application of logic to systematically collected data. Its steps are (1) stating the problem,

(2) formulating a hypothesis, (3) observing and experimenting, (4) interpreting data, and (5) drawing conclusions. The human mind does not always methodically follow the steps outlined in the solution of problems, but the scientific method provides us with an approximation of the intellectual process of the researcher in his creation of knowledge.

Researchers disagree on the validity of applying the scientific method to both the natural and social sciences.[3] Some researchers maintain that the scientific method can only be used in the natural sciences, and other researchers question the existence of a single methodology applicable to both divisions of the sciences. A study of the various sciences, natural and social, indicates that their differences in purpose and function have produced significant variations in techniques of data collection, but both the natural and social sciences rely in principle on the five-step scientific method outlined above.

Other significant areas of agreement common to the natural and social sciences are those underlying the scientific method and the goals of sciences. This writer advocates that researchers in world study in librarianship, along with their colleagues in other sciences, assume (1) uniformity of nature and (2) the reliability of the psychological processes.[4] John Stuart Mill expressed the principle of the uniformity of nature as follows: "there are such things in nature as parallel cases; that what happens once, will, under sufficient degree of similarity of circumstances, happen again, and not only again, but always."[5] The assumption concerning the reliability of the psychological processes signifies that man "can gain knowledge of the world through the psychological processes of perceiving, remembering, and reasoning."[6] Traditionally, scientists have maintained three goals with regard to the phenomena they encounter: (1) explanation, (2) prediction, and (3) control.[7] At this writing, researchers in world study in librarianship have shared with other scientists the goal of explanation of library phenomena, but they have almost completely disregarded the other equally important, but more difficult to attain goals of prediction and control. This writer advocates the adoption of the goals of prediction and control by researchers in this field.

TYPES OF RESEARCH METHODS

Presently the bulk of contributions to world study in librarianship includes narratives of the experiences of practicing librarians or library consultants in a host country. Although the work of well-intentioned individuals, many of these studies are so weak in research methodology that their conclusions constitute descriptions of particular instances of foreign library experience rather than analytical studies with findings that may be generalized. Serious researchers in world study in librarianship, however, have at their disposal seven research methods: (1) historical method, (2) survey method, (3) case method, (4) statistical method,

(5) experimental method, (6) composite methods which include any or all of the methods described above, and (7) comparative method. This writer advocates that researchers in comparative study in librarianship rigorously employ comparative method, a procedure that facilitates the study of data concerning two or more comparable library phenomena, collected through any of the seven methods described above, juxtaposed, and analyzed for the purpose of formulating logical hypotheses and conclusions.

PRELIMINARIES TO INITIATING RESEARCH

Although the first step of the scientific method is stating the problem, the researcher must initiate his inquiry with the preliminary activity of selecting a topic. For the student, the topic usually results in a report, master's thesis, or doctoral dissertation, research for which is often conducted in the university library; for the librarian or library consultant the research topic most likely results from a practical problem encountered during the course of the researcher's foreign assignment.

In selecting a topic for research in world study in librarianship, the following suggestions may prove helpful: (1) choose a field or an area in which you are interested or experienced; (2) duplicate an earlier study which is of interest or the conclusions of which seem doubtful (such a study is usually not acceptable for a doctoral dissertation); (3) examine the final chapters of studies or dissertations for the purpose of locating areas of librarianship requiring further research; (4) examine data of existing studies to determine whether a better hypothesis may be formulated; (5) choose an assumption of current practice and test it; and (6) read exhaustively in the literature of world librarianship.[8] George J. Mouly suggests that students who are specifically searching for a thesis or dissertation topic will be interested in the following five criteria: (1) the topic should be of interest to the student; (2) it should be "sufficiently original" to avoid "objectionable duplication;" (3) it should be amenable to research, that is, oriented toward a criterion and stated as a testable relationship; (4) it should contain the possibility of adding to the present state of knowledge of librarianship as a science or discipline, as opposed to a trivial problem; and (5) it should be feasible, in the sense that data are available to the student within practicable limits.[9]

In addition to applying criteria in selecting a topic, the researcher in world study in librarianship should bear in mind four requirements of research in this field: (1) knowledge of the language of the area to be studied; (2) knowledge of the area's history, economy, politics, and sociology; (3) residence, at least temporarily, in the country whose librarianship is being studied; and (4) control of one's own cultural and personal biases.[10] In his book *Comparative Method in Education*, George Z. F. Bereday, after discussing the requirements imposed on the student of comparative education, concludes, "Failure to comply with these prerequisites cuts one off from the true nature of the educational system under observation as effectively as blindness. Only in exceptional cases are the writings of people who have not complied with these requirements trustworthy."[11] In the opinion of this writer, Bereday's statement is equally valid when applied to the writings within world study in librarianship.

The librarian, or library consultant, who conducts his investigation while residing in a foreign country may choose a topic as the result of a practical problem because the subject to be studied usually presents itself as an obstacle to the proper functioning of the researcher. The librarian who travels to another country to investigate, for example, the topic of the development of that country's librarianship, may be frustrated in his attempt to carry out the prelude to his study, conducting an exhaustive literature search. Complicating his search may be local library practices, such as the cataloging practice of that country. Accustomed to entries for books by author, title, and subject, the researcher may be surprised to discover that only author entries are made in the catalog of the country's national library. His alternative approach for locating subject entries for books on his research topic through the country's national bibliography may lead him to discover that such a reference tool is nonexistent. The investigator's surprise is compounded when he discovers that the country has no trade bibliography either. Completely frustrated in his professional approach, the researcher is confronted with his first experience of culture shock. The broad topic of a country's librarianship, choice of which resulted as an academic exercise, might become modified through experience of culture shock to the topic of the country's bibliographic control.

Deobold B. Van Dalen summarized the steps of the reflective thinking as defined by John Dewey in his book *How We Think*. The process which Dewey described is an activity similar to problem solving in world study in librarianship. The process may be outlined as follows:

1. A felt difficulty. Man encounters some obstacle, experience, or problem that puzzles him.
   a. He lacks the means to get to the end desired.
   b. He has difficulty in identifying the character of an object.
2. Location and definition of the difficulty. Man makes observations—gathers facts—that enable him to define his difficulty more precisely.
3. Suggested solutions of the problem—hypotheses. From his preliminary study of the facts, man makes intelligent guesses about possible solutions of the problem. The solutions—generalizations he offers to explain the facts causing him the difficulty—are called hypotheses.
4. Deductively reasoning out the consequences of the suggested solutions. Man deductively reasons that if each hypothesis is true, certain consequences should follow.
5. Testing the hypothesis by action. Man tests each hypothesis by searching

for observable evidence that will confirm whether or not the consequences that should follow actually occur. By this process, he finds out which hypothesis is in harmony with observable facts and thus offers the most reliable answer to his problem.[12]

The sources the researcher uses to identify significant problems in world study in librarianship may be divided into (1) professional experiences and (2) professional and library-related literature.

Since, as John Dewey indicated, problems arise from felt difficulties, the importance for the researcher in world study in librarianship to have meaningful library experience outside of his own country cannot be overemphasized. In addition to foreign residence, immersing oneself in the professional and library-related literature is extremely important.[13]

Immersing oneself in the literature of the field may reveal topics of genuine research potential. Examples illustrating the various research methods are (1) study of the public library movement in the United States (historical method), (2) examination of book selection procedures of libraries in Cuba (survey method), (3) a librarian of South Africa (case method), (4) economic status of readers as reflected in student use of academic libraries in Australia (statistical method), (5) the introduction of public library service at the Delhi Public Library (experimental method), (6) librarianship in Colombia (composite method), and (7) library education in Pakistan and the Philippines (comparative method).[14]

After selecting his topic, for example, a comparison of library education in Pakistan and the Philippines, the researcher must define it; for example, the purpose of this study was to determine the causative or influential elements involved in the development of library education in Pakistan and the Phillipines.

Douglas Waples advised researchers to outline the proposed investigation with reference to each of the following elements: (1) title and full statement of the problem, (2) definition of terms and limitations of scope, (3) previous studies in the general field, (4) analysis of subproblems and hypotheses, (5) designation and evaluation of sources, (6) types of evidence desired and method of obtaining data from the appropriate sources, (7) rough topical organization of manuscript, (8) estimate of costs, and (9) tentative time schedule.[15] This type of outlining is useful for initiating research in world study in librarianship.

Prior to comparing library phenomena, the researcher must gather relevant data on the basis of a systematic literature search. In order to guide the researcher in a total approach to a country's librarianship the following checklist, quoted by S. Simsova from a course outline of the Columbia University School of Library Science, is suggested. (When doing a study of one aspect of a country's librarianship, the researcher will select only the relevant part or parts of the outline, or devise his own checklist.)

I. Brief historical review
   A. Library tradition and historic beginnings
   B. Landmarks in library development
   C. Most recent statistics by number and type of library
II. Current statements of library objectives and standards
III. Patterns of library government
   A. National responsibilities for library service
      1. Laws and legislation
      2. Financial support or assistance
      3. Control and supervision
      4. Centralized services to libraries
      5. Other direct or special services
   B. The role of state or province in library development
   C. Local responsibilities for library service
IV. Brief survey of existing library resources
   A. National libraries
   B. Public libraries
   C. School library provision
   D. College and university libraries
   E. Special libraries
   F. Foreign libraries
V. Library materials (extent and characteristics)
   A. Books and pamphlets
   B. Periodicals and newspapers
   C. Government publications
   D. Films and other audio-visual materials
   E. Materials for children and young people
   F. Special problems
      1. Language problems
      2. Materials for illiterate and newly-literate adults
      3. Other
VI. Library services
   A. Acquisition, cataloging, and bibliographic controls
   B. Reference and information services
   C. Adult and fundamental education services
   D. Services to children and young people
   E. Services to special groups (e.g., minorities, the blind)
VII. Existing library personnel
   A. Existing library personnel
      1. Number and qualifications
      2. Salaries and status
   B. Professional training programs in the country
      1. Curricula
      2. Materials and methods of instruction
      3. Teaching staff
      4. Research and publications

      C. Apprenticeship and other inservice training programs
      D. Foreign study and visitation
         1. Opportunities for, and extent of, foreign study
         2. Certification and degrees
         3. Equivalences of foreign study programs
         4. Advantages and limitations of study abroad
VIII. Aspects of library development
      A. Analysis of existing national or other library plans and studies
      B. Library coverage: quantitative: qualitative
         1. Size and types of library units
         2. Techniques for coordination and cooperation
      C. Library finances
         1. National, state, and local
         2. Other (e.g., philanthropic foundations)
      D. Library buildings and equipment
      E. Library personnel and training
         1. Professional
         2. Other
      F. Opportunities for international assistance and cooperation, for example,
         1. Exchange or training of library personnel
         2. Operation of demonstration or other field programs
         3. Supply (including translations or adaptations) of publications, films, or other material
         4. Grants-in-aid or other financial assistance
  IX. Summary and recommendations
      A. Main characteristics and achievements of the library system
      B. Outstanding problems and needs
      C. Suggested topics for research and investigation
   X. Selected bibliography
      Systematic listing of main sources of information, including statistical data, preferably annotated.[16]

If the researcher finds the above checklist too general for his needs, he may decide to devise a checklist of the components of the phenomena being compared; for example, the researcher investigating library education in Pakistan and the Philippines decided to search for data related to twelve items: (1) date for starting of library education, (2) level of courses, (3) admission requirements, (4) curriculum, (5) status of library schools and physical facilities, (6) faculty, (7) methods of instruction, (8) teaching and reading materials, (9) tuition fees and other expenses, (10) requirements for graduation, (11) accreditation, and (12) library legislation.

LITERATURE SEARCHING

Another step preliminary to comparing library phenomena is reading widely on the topic to be investigated. Serious research in world study in librarianship potentially requires searching three categories of material: (1) the literature of librarianship, (2) background information about the country involved, and (3) where the phenomena being investigated have involvement in fields other than librarianship, interdisciplinary material from the various topics having bearing on the aspects of the subjects being studied.

Sources indispensable to searching the literature of librarianship are the following:

Cannons, Harry George Turner, *Bibliography of Library Economy. A Classified Index to the Professional Periodical Literature in the English Language Relating to Library Economy, Printing, Methods of Publishing, Copyright, Bibliography, etc. from 1876 to 1920* (Chicago: American Library Association, 1927), 680 pp.

Internationale Bibliographie des Buch-und Bibliothekswesens, 1904-1912, 1922-1939 (Leipzig: Harrossowitz, 1905-1940), 13 vols. and n.F. 1-14.

Library and Information Science Abstracts. No. 1-, Jan.-Feb. 1969- (London: Library Association, 1969-). Bimonthly.

Library Literature, 1921/1932 (New York: Wilson, 1934-).

Library Science Abstracts, vol. 1-, No. 1-, 1950- (London: Library Association).

Effective literature searching is dependent upon the researcher's knowledge of subject headings, familiarity with which may be gained through card catalogs, indexes of monographs, reference books, and lists of subject headings.

Researchers should develop techniques for reducing the amount of searching time required, one example of which is isolating the date or period when the library phenomenon being investigated was of significance; for example, knowing that the history of library education in Pakistan dated from 1915 and that education for librarianship in the Philippines began in 1914, the researcher began his literature searching in library literature with bibliographic sources whose chronological coverage corresponded to the first quarter of the twentieth century; a search through the index *Library Literature* under the subject heading "Education for Librarianship—Pakistan" and "Education for Librarianship—Philippines" revealed various relevant entries, among which were the following: Anis Khurshid, "Library Training in Pakistan," *UNESCO Bull. Lib.*, 15, 31-33 (January 1961); and C. Damasao, "Library Education in the Philippines," *J. Educ. Lib.*, 6, 310-317 (Spring 1966); a bibliographic search for background information about Pakistan and the Philippines uncovered the following sources: Herbert Feldman, *Pakistan: An Introduction*, 2nd ed. (Lahore: Oxford University Press, 1968); and Onofre D. Corpus, *The Philippines* (Englewood Cliffs, N.J.: Prentice-Hall, 1966); because the researcher needed interdisciplinary material for study he searched more extensively until he found D. N. Wilber, Pakistan, *Its People, Its Society, Its Culture* (New Haven, Conn.: Human Relations Area Files Press, 1964); and Wolfe Management Services, *Developmental Book*

Activities and Needs in the Philippines (New York: Agency for International Development Contract No. AID csd-1162, 1966).

Searching in secondary sources in the literature of librarianship and in auxiliary sources in areas cognate to the problem being investigated represents the first two phases of data collecting, providing the researcher a framework of information upon which he can plan the final phase of data gathering. In order to produce a genuine research study, one contributing new knowledge to world study in librarianship, the investigator must analyze the information drawn from secondary and auxiliary sources in terms of its gaps, contradictions, and authenticity in order to determine the types of primary sources needed to furnish the raw data for his research. S. Simsova described the sources useful for investigation in this field as follows:

> Primary historical sources in librarianship are annual reports of libraries, annual reports of central authorities, plans for future development, government and other reports, library legislation, conference reports, library textbooks and other professional literature, publications of individual libraries, descriptions of other professional literature, publications of individual libraries, descriptions of libraries in fiction.

> The second group consists of particular information from living individuals (interviews) and direct observation of behavior in process (visiting).

> The primary field sources in librarianship are descriptive accounts written by observers, native or foreign, material collected through interviews, visits, correspondence.

> The third group of sources giving "data from enumerations" includes library statistics, international and national library surveys.[17]

Regardless of the skill in the researcher's use of primary and secondary sources, no thorough investigation in world study in librarianship is complete without on-site visiting of the agencies of librarianship being studied. A serious comparative study of library education in Pakistan and the Philippines would include tours of libraries and library schools in both countries.

METHODOLOGY OF COMPARATIVE STUDY IN LIBRARIANSHIP

To interpret the term "comparative study" as denoting a discipline having one particular research methodology is a fallacy. The methodologies used to investigate the comparative aspects of, for example, religion, anatomy, economics, politics, psychology, government, anthropology, and literature are similar in their common purpose of analyzing phenomena in terms of their patterns, similarities, and differences, but the methodologies are necessarily dissimilar because of the differences inherent in the problems to be analyzed in these disciplines; for example, comparative anthropology includes the variable of geography, while comparative anatomy does not; comparative literature is preoccupied with qualitative judgments, while comparative psychology's preoccupation is with judgments of a quantitative type. Librarianship, because of its interdisciplinary nature, includes problems which involve variables of subject, time, geography, quantity, and quality; therefore, the researcher in comparative study in librarianship must draw from an arsenal of comparative methodologies developed previously in other disciplines; or, where the problems of librarianship are unique or have a unique configuration of components, the researcher must devise a methodology whose uniqueness lies in its composite nature. (For a discussion of some comparative methodologies used in disciplines other than librarianship, the reader is directed to the works of George Z. F. Bereday, Jean Blondel, Gunnar Hecksher, and William N. Loucks and William G. Whitney listed in the Bibliography.)

If the researcher were studying comparative library education, for example, he would be wise to study thoroughly the methodology of comparative education whose sophisticated development is attributable to over a century of testing. The methodology of comparative library education based on the methodology of comparative education includes four steps: (1) description, (2) interpretation, (3) juxtaposition, and (4) comparison.[18] Description is the systematic statement of information concerning library phenomena in two or more cases or geographical areas. The second step, interpretation, involves the analysis of these data in terms of the social sciences. In juxtaposition the researcher places comparable data side-by-side for the purpose of formulation of one or more hypotheses. Finally, comparison, the analytical presentation of data concerning the library education in two or more cases or geographical areas, takes place in one integrated report. These steps may be represented graphically as in Figure 2.1.

Description

The descriptive phase of the comparative method consists of the presentation in narrative form of data relating to the library phenomenon being studied. In order to guide his data collecting, the researcher must have a logically devised preliminary topical outline of his subject. He may either use an existing scheme or he may devise his own scheme. Because of the understanding of the components of the research topic being investigated which devising one's own scheme provides, it is preferable to using a ready-made scheme. The pleasure which taxonomy provides the researcher, however, depends solely on his analytical powers. For the researcher with a logical mind, devising a taxonomical sequence is as pleasant a process as sectioning an orange; to the person with the illogical mind taxonomy is as irritating as peeling an onion. Once the scheme is devised, the researcher must collect appropriate data and present them in narrative form. This presentation must be elaborated in accordance with a systematic outline, arranged in tabular form, and completed with a list of bibliographic

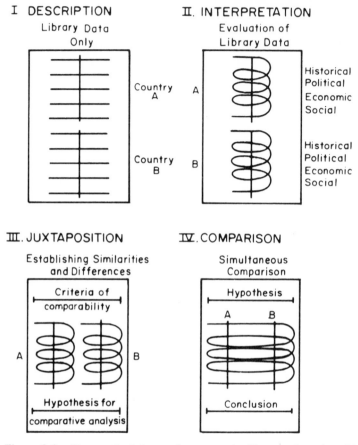

Figure 2.1   The methodology of comparative library education. (Adapted from Note 1.)

sources from which the data were drawn. In organizing the descriptive information the same preliminary checklist used for data gathering may also serve as the sequence for the data in narrative form. With regard to the study of library education in Pakistan and the Philippines, the same twelve items that guided the data collection also served as the outline for the study's descriptive section.

Interpretation

Interpretation is the analysis of tabulated data in terms of the social sciences. Ideally, the relevant information should be scrutinized in accordance with all the factors which affected the phenomenon being investigated, but in reality the investigator will be limited by the the subject areas in which he has had education and experience. The following outline from a course outline of the Columbia University School of Library Service lists the factors relevant to the development of librarianship.

  I. Main historical and political factors
 II. Geography and climate
III. Population factors
   A. Total number of inhabitants
   B. Racial and national groups (where significant)
   C. Sex and age groups (adults, children of school age, children under 6)
   D. Educational levels (years of schooling completed, extent of illiteracy)
   E. Urban-rural distribution
 IV. Economic factors
   A. National and average income
   B. Main occupations and industries
  V. Cultural factors
   A. Language and dialects
   B. Main religions
   C. Other (e.g., segregation by race or sex)
 VI. Governmental structure (national, state, local)
   A. Extent of centralization
   B. Sources and amounts of tax and other revenues
VII. Educational factors
   A. The educational system
   B. Agencies and programs of adult and fundamental education (e.g., agricultural extension services, library campaigns)
VIII. Existing patterns of communications
   A. Number and circulation of newspapers
   B. Production and distribution of books and magazines
   C. Film production and attendance
   D. Radio and television[19]

In the study of library education in Pakistan and the Philippines, the researcher analyzed the relevant data in terms of four factors: (1) historical aspects, (2) political aspects, (3) economic aspects, and (4) social aspects.

Juxtaposition

The third step of the comparative method, juxtaposition, is the side-by-side placement of interwoven reports of comparable data, and relevant social science elements, a process which has two purposes: (1) discovering similarities and differences in the data compared and (2) formulation of a hypothesis; for example, in the comparative study of library education in Pakistan and the Philippines, the twelve elements enumerated previously were related to factors of the countries' history, politics, economics, and sociology. The four interwoven reports were then placed side-by-side in two columns. This arrangement of information makes evident—in all comparisons—similarities and differences, and in some cases enables the researcher to discover a unifying concept and hypothesis which explain the phenomenon being studied. Juxtaposing information about the historical aspects of library legislation in Pakistan and the Philippines, for example, produced the following statements:

> Library legislation in Pakistan provided for the establishment of municipal, district, and school libraries, and copyright law is enforced. Presently, no library legislation in Pakistan guarantees an annual budget for the continuous support of libraries.

> Library legislation in the Philippines provided for the establishment of national, provincial, and municipal libraries. Depository laws are not enforced in the Philippines, and no legal provision exists for continuous financial support of the country's libraries.*

The reader will note that in juxtaposition no comparison has been made; instead, the researcher has presented two statements from which similarities and differences become apparent. The comparison does not begin until an introductory statement is made whose purpose is to serve as the criterion of comparability. Once this criterion is established, the statements concerning the countries' library legislation are then reconsidered in terms of the criterion of comparability and restated in a hypothesis which contains the subject of the comparative study being conducted. Juxtaposition, then, requires statement of a criterion of comparability, restatement of the data being compared, and a hypothesis. In one example of juxtaposition the statements relating to the historical aspects of library education in Pakistan and the Philippines, when interwoven with data about library legislation in the countries, reveal the following paragraph:

> Investigating the conditions accompanying the development of library education in a country, this researcher noted the following situations with regard to library legislation:

> Library legislation in Pakiston provided for the establishment of municipal, district, and school libraries, and copyright law is enforced. Presently, no library legislation in Pakistan guarantees an annual budget for the continuous support of libraries. Library legislation in the Philippines provided for the establishment of a national, provincial and municipal libraries. Depository laws are not enforced in the Philippines, and no legal provision exists for continuous financial support for the country's libraries.

*This example of juxtaposition was developed by Mr. Naimuddin Qureshi in consultation with the author of this chapter. Relevant information was drawn from primary sources of data in the International Library Information Center of the School of Library and Information Science at the University of Pittsburgh.

In this comparison, limited in scope to two countries, these situations suggest a positive correlation between the state of library legislation in a country and the development of its library education.

Comparison

Comparison, the final step of the comparative method, is a report of the conclusions of the study. Since this report is the only part of his work that the researcher publishes—the first three steps, description, analysis, and juxtaposition, are done for the researcher's benefit alone—comparison may be likened to the tip of an iceberg; it is the only part of the researcher's work which the reader sees, and it rises, or falls, with the bulk of the research which supports it.

In a comparison of librarianship in two or more countries a researcher would be likely to present various hypotheses and conclusions, which by synthesis may eventually result in formulation of theories or laws of librarianship; in an aspect approach the investigator would present only the hypotheses and conclusions related to the aspect of librarianship under investigation.

A statement relating to library legislation in the study of factors involved in the development of library education in Pakistan and the Philippines might be worded as follows in the comparative step of the comparative method:

A positive correlation appears to exist between library legislation and the development of library education in a country. Well developed library education, meeting the needs of a country in terms of numbers of librarians educated, training programs resulting in levels of professional competence, and locally produced teaching materials of high quality, is accompanied by effective library legislation, providing adequate and continuous support of libraries. Our study indicated that in Pakistan library legislation provides for the establishment of libraries, but does not provide for their continuous support. In the Philippines depository laws are not enforced, and no legal provision exists for continuous support of the country's libraries. The inadequate and ineffective library legislation in Pakistan and the Philippines are symptomatic of the state of development of their library education.

This illustration of the comparison phase of the comparative method indicates its usefulness as an approach to creating new knowledge in the field of world study in librarianship while making obvious its weaknesses: the hypotheses formulated are merely tested in the study itself and cannot be accepted as valid until they have been verified in the arena of librarianship throughout the world. Of all the phases of comparative method, comparison is, according to Bereday, "the newest and least well-worked-out state of comparative procedures."[20]

CONCLUSIONS

World study in librarianship has experienced a continuous development, paralleling the development of librarianship from antiquity. Considerable progress has been made from early comparative study in librarianship to today's incipient world study in librarianship. Greater progress, as evidenced by improved explanation, prediction, and control of librarianship, are anticipated when rigorous application of research methodology to international and comparative topics will make possible the creation of a true international and comparative library science. Although the comparative method holds considerable promise for the progress of librarianship, researchers in the field should not become so enamored of methodology and blind to the limitations of comparative method as to forget an extremely significant question: What lies beyond comparative method in library research? Researchers who consider the question rhetorically will be guilty of the same blunder committed by ancient and medieval philosophers who considered deductive reasoning the ultimate method to arrive at truth. So this writer repeats, what lies beyond the comparative method in library research?

NOTES

1. Deobold B. Van Dalen attributed man's attempt to acquire knowledge to solve his problems to five sources: (1) authority, (2) personal experience, (3) deductive reasoning, (4) inductive reasoning, and (5) the scientific method. By extrapolation, this researcher applies them to the acquiring of new knowledge in librarianship. For Van Dalen's explanation of the role of these sources in the research process, see his chapter on "Methods of Acquiring Knowledge" in *Understanding Educational Research* (New York: McGraw-Hill, 1966).
2. George Z. F. Bereday, *Comparative Method in Education* (New York: Holt, Rinehart and Winston, 1964), p. 25.
3. Note 1, p. 32.
4. Deobold B. Van Dalen discusses the assumptions underlying the scientific method in Note 1, pp. 33-40.
5. Note 1, p. 34.
6. Note 1, p. 38.
7. Deobold B. Van Dalen discusses the goals of science in Note 1, pp. 40-44.
8. Herbert Goldhor makes suggestions for choosing a research topic in librarianship in *An Introduction to Scientific Research in Librarianship* (Champaign, Ill.: Illini Union Bookstore, 1969), pp. 33-36.
9. Note 8, p. 36.
10. For a discussion of the demands imposed upon the student of comparative education, requirements which in the opinion of this researcher apply with equal validity to the student of world study in librarianship, see Note 2, pp. 10-11.
11. Note 2, p. 10.

12. Note 1, pp. 28-29.
13. A bibliography of examples from the literature of international and comparative study in librarianship is included in Dorothy G. Collings' article "Comparative Librarianship," in *Encyclopedia of Library and Information Science*, Vol. 5, A. Kent and H. Lancour, eds. (New York: Marcel Dekker, 1971), pp. 492-502.
14. Herbert Goldhor discusses the various research methods available to researchers in librarianship in Note 8.
15. Douglas Waples, *Investigating Library Problems* (Chicago: University of Chicago Press, 1939), p. 106.
16. S. Simsova and M. MacKee, *A Handbook of Comparative Librarianship* (London: Bingley, 1970), pp. 401-403.
17. Ibid.
18. The research methodology proposed here for the study of comparative library education is derived from the model for research in comparative education devised by George Z. F. Bereday. See Note 1, pp. 3-51.
19. S. Simsova and M. MacKee, *A Handbook of Comparative Librarianship*, pp. 400-401.
20. George Z. F. Bereday, *Comparative Method in Education*, p. 42.

3
The Research Methodology
Underlying this Study

Richard Krzys and Gaston Litton

OBJECTIVES OF WORLD STUDY IN LIBRARIANSHIP

To maximize the benefits of our study, it is important that students and instructors clearly define their objectives. Ideally, these statements of anticipated behavioral outcomes should be decided upon through a consensus of participants during the early sessions of the course.

As a starter to discussion for achieving the desired consensus, we propose as suggestions eight tentative objectives: (1) to analyze the nature of librarianship, (2) to compare its processes within the same country, (3) to compare them in various regions of the world, (4) to formulate generalizations about world librarianship, (5) to explore possibilities for application of "lessons of world librarianship" to a particular professional problem, (6) to afford students an opportunity to discuss with their colleagues from abroad the library situations in their countries, (7) to provide the background information about practicing librarianship there, and (8) to formulate suggestions for developing a global librarianship, that phase of library development to be characterized by decision-making for the purpose of satisfying humanity's information needs rather than purely regional or national needs. These objectives are intended, of course, only as suggestions. Readers of this book may wish to devise their own objectives. For illustrations of each type of objective suggested here, see Table 3.1.

Table 3.1 Illustrations of Objectives of World Study in Librarianship

Objective	Illustrations
1. Analyze the nature of librarianship.	1. Does it have theoretical knowledge? 2. Does it have authority emanating from education and theory? 3. Does it have community sanction and approval of this authority? 4. Does it have a functional code of ethics? 5. Does it have a professional college? 6. Does it have a service orientation?
2. Compare its processes within the same country.	1. Compare reader services to blacks in the North and the South of the United States. 2. Compare reader services to the English-speaking and French-speaking communities within Canada.
3. Compare its processes in various regions of the world.	1. Compare British and U.S. Reference Service. 2. Compare cataloging practices in the United Kingdom and United States.
4. Generalize about world librarianship.	1. Technical services appear to be better developed throughout the world than reader services. 2. School libraries are the least developed type of library throughout the world.
5. Apply "lessons of world librarianship" to a particular professional problem.	1. Developing countries attempting to compile national bibliography should encourage agencies or companies to develop them rather than individuals. 2. Library architecture should incorporate the principal features of architecture of the locale in question.
6. Provide students opportunities to discuss with their colleagues from abroad the library situation in their countries.	1. Students should be ready to compare the librarianship of their countries to the country being studied.
7. Provide background information about the librarianship in a particular area of the world for students contemplating practicing librarianship there.	1. Provide information about a country's history, economy, politics, and social composition.
8. Formulate suggestions for a global librarianship.	1. Librarians throughout the world should use ISBD and ISBN.

AREAS AND ASPECTS OF LIBRARIANSHIP

In order to acquaint our readers with the varieties of professional practice throughout the globe, we shall attempt to divide the five continents into nine comprehensible areas of library activity as follows:

Asia
1. Middle East
2. Central, South, East, and Southeast Asia

Africa
3. Africa

Europe
4. Western Europe
5. Union of Soviet Socialist Republics
6. Eastern Europe

America
7. Latin America
8. United States and Canada

Australia, New Zealand, and Oceania
9. Australia, New Zealand, and Oceania

Within each geographical area eleven aspects of librarianship will be examined. They are:

1. Bibliographic control
2. Legislation
3. Financial support
4. The profession
5. Practitioners
6. Associations
7. Educational agencies
8. Literature
9. Service agencies
10. Services
11. Planning for the future

To clarify the scope of the eleven aspects of our profession, we shall define each aspect as intended throughout this textbook. The definitions are as follows:

Bibliographic control is the capability to recall through the use of prescribed and uniform descriptive techniques data essential to the identification of each item of the total production of publications of a political unit, for example, a city, state, province, etc. of a country, region, continent or area of the world.

Library legislation is composed of those statutes and laws which define, establish, facilitate, or support librarianship, its agencies, activities, processes, or services.

Financial support is the provision of the monetary base essential for the establishment, maintenance, and development of libraries or the library profession.

The profession denotes librarianship, ". . . the collection, preservation, organization and use of recorded communications."[1]

Practitioners are defined as individuals involved in the essential activities of librarianship, regardless of whether or not these individuals hold the professional library degree.

Associations refer to organizations of persons or agencies that band together for the improvement of library service and the status and salaries of the profession's practitioners.

Educational agencies are the various schools and programs through which the practitioners of librarianship learn the theory and practice of the profession. These agencies may include: (1) schools which have college or university affiliation, (2) technical institutes, (3) libraries which provide in-service training, and (4) agencies that provide correspondence courses in librarianship.

Literature, according to Jean Key Gates, refers to the body of writings by or for librarians that concern themselves with: (1) the historical bases of the profession, (2) library functions, techniques, and activities, and the principles underlying them, and (3) the profession itself.[2]

Service agencies denote those establishments maintained by the profession's practitioners for the care, lending, and administration of graphic records essential for the provision of information services to the agencies' users.

Services, according to Leonard Montague Harrod, are "the facilities provided by a library for the use of books and the dissemination of information."[3]

Planning for the future, specifically library planning, has been defined within the *A.L.A. Glossary of Library Terms* as the "formulation of comprehensive integrated plans for library objectives in city, county, region, state, or nation."[4]

THE AREA CONCEPT OF LIBRARIANSHIP

World librarianship represents a professional response to humanity's need to preserve and consult the cumulative graphic record of mankind. Although our profession is a world phenomenon, significant differences of philosophy and practice are evident throughout the world. These differences make it proper at this writing to conceptualize an area librarianship.

RATIONALE UNDERLYING THE CONCEPT

We predicate the validity of the concept on the following bases:

1. The distinct professional philosophies and services that are culturally determined are present in each area.

2. Common characteristics of library development have been applied to each area by writers within our professional literature.

A PREVIEW OF A STUDY PROBLEM

Because the fundamental problems underlying world study in librarianship are library development and the advancement of the profession itself, let us consider some typical study problems relating to these concepts. For demonstration purposes, the following historical problems are seen distantly as if viewed from the wrong end of a telescope.

If an extraterrestrial spaceship had been stationed high above the region of the Tigris, Euphrates, and the Nile for the past five thousand years and its sights had been directed toward libraries, the interpreters of the data would have observed remarkable changes. Clay tablets of Mesopotamia and papyrus rolls of Egypt would have given way centuries later to parchment and paper codices and then to microforms and computer tape. The buildings that house these bibliographic records would have changed from monumental archives to modest private collections and functional public, academic, school, and special libraries. Lastly, the users of the collections would have enlarged in scope from a few priests, royalty, and scribes to masses of students, researchers, and ordinary citizens.[5]

From this series of statements expressing change, the interpreters of data would have to isolate the modifications in our professional practice, identify the forces that influenced the modifications, and hypothesize about them in terms of relationships to variables that interact with library phenomena. Finally, the interpreters of these data would, after rejecting invalid hypotheses, assemble the valid hypotheses in a meaningful way to formulate a component part of the theory of library science.

NATURE OF THE REASONING PROCESS USED IN WORLD STUDY IN LIBRARIANSHIP

Basically, searching for explanations involves sleuthing among primary and secondary sources relating to an aspect or problem of our profession. For the best possible explanation of this process, rather than consult our professional literature, we proceed to a most unlikely source, the apartment at 221 Baker Street in London. Within its large "airy sitting-room, cheerfully furnished, and illuminated by two broad windows,"[6] the famous John H. Watson, M.D. heard an explanation of the deductive reasoning process as utilized in "The Study in Scarlet" by the even more famous Sherlock Holmes. He stated:

"I have already explained to you what is out of the common is usually a guide rather than a hindrance. In solving a problem of this sort, the grand thing is to be able to reason backwards. That is a very useful accomplishment, and a very easy one, but people do not practice it much. In the everyday affairs of life it is more useful to reason forwards, and so the other comes to be neglected. There are fifty who can reason synthetically for one who can reason analytically."

"I confess," said I, "That I do not quite follow you."

"I hardly expected that you would. Let me see if I can make it clearer. Most people, if you describe a train of events to them, will tell you what the

"In solving a problem of this sort, the grand thing is to be able to reason backwards," said Sherlock Holmes to Dr. Watson.

result would be. They can put those events together in their minds, and argue from them that something will come to pass. There are few people, however, who, if you tell them a result, would be able to evolve from their own inner consciousness what the steps are which led up to that result. This power is what I mean when I talk of reasoning backwards, or analytically."

"I understand," said [Watson].[7]

Because of the strong similarities of the reasoning process of both activities—crime detection and world study in librarianship—Holmes's comments are equally applicable to both fields. If we were to substitute within the theory of crime detection the term "graphic records" for the indispensable "clues" of sleuthing, then the analogy would become even stronger. In short, a researcher in world librarianship is a social science detective who investigates events related to the development of librarianship throughout the world.

SUGGESTIONS FOR WORLD STUDY IN LIBRARIANSHIP

In order to deepen one's understanding of world librarianship, it is suggested that each of its aspects be analyzed, whenever possible, in accordance with seven elements:

1. Nature of the Aspects
2. Purposes
3. Origin
4. Categories
5. Variables
6. Development
7. Demise

To illustrate this study technique, let us consider the aspects of libraries in terms of seven questions as illustrated in Table 3.2.

When a researcher has answered the questions above and has related them to

Table 3.2 Analyzing an Aspect of Librarianship

Question	Type
1. What is a library?	Nature
2. Why is it established?	Purpose(s)
3. Which element(s) initiate a library?	Origin
4. Which types of the aspect are evident?	Categories
5. Which forces influence its development?	Variable(s)
6. Which phases does a library experience?	Development
7. What ends a library's existence?	Demise

explain the phenomenon under investigation, we can say that the researcher has formulated a theory. The eminent researcher, writer, and library educator, Dr. Jesse Shera, expressed his theory of library development in the following terms:

> The library is a product of cultural maturation. It came into being when societies ceased to be nomadic and became urbanized, and when graphic records became important to the effective operation of organized human relationships. There is no record of when, or how, libraries began, but one can assume, from the scattered and fragmentary evidence that has survived, that early libraries were essentially archival-storage places for the preservation of records that were necessary for the transaction of business or commerce, the administration of the state, and the communication of belief to succeeding generations.[8]

When a researcher's explanations transcend the "what" and "why" of hypothesizing and begin to *predict* the occurrence of a phenomenon, as Shera's did, we have theory. If the researcher goes beyond prediction to stating information that will allow us to control phenomena, then we have law.

FORMULATING TENTATIVE THEORIES

A major objective of world study in librarianship is the formulation of a descriptive and analytical statement regarding all nine geographical areas of our profession throughout the world. Much of the material for these statements will emanate from the reading of *World Librarianship*; however, additional data will be found in the relevant literature of librarianship, especially where the data in this book may be lacking, incomplete, or outdated. Such searching through the current literature is necessary because data regarding world librarianship shift as regularly as activity within a giant aquarium. Because the profession is dynamic and changing, relevant data will reflect the shifts in professional activity.

This study will include, wherever possible, answers to the questions posed previously regarding the nature, purpose, origin, categories, variables, development, and demise of the aspect of bibliographic control, the questions read as follows:

1. What is bibliographic control?
2. Why is it established?
3. Which elements give rise to bibliographic control?
4. Which types of attempts at bibliographic control exist?
5. Which forces influence its development?
6. Which phases does bibliographic control experience?
7. What terminates bibliographic control?

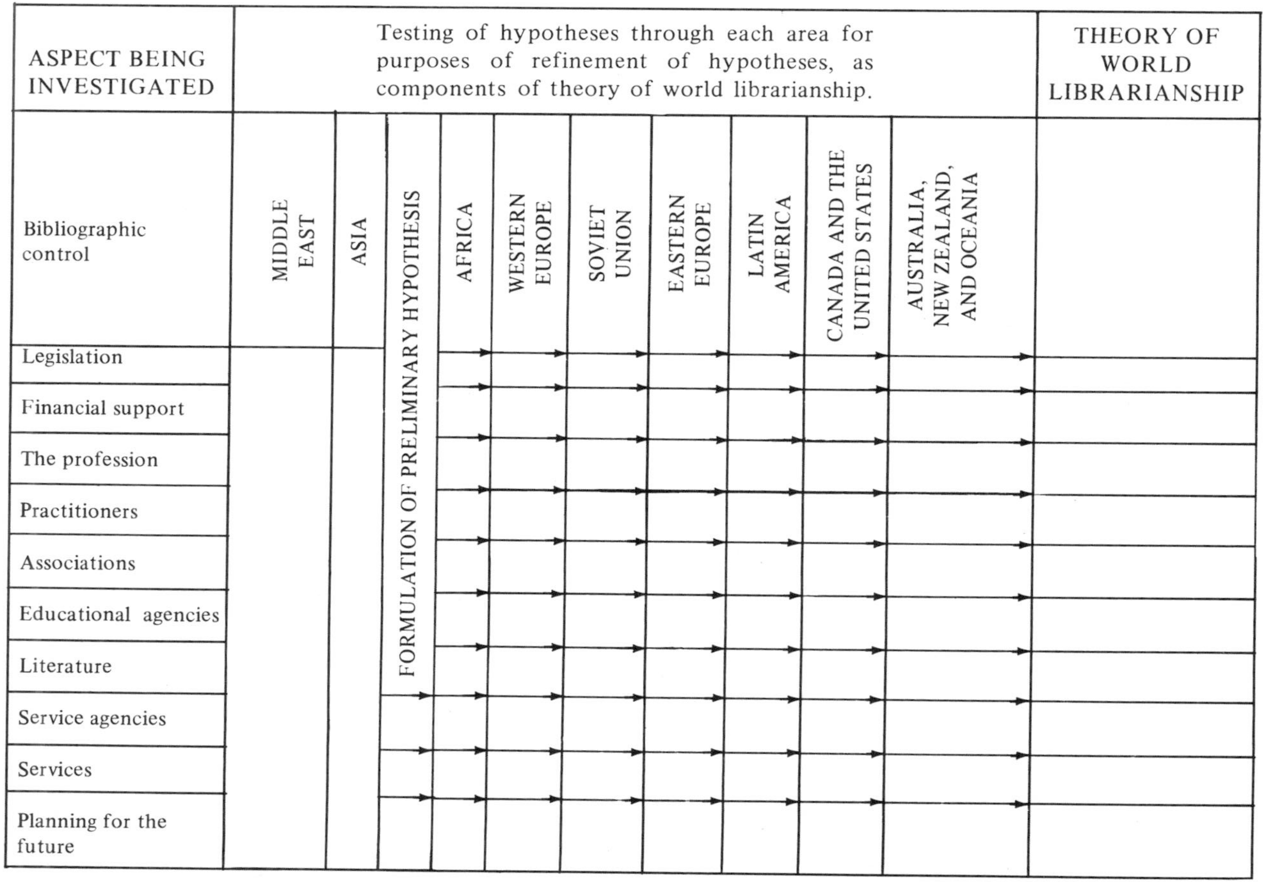

THEORY OF WORLD LIBRARIANSHIP

Testing of hypotheses through each area for purposes of refinement of hypotheses, as components of theory of world librarianship.

ASPECT BEING INVESTIGATED	MIDDLE EAST	ASIA	FORMULATION OF PRELIMINARY HYPOTHESIS	AFRICA	WESTERN EUROPE	SOVIET UNION	EASTERN EUROPE	LATIN AMERICA	CANADA AND THE UNITED STATES	AUSTRALIA, NEW ZEALAND, AND OCEANIA	THEORY OF WORLD LIBRARIANSHIP
Bibliographic control											
Legislation											
Financial support											
The profession											
Practitioners											
Associations											
Educational agencies											
Literature											
Service agencies											
Services											
Planning for the future											

Figure 3.1 Model for theory formulation for world librarianship.

The procedure for formulation of hypotheses that may become components of a theory of world librarianship is illustrated by Figure 3.1.

INITIATION OF OUR TOUR

Having explored the concepts of world librarianship, world study in librarianship, the geography of world librarianship, and the potential they hold for the future development of knowledge within our field, we proceed to Chapter 4 entitled "The Historical Bases of World Librarianship." We begin with a look at the library history of the Middle East. We start there because scholars preoccupied with the beginnings of civilization are generally agreed that the Mesopotamian Valley, located in the country today called Iraq, is where civilization—as well as writing and graphic records—first arose. That region of the world has long been known as "the cradle of civilization." On the basis of today's knowledge, Mesopotamia also deserves to be called "the cradle of librarianship."

NOTES

1. Thomas Landau, ed., *Encyclopedia of Librarianship*, 3rd ed. (New York: Hafner, 1966), pp. 248-249.
2. Jean Key Gates, *Introduction to Librarianship* (New York: McGraw-Hill, 1968), p. 133.
3. Leonard Montague Harrod, *The Librarians' Glossary of Terms Used in Librarianship and the Book Crafts* (London: Andre Deutsch, 1959), p. 387.
4. American Library Association, Editorial Committee, Subcommittee on Library Terminology, *A.L.A. Glossary of Library Terms* (Chicago: American Library Association, 1943), p. 82.
5. Richard Krzys, "Library Historiography," *Encyclopedia of Library and Information Science*, Vol. 15, A. Kent, H. Lancour, and J.E. Daily, eds. (New York: Marcel Dekker, 1975), p. 294.
6. Sir Arthur Conan Doyle, *A Sherlock Holmes Reader* (New York: Berkeley Publishing Corp. 1975), p. 4.
7. Ibid., p. 92.
8. Jesse H. Shera, *The Foundations of Education for Librarianship* (New York: Becker and Hayes, 1972), p. 103.

THE STUDY

4

The Historical Bases of World Librarianship

Richard Krzys, Gaston Litton,
and Area Research Associates

A PRELIMINARY OVERVIEW

It is since man became literate that we are concerned in world librarianship. Our study begins properly after man had started to record his thoughts, actions, aspirations, and ideals, and when he had decided to organize his graphic records for referral and dissemination, as he understood those activities at that time.

By roughly 3000 B.C. the documentation of man's existence became of increasing importance to him, and as he collected it, its volume increased in size and importance. Thus ancient man found it necessary to create archives alongside his temples of worship and in the palaces of kings, their contents being religious first, and governmental thereafter. Later, the contents and work of the archives began to be shared with a related agency, the library, the division between the two being at first unclear and even today overlapping and confusing.

Man's first writing materials were made from commodities that were found in abundance in a region—papyrus in the Nile Valley and clay in the Mesopotamian Valley. These materials were often so perishable that, except for clay tablets, few specimens are extant. Then, around A.D. 100, when China made its unique contribution to man's cultural development, in the invention of paper, man was also ready first in the Orient and centuries later in the West with the technology to print from movable type. This happy combination not only faciliated documentation and communication, representing a quantum leap for man on the road to cultural development, but it was also an overpowering force which changed the form, contents, and service previously performed by libraries.

By the nineteenth century these agencies the world over began to reveal characteristics easily identifiable and amenable to study, serene judgment, and constructive comparison.

Comparative librarianship had become a worldwide possibility. In our time, instantaneous international communication, and equally remarkable transportation have made world study in librarianship a necessity, as man moves through librarianship and other institutions toward a One World.

The Prehistoric Period

Anthropologists are generally inclined to believe that man has been on this planet for approximately 1.3 million years.[1] For more than 99 percent of that time he made very little progress toward the advances in communication essential to the development of libraries and librarianship; however, one such essential advance was reached when man began to gesture, and greater progress was made when he began to speak. Around 30,000 B.C. cave paintings appeared in Europe, created by prehistoric men called Cro-Magnon.[2] Why they produced these paintings is a question that has absorbed scores of prehistorians in fascinating arguments ever since the discoveries in Altamira, Spain in 1879[3] and similar finds decades later in Dordogne and Lascaux, France.

Man's Creation of Graphic Records

Based on the theory that anthropologists have laboriously pieced together, it appears that cave paintings had a kind of magical significance; once drawn by the shaman artists, the animals depicted were thought to be destined to be killed during the cavemen's hunts. As the millenia advanced, man slowly decreased his absolute dependence on hunting by learning to grow crops and domesticate animals. This progress achieved, man pushed ahead to another significant advance; he began to live communally.

Antiquity

Along with the advantages that communal living brought—government, commerce, and formal education—arose a need for some method to record ideas, so that they might endure with some degree of permanence. And after many phases of development writing emerged.

The separate developments of writing that arose in Mesopotamia and Egypt probably started as mnemonic devices; for example, a series of lines incised on a bone could have represented the number of animals that a Sumerian or Egyptian farmer owned. This proto writing served much the same purpose as tieing a string around one's finger might be used today as a reminder to do something.

The first stage of writing in every major civilization, including the Mesopotamian and Egyptian, was pictographic, the use of drawings of objects to represent the objects themselves.[4]

MIDDLE EASTERN LIBRARIANSHIP: ITS BACKGROUND, EMERGENCE, AND DEVELOPMENT
Richard Krzys and Mohammed Aman

According to Jesse Shera's theory of library development, libraries arise when a people abandon nomadism for civilization and begin to need graphic records for government, commerce, and education.[5] Early convergence of these elements probably occurred in Mesopotamia; however, as Elmer Johnson stated, the exact site of the origin of library development has not yet been established, although historians favor Mesopotamia and Egypt.[6]

We know with certitude, however, that within Mesopotamia a remarkable library was developed by Ashurbanipal, king of Assyria (ca. 668-627 B.C.) in Nineveh. There he assembled a collection of over 30,000 clay tablets in the various rooms of his palace. From the evidence of these tablets many subjects were included in this collection, among which were at least the following: history, government, biography, geography, business, law, taxation, legends, mythology, religion, science, astronomy, astrology, biology, mathematics, medicine, and natural history.[7]

Owing to the official sponsorship of Ashurbanipal's library, the government-related nature of its collection, and its wide scope, we can attribute the creation of the concept of the national library to Middle Eastern librarianship of antiquity.

From an inscription on a clay tablet dating from Ashurbanipal's reign, we learn furthermore that the Assyrian monarch had a high regard for libraries:

> Palace of Sardanapalus,* King of the world, King of Assyria, to whom the God Nebo and the Goddess Ourmit have given ears to hear and eyes to see what is the foundation of government. They have revealed to the kings, my predecessors, this cuneiform writing. The manifestation of the God Nebo, . . . of the God of the intellect.—I have written it upon clay tablets, I have placed it in the midst of my palace for the instruction of my subjects.[8]

Egypt

Since the fourth millenium B.C. when books of papyrus were produced in quantities large enough to form collections, libraries in Egypt have had a continuous history to the present day.

*Sardanapalus was the Greek name for Ashurbanipal.

Commenting on them, Johnson stated:

Although we have reliable evidence that libraries did exist in ancient Egypt, the archeological evidence for specific collections is much scarcer than in Babylonia. Instead of the thousands of tablets found in the Mesopotamian ruins, we have only fragments of texts, tomb illustrations, and inscriptions from walls and monuments to rely on for the history of Egyptian libraries. There is, for example, evidence that Khufu (Cheops), a monarch of the Fourth Dynasty (ca. 2600 B.C.), had a "House of Writings," and this practice continued under his successors.[9]

The most famous ancient library in Egypt was the Alexandrian Library, actually a Greek library of the empire of Alexander the Great who reigned approximately from 336 to 323 B.C. The Alexandrian Library had as its purpose amassing an exhaustive collection of ancient writings from all over the known world.

Arab-Islamic Libraries

By the sixth century B.C., Babylon was destroyed by the Persians. Centuries later the Middle East was overrun, conquered, and occupied first by the Greeks and then by the Romans. Following the disintegration of the Roman Empire in the fifth century A.D., various regions of the Middle East emerged as autonomous nations and empires; for example, the Byzantine Empire claimed a vast area of land and, through its capital of Constantinople (Istanbul), maintained sovereignty over the area for a millennium.

Roaming the desert were thousands of Bedouin nomads who pledged allegiance to no leader until the seventh century A.D., when the Prophet Mohammed, through his teachings that subsequently constituted the Koran, spiritually united the Arabs into the nation of Islam. After the Prophet's death in A.D. 632, driven by their religious faith and the belief that creating an Islamic Empire was carrying out a divine plan, the Arabs gained control of most of the Middle East. By the eighth century they amassed a vast empire extending from India to northern Africa and almost the entire Iberian Peninsula; however, throughout the period of Arab occupation a succession of invaders—the Seljuk Turks, the European Crusaders, and the Mongols from Asia—made the Arab domination less than absolute.

Despite these incursions, the Arabs were able to develop a high state of culture and create a number of outstanding libraries. Islamic libraries in the Middle Ages thrived in the main centers of Arab learning, for example, Cairo, Mecca, Medina, Kufa, Damascus, Basra, and Baghdad. As Alfred Hessel suggested, the cultural confrontations that the Islamic Empire experienced generated a stimulating climate for the development of libraries.

The great rise of literary and scientific activity in the Islamic world set in toward the end of the eighth century. It was promoted by the manufacture of paper, introduced at that time from the Far East, which provided a cheap material for the production of books. The libraries of the Eastern Roman Empire seem to have been used as models in building. Thus we hear that Harun-al-Raschid founded a library in Baghdad and received manuscripts from Byzantium and elsewhere as tribute. His son Mamun (d. 883) was an even more ardent collector. He is credited with having investigated the scholarly enterprise of translating the masterpieces of Greek and Oriental literature into Arabic. In addition to Baghdad, there were libraries at Kufa and Basra; in fact, before long all the larger mosques, as well as the universities established throughout the caliphate, acquired their own book collections.[10]

The glorious days of the Arab Empire were threatened when the Mongols invaded Islam in the thirteenth century. Halagu Khan, the grandson of Genghis Khan, captured Baghdad, burning and destroying all books in its libraries. Then, and for centuries afterward, Cairo stood alone as the center of the preservation and dissemination of Islamic culture.

By the seventeenth century, the Islamic Empire was conquered by another Muslim people, the Ottoman Turks. Eventually the Ottoman Empire declined to the extent that European statesmen referred to it as the "Sick Man" of Europe and Asia. After World War I the Middle East became nothing more than a group of European colonies, and Middle Eastern library development was influenced accordingly by the Turkish, French, and British colonizers.

Especially noticeable was the colonizers' influence in Egyptian libraries where foreign books, the majority in English and French, were introduced. Through their domination of Egypt, the cultures of various nations significantly influenced the Egyptian library scene.

Unfortunately the French and British domination also had adverse effects, especially from exploitation. Rather than information agencies designed in accordance with local needs, the libraries created by the colonial powers generally took the form of reading rooms for the use of expatriates. After World War II the European powers deserted the Middle East, leaving behind problems of health, welfare, and education that were worse than they had inherited from the Ottoman Empire.

Today the Middle East has experienced a rebirth because of the discovery of vast oil reserves. Through them millions of dollars are brought daily into the Arab economies. Especially favored have been Saudi Arabia and Kuwait which because of their newly acquired wealth and progressive governments have been converted since World War II from patches of sand in the desert to sparkling oases. Judging from the progress in their national and academic library development, the Arab countries of the Middle East may witness once more a renaissance of Islamic libraries and cultural centers reminiscent of the era of Harun-al-Raschid.

ASIAN LIBRARIANSHIP: ITS BACKGROUND, EMERGENCE, AND DEVELOPMENT
Hedwig Anuar

Libraries in Asia were among the earliest in the world, with surviving collections representing a wide variety of writing materials such as bone, bamboo, palm-leaf, gold, wood, stone, bronze, pottery, and silk. These ancient libraries, archival or religious in character, included repositories of official government records as well as temple and monastery libraries containing collections of palm-leaf manuscripts of Buddhist and later of Hindu and Muslim scriptures, and found in Sri Lanka, India, Burma, China, Korea, and Japan as well as in Thailand, Nepal, and other Asian countries. These temple libraries were also seats of learning and developed as university libraries.

Private libraries were gradually developed, first by royalty and then by government officials and nobles, some of whom opened their libraries to the public. These early libraries which served ruling or religious elites gradually fell into neglect and decay as empires, kingdoms, and princedoms fell, although some of their collections have survived up to the present.

The next impetus to the development of libraries in Asia was the advent of Western exploration and discovery from the fifteenth century, followed by colonialism in various indirect and direct forms, and the gradual development of modern economic and political systems. Administrators, missionaries, educationalists, and scientists set up new libraries, usually patterned after libraries in their own countries, and sometimes paralleling their library development.

Research libraries and museums of learned societies, such as those which began in Europe from the seventeenth century, were also founded in French Indochina, in the Netherlands East Indies, and in British India and the eastern colonies. One of the oldest was the library of the Royal Batavian Society of Culture and Sciences (Koninklijk Genootschap van Kunsten en Wetenschappen) established in 1778, and now the Perpustakaan Museum Pusat (Central Museum Library) in Jakarta, Indonesia. The Royal Asiatic Society of Great Britain and Ireland was founded in 1823, and developed a number of branches in Asia, including those of Ceylon (1845), Shanghai or North China (1857), Malaysia (1877), and Korea (1900). Other learned societies founded in the early twentieth century were the Siam Society (1904) and the Burma Research Society (1910).

Proprietary and subscription libraries, which were the predecessors of public libraries in Asia, were formed during the late eighteenth and the nineteenth centuries, which also saw the beginnings of modern university library development. Some of the early libraries of learned societies as well as subscription libraries later formed the nucleus of national libraries. However, the greatest impetus to the development of public and national libraries was the transformation of the colonial territories into newly independent nations after World War II.

Special libraries, apart from those of research societies mentioned earlier, developed mainly during the nineteenth and early twentieth centuries, attached to government ministries and research institutes, particularly those concerned with agriculture, health, and the exploitation of natural resources. One of the most famous is the Bibliotheca Bogoriensis founded in 1842 as the library for the Botanical Gardens in Bogor, Indonesia. More recently, special libraries have also been developed in support of industrial research as well as economic and social planning services.

Before World War II, education in Asia was generally confined to an elite group and the movement towards universal primary education was a response to the political demands arising from postwar independence. It is therefore hardly surprising that school libraries have been and still are the most neglected and weakest of all types of libraries in the Asian continent.

While this bird's-eye view of the history of Asian libraries is of general application, it must be borne in mind that the periods of library history vary from country to country, stretching over centuries in some countries, while starting in the twentieth century for others. An outline of the library history of some of the major countries of the region is given as an example of the immense antiquity and complexity of their patterns of library development.

"Libraries in China, as in Greece, were first organized as official archives, followed by the establishment of centralized libraries by the government and private collections. The earliest known Chinese documents surviving today are those written or incised on animal bones and tortoise shells, which formed part of the royal archives in the latter part of the Shang Dynasty 1765?-1123? B.C.)."[11] The establishment of royal archives and state archives during the Chou dynasty (1122?-256 B.C.) was followed by the growth of writings by individual authors and the development of private libraries by government officials and nobles. A unified empire under the emperor Shih Huang Ti (Chin dynasty, 221-207 B.C.) saw the destruction of books, with certain exceptions, in 206 B.C. Books and libraries began to develop again during the Han dynasty (206 B.C. - A.D. 220), aided by the invention of paper around A.D. 100. Block printing began in the seventh century during the Tang dynasty (618-907) when literature and libraries flourished, and continued to do so during the Sung dynasty (960-1279) which succeeded it. After the Mongol conquest and establishment of the Yuan dynasty (1260-1368), the Ming dynasty (1368-1644) was a period of further establishment and development of imperial and private libraries. The long Chi'ing dynasty (1644-1912) founded by the Manchus saw the founding of the Capital or National Library in 1909 and marked the beginnings of modern library development in China.

In India, the earliest libraries were collections of manuscripts of birchbark and palm-leaves and were associated with temples, monasteries, and places of learning, such as those of Nalanda and Taxila. Buddhism was established in the fifth century B.C. and famous Buddhist libraries attracted scholars and pilgrims from other parts of India as well as from Sri Lanka, Burma, and China. For example, Fa-Hsien, a Chinese traveller in the fourth century A.D., stayed three years learning Sanskrit and copying the texts in Pataliputra, in Central India. Other travellers were Huen-Tsang who journeyed in India between A.D. 629 and 642 and I-Tsing who came to India about A.D. 672 and stayed in Nalanda for ten years.[12] Many royal and private libraries were developed during the medieval period, while the Mughal empire also saw the development of great Muslim libraries set up in palaces and mosques. An Imperial Library was created by Babur in Delhi, while a separate department for libraries was set up during the reign of Akbar (1556-1605).[13] Western influence began from the time of the later Mughals. Early libraries were started by the Jesuits in Agra and Delhi. "The English Company in Madras started a library as early as 1662. The Society for Promotion of Christian Knowledge sent out a circulating library to Calcutta . . . in 1709."[14] Public libraries gradually developed in the provincial capitals, while Baroda State pioneered public library provision on a statewide basis in 1906. The foundations of India's National Library were laid in 1903 by the amalgamation of the Calcutta Public Library (founded 1836) and the Imperial Library (founded 1891).

The great cultural and literary influences of China and India are clearly reflected in the history of libraries of their neighboring countries. In Sri Lanka, the earliest Buddhist inscriptions date from the third century B.C. and by the first century B.C., Buddhist texts and their commentaries were written by monks. Early temple libraries flourished in Sri Lanka and were visited by Fa-Hsien and others. Libraries continued to be developed under successive Sinhala rulers, apart from periods of invasion and of destruction of books, such as that by the Kalingas in the thirteenth century A.D. and by the Portuguese in the sixteenth century. Literary activity declined up to the seventeenth century but revived in the eighteenth century. In the nineteenth century, missionary activity and the founding of societies and institutions led to the establishment of research and subscription libraries and to the beginnings of modern library development.[15]

In Burma, the earliest libraries date from the eleventh century A.D. As in Sri Lanka, these were libraries of Buddhist manuscripts on palm-leaf or bamboo, and places such as Pagan developed into seats of Buddhist learning. Buddhist monasteries also developed village schools which were well-established in the precolonial era. The Burmese literacy rate in the late eighteenth century has been estimated to be higher than that at the time in the United States and Western Europe.[16] In 1795, the Royal Library was estimated to be "the largest royal collection between the Danube and the borders of China."[17] British rule was gradually extended over the whole of Burma between 1826 and 1886. The

Bernard Free Library, the first public library in Burma, was established in 1883 by Charles Bernard, the Chief Commissioner of British Burma, and became a nucleus of the National Library, established in 1952. Burmese libraries were almost totally destroyed during World War II, when Burma was overrun, first by the Japanese and then by the returning Allied forces. The development of libraries since independence has been assisted by literacy campaigns and the promotion of indigenous publishing.[18]

Chinese influence is a feature of the development of libraries in Korea and Japan. Korea has a very long library history, since the first Korean library described dates back to the period 195-57? B.C. - A.D. 313. The first important royal library was established in A.D. 682, while the tenth century saw the creation of a national policy for the promotion of books and libraries. Papermaking and printing techniques, first introduced from China in the fifth century A.D., reached their height in the thirteenth century, which also saw the perfection of the Korean alphabet. These developments led to the further expansion of libraries in the fifteenth and sixteenth centuries, including libraries for the common people, a remarkable and uncommon feature in the history of Asian libraries. Western influence began at the turn of the nineteenth century. Modernization of the Korean library system was retarded by Japanese rule from 1910 to 1945, military occupation and the division of Korea into North and South between 1945 and 1948, followed by the Korean War from 1950 to 1953. A dynamic resurgence of libraries in South Korea has taken place since then, beginning with the reorganization of the Korean Library Association in 1955 and the passing of a Library Law in 1963.[19]

The earliest libraries in Japan date from the early seventh century A.D. and were temple or archival libraries. Private libraries of nobles gradually developed during the Heian Period (A.D. 794-1185) when the capital was moved from Nara to Kyoto (then called Heian). Although printed materials on Buddhism and Confucianism had been known from China directly or via Korea for a long time, the printing process became popular in Japan only from the eleventh century. The first feudal period of the Shogunate established in 1185 saw the further development of Buddhist libraries, while the Tokugawa Shogunate of the second feudal period from 1603 marked the setting up of libraries by scholars and rich merchants as well. Gradually, from the mid-eighteenth to the mid-nineteenth centuries, these private libraries were opened to the public, but usually on payment of high fees.

Free library services impressed the educationalist, Yukichi Fukuzawa, when he visited national and public libraries in the United States and Europe in 1860 and 1863, respectively. The Meiji Restoration of 1867 began the abolition of the feudal system and class distinctions. In 1872, the Shojakukan, later the Imperial Library, was established, becoming the first modern library in Japan open to the public. Local governments began to establish prefectural libraries and the Japan Library Association was founded in 1892. A number of important special libraries, such as that of the Toyo Bunko (1917), were also founded in the earlier decades of the twentieth century before World War II. The postwar reconstruction of libraries was assisted by American library advisers and consultants. The National Diet Library was set up in 1948, closely modelled on the Library of Congress, and absorbing both the Imperial Library and the Toyo Bunko. A Library Law (for public libraries) was enacted in 1950 in Japan. Because of the country's vast economic and industrial development since World War II, libraries and documentation services in the fields of science and technology have experienced extensive growth during the last three decades.[20]

AFRICAN LIBRARIANSHIP: ITS BACKGROUND, EMERGENCE, AND DEVELOPMENT
Harry Kibirige

Undoubtedly, in ancient times Africa was one of the leading centers of civilization with much larger libraries than in Europe. This fact is not surprising when one realizes that archeological discoveries by Dr. Louis Leakey have revealed positive evidence that the earliest man may have originated in Africa.[21] More archeological studies of Africa might unveil even more surprises for the archeologist and librarian alike. Although the Middle Ages were not as flourishing for Africa as the ancient times, several parts of the continent had literary civilizations, and private collections must have existed. For instance, Ethiopia had a script in the pre-Christian era. According to Rita Pankhurst, an ancient literary tradition has thus continued without interruption to the present day although the languages and the alphabets have changed.[22] It is now well known that literary African empires flourished in West Africa during this period. The Mali Empire which covered much of West Africa in the fourteenth century used the Arab script. During this period, Timbuctu became a renowned center of scholarship with a famous university at Sankore. According to Felix Dubois, "Poetry and works of imagination were not lacking, nor compositions of a kind peculiar to Arabian literature; such as the Hariri and the Hamadani. . . . The historical and geographical works of Morocco, Tunis and Egypt were well known in Timbuctu . . . and the pure sciences were represented by books on astronomy and medicine. In short, the libraries of Timbuctu may be said to have included almost the whole of Arabian literature."[23]

Along the East African coast, Arab influence resulted in the emergence of successful medieval commercial cities like Mombasa, Kilwa, and Malindi. Robert Munn suggested that these cities were likely to have had libraries.[24] Similarly, Wilfred Plumbe concluded that "It is likely, in fact, that libraries were established whenever the tide of Islam surged."[25] Medieval Egypt continued this literary tradition uninterrupted to the present day.

Modern times were ushered in by the nineteenth century industrialization of Western Europe and America. The African continent lagged behind as the world was overtaken by new technologies. For instance, while Egyptian libraries continued to grow, their rates of growth were much slower than European and later North American collections. As regards the rest of Africa, the advent of Europeans in the fifteenth century spelled four centuries of doom manifest in slavery, slave trade, and slave wars. It would be most unrealistic to expect centers of learning and libraries to have continued under such circumstances. When colonization replaced slave trade, scanty libraries were established, usually to satisfy the interests of the colonial staff from the metropolitan powers. The few international surveys which were made did not seem to favor services for the indigenous populations. For instance, in 1928-1929, the Carnegie Corporation of New York sponsored such a survey on libraries in the Union of South Africa, Rhodesia, and Kenya Colony. In its final report on Kenya, it recommended inter alia thus: "While natives are, no doubt, making appreciable progress toward civilization, it will be many years before they require a considerable amount of library service. The problem, therefore, is how to bring books to a small number of white persons—and to a somewhat lesser degree to a large group of Indians who are scattered very widely over a wide sweep of country."[26]

Another feature which characterized colonial, especially public, libraries was the need for subscriptions. Commenting on the Kenya libraries, John Strickland intimated that charging an annual subscription of 35 shillings (approximately $5.00) kept the membership predominently European.[27] This pattern was common in most of Colonial Africa, and Wilfred Plumbe's study mentions several subscription libraries.[28]

With regard to academic libraries, colonial Africa had few colleges until a few years prior to independence. After World War II, the European powers realized that they could not hold on to their colonies for much longer. Colleges were thus established to educate natives who might take over the administrative responsibilities. Thus, university colleges sprouted in several British colonies. Those in Achimoto (Ghana), Ibadan (Nigeria), and Makerere (Uganda) were all founded in 1948. The former Belgian Congo (now Zaire) had the Université Lovanium established in Leopoldville (now Kinshasa) in 1954,[29] only six years before independence. These colleges started with small university collections which have gradually developed into large libraries.

Most of the library systems in Africa today are results of postindependence efforts. Admittedly, many of them had their foundations laid a few years before independence, but where accelerated growth has been attained, it has been more manifest in the postcolonial era.

WESTERN EUROPEAN LIBRARIANSHIP: ITS BACKGROUND, EMERGENCE, AND DEVELOPMENT*

Jean-Pierre Clavel

Librarianship is a profession which developed only after certain of its supporting elements had come into being. The printed word gave the impetus to modern

*This section was written without references.

librarianship; it was printing which brought about the abundance of libraries in the first place, then caused the publication of bibliographies, the formulation of classification schemes, the codification of cataloging rules, and other requisites for the provision of library service.

In Western Europe, libraries have passed through successive stages of development. Monastery libraries, which had existed centuries before the invention of printing, were joined in the sixteenth century by more numerous and greatly expanded university libraries. The Enlightenment saw the creation of a large number of public libraries, which subsequently benefitted greatly from the French Revolution; these libraries increased greatly in number during the nineteenth and twentieth centuries. This same period also saw the appearance of the first special libraries and the formation of the first book collections in schools. Thus, in Western Europe, from the outset a symbiotic relationship existed between the printed word and libraries.

Another evidence of this parallel development was the appearance of bibliographies. It would seem that the first of such works was that of J. Tritheim (1462-1516), *Liber de Scriptoribus Ecclesiasticis* (Basel, 1494). However, the first bibliography of importance was that of Conrad Gesner, *Bibliotheca Universalis* (Zurich, 1545). The increasingly greater output of the printing press forced scholars to compile bibliographies of an even more specialized nature. At the apex of this pyramid are the national bibliographies, the larger number of which have been produced since the nineteenth century.

The sixteenth century also saw the appearance in Western Europe of the first scholar librarians, such as G. Budé (1467-1540), royal librarian to Francis I. He and others of his period were actually scholars who presided over libraries rather than librarians in the modern sense of the word. Others who followed them defined and created foundations of the profession, men such as Gabriel Naudé (1600-1653), the author of *Avis pour Dresser une Bibliothèque*. In this work, published in 1627, Naudé proposed the basic principle that libraries should be open to all. Gottfried Leibniz (1646-1716) advanced Naudé's work by formulating the following tenets of librarianship: (1) libraries should contain all of the original ideas written by the human species; (2) they should operate under an annual budget reviewed at regular intervals to cover increasing expenses; (3) each library should have a catalog with entries arranged by author, year of publication, and subject matter; (4) libraries should be open to the public and offer all that is necessary, such as heating, lighting, seating arrangements, and fixed hours of opening, for the convenience and comfort of users.

The first library to put these principles into practice was founded at the University at Göttingen, in 1735. Johann Gesner, who directed this institution from 1736 to 1761, was followed by J. D. Rouss who lived until 1837. These librarians devised a system by which books were arranged on the shelves by their accession number. This system was adopted throughout the greater part of the continent of Europe during the nineteenth century.

The considerable increase in library holdings at the turn of the twentieth century induced many librarians to replace this arrangement by accession to another based on the book's subject, a system introduced by booksellers for ease of selection. This system became quite common in Europe following World War I, when libraries also abandoned the publishing of book catalogs in favor of card catalogs. Today only a few national libraries continue to issue their catalogs in printed form.

The current trend among the university libraries of Western Europe is to place parts of their holdings on shelves open to the public. They employ generally either the Universal Decimal Classification (UDC) or a classification scheme of their own design. German librarians are in the throes of developing a classification system, which its creators hope may be useful on a wider basis, but their project has not yet been concluded.

In the development of cataloging, English librarians were the first to codify rules for the practice. This event occurred in 1841, when Anthony Panizzi edited his *Ninety-one Rules* for use at the British Museum. Forty years were to pass, however, before other European countries were also to codify their cataloging rules. The librarians mainly responsible for this were Karl Dziatzko in Germany in 1886 and Léopold Delisle in France in 1889, whose joint efforts led to the publication of the *Preussische Instruktionen*, a first edition appearing in 1889 which was republished in 1906. These rules became used widely in Europe during the first half of the twentieth century.

The necessity for cataloging rules, intensified by the increased quantity of printed material to be described bibliographically, led to the offering of courses for the training of professional librarians. In 1879, an examination was held in France which certified librarians. Great Britain followed with courses given in 1885. Germany created in 1886 the first chair in librarianship, which was filled by Dziatzko in Göttingen University.

As libraries expanded and their holdings became more numerous, the technical problems involving the organization of materials became more complex. Librarians were obliged to broaden their knowledge. Following the offering of professional training courses, library associations were established. Their meetings provided a forum for ideas and experience, which when recorded were disseminated through professional journals.

These library associations began in Great Britain, whose association founded in 1877, was followed by that of Switzerland (1898), Germany (1900), and France (1906). The appearance of professional journals often preceded the formation of library associations, as will be seen in the following list of bulletins with the year of their founding: *Serapeum* (Anzeiger für Literatur der Bibliothekswissenschaft), also in Germany, which began publication in 1840; *Zentralblatt für Bibliothekswesen*, since 1884 in Switzerland; *Revista delle Bibliotheche*, in Italy since 1888; *Revue des Bibliothèques*, published in France since 1891; the *Library Association Record* of England, from 1899; and the *Nordisk Tidskrift für bol-och Bibliotheksväsen*, published in Sweden since 1914.

It should perhaps be noted that all of the efforts related above were undertaken at the national level. Some of these have had an effect on librarianship at the international level, such as the Göttingen system, but such influence resulted from local success. Not until the second half of the twentieth century did a true Western European librarianship emerge, recognizable by its ability to resolve problems on a continental level, or at least for Western Europe. Without doubt, the International Federation of Library Associations (IFLA) was created with a view to addressing such problems; certainly IFLA's establishment was purely a European movement. Upon attaining worldwide scope during the sixties, IFLA has endeavored to address global concerns. This broadening of interest has not only led to a greater participation in its activities by librarians from various places throughout the world, but it has also revealed that the global solutions advocated by IFLA were not necessarily the best answers to European library problems. With regard to libraries, the continent of Europe enjoys a very special position, having a great number of libraries which for four centuries or more have been developing important collections, even though their losses from war have been great. At the present time more than 300 libraries in Western Europe possess a million or more books each. In spite of Europe's numerous political divisions and the multiplicity of national languages which weakens any concerned effort, there has been a steady development of librarianship which may be termed distinctly Western European.

This situation has led some Western European librarians to the inevitable conclusion that unified action on a continental scale has become necessary, particularly of a kind that is directed towards uniting libraries belonging to the same class. This awareness resulted in the creation of the League of European Research Libraries (LIBER), an association of 180 large Western European libraries whose aim is to record their experiences and arrive at solutions to common problems, devising different efforts to improve reader services. For practical purposes LIBER limits its activities to the libraries of Western Europe, maintaining contact with the Council for Cultural Cooperation. Among the first problems to be studied by LIBER was the acquisition of publications from the countries of the "Third World," staff exchanges, securing and making available doctoral dissertations, and computerized library networks. Undoubtedly, LIBER will contribute to the development of Western European library policy within the framework of the World Science Information System (UNISIST).

The need to formulate specific library policies for Western Europe was felt in the 1970s when a few of its national libraries began to publish their national bibliographies by computers. The adoption of the MARC II by the British Library, followed by attempts of French and German libraries to adapt this system to their own needs, based especially on the work done at the Bibliothèque Universitaire de Grenoble, and called "Mise en Ordinateur de Notices Catalographiques de Livres" (MONOCLE), have fostered studies envisaging an operational format appropriate for Western Europe. This format was defined by a team of librarians and computer experts drawn from the following institutions: the Bibliothèque Nationale de Paris, the Bibliothèque Royale de Bruxelles, the Bibliothèque Universitaire de Grenoble, the Bibliothèque Cantonale et Universitaire de Lausanne, the Bibliothèque Universitaire d'Utrecht, and the Council of the British National Bibliography in London. After publishing the format INTERMARC in February 1974, the team developed a manual for serial publications INTERMARC[S]). Subsequently, other Western European national libraries have become interested in this enterprise, notably the Deutsche Bibliothek of Frankfort, as well as the Bibliotheca Nazionale of Florence, the Biblioteca Nacional of Madrid, the Royal Library in Copenhagen (Denmark), and the National Bibliography of the Netherlands.

In order to achieve the standardization of bibliographic procedures necessary for the computerized exchange of bibliographic information on the continent, it will be necessary to face realistically the various difficulties which prevent full cooperation among Western European libraries. As previously mentioned, these difficulties include the differences in political structures, the variety of national languages, and, not least, the absence of a central governmental authority. While these obstacles are difficult to overcome, the success of INTERMARC should stimulate the cooperation of Western European librarians who in the years to come must select those problems which should be resolved for their entire continent despite national, cultural, and linguistic differences. As far as the methods themselves are concerned, we know that such an agreement is feasible.

Though the overall situation is encouraging, an important consideration is the establishment by Western Europe of library relations with the socialist countries of Eastern Europe. It may be assumed that agreements will eventually be reached among those countries, probably first with nations having library traditions and resources that are similar to those of the Western European countries.

The librarians of the socialist countries have maintained contacts with each other since 1964, which were fostered not by any agreement among the librarians themselves but from a decision of the cultural ministers of the Council for Mutual Economic Assistance (COMECON). These meetings, while devoted originally to various topics unrelated to librarianship, have dealt more recently with library related problems.

The Organization for Economic Cooperation and Development (OECD) set up a commission which deals with a subject of interest to librarians involved in a larger perspective, the flow of scientific information. The beginnings of OECD have been similar to those of COMECON, in that they did not originate with the librarians themselves but sprang from the milieu of economic technocracy. It is thus in the field of economic studies that problems of scientific information are being examined, such as ways of reducing costs and promoting economic goals. Obviously, the interests and methodology of economists and librarians are dissimilar. Western European librarians are not as yet agreed on a major goal;

consequently, commissions which have been created recently pursue different objectives. The OECD commission could avail itself of the assistance of library experts for advice on certain problems; however, the commission is concerned only with library problems within the framework of the general policy regarding scientific information. Its recommendations may eventually have a beneficial effect on the profession if the governments which are members of the OECD could assure enforcement of certain measures affecting publications and data banks. IFLA and LIBER have never been able to secure agreement for the passage of resolutions concerning work methods of libraries. Now, perhaps, through the intermediary of UNESCO or the Council of Europe, IFLA and LIBER may be able to ensure the adoption of measures that will modify cultural policy, accelerate the diffusion of scientific information, and solve practical problems plaguing the profession in Western Europe.

It is not for us to pass judgment on the merits of these various movements; it seems, however, that for individual libraries and librarians, LIBER as an association permits the fullest participation in projects of common interest. On the other hand, the formulation of a global policy in librarianship is obviously much more difficult.

In another area—the application of the International Standard Book Number (ISBN)—an agreement among European libraries should be sought. Great Britain and Germany now lead in this field; the Nordic countries, the economic union of Belgium, the Netherlands, and Luxembourg (Benelux), France, and Switzerland follow behind at some distance, with the Latin Countries of Western Europe in the rear.

Differences within librarianship between the countries of Western Europe can be observed, for example, in their approaches to library education, the development of facilities for reading, and the comparative wealth of university collections.

One of the gravest problems facing librarians in Western Europe is that of a proposed tax on reading which societies for the protection of authors' rights are attempting to have introduced into the legislation of various countries. For each book lent by any library, those organizations seek the payment of a tax (presumably very modest, at the outset) to be made to the treasury of the authors' society. Rightfully, librarians regard the introduction of this tax with grave misgivings as a formidable deterrent to reading and the use of libraries.

SOVIET LIBRARIANSHIP: ITS BACKGROUND, EMERGENCE, AND DEVELOPMENT*
B.P. Kanevsky

The first book repositories in the area of the present Soviet Union appeared as early as the fourth and fifth centuries in the monasteries of Georgia and Armenia.

*Because the references provided by Mr. Kanevsky are in the Russian language, and are unavailable to the large majority of Western readers, except for Note 30, we have deleted all other references from this text.

In ancient Russia a written language appeared in the seventh century, prior to the country's acceptance of Christianity at the end of the ninth century. Then the foundation of the modern Russian alphabet emerged from the Glagolithic and Cyrillic alphabets. By the eleventh century literacy was rather widespread, and the embryo of the country's bibliography appeared.

The oldest extant writings in Russia date back to the eleventh century, when in 1037 Yaroslav the Wise established the first library in ancient Russia. By the twelfth century other libraries appeared in monasteries and churches in Novgorod, Chernigov, and Vladimir, located in what is today the south-central European part of the USSR.

The fifteenth to seventeenth centuries were notable for the growth of book repositories, private collections, and libraries belonging to the czars, church authorities, and various state institutions. In Moscow a number of monasteries developed rich collections of manuscripts that were mostly religious literature.

The earliest known Russian incunabulum was *The Book of the Apostles* printed by I. Fyodorov in Moscow in 1564. Ten years later Fyodorov printed in Lvov (formerly in Poland) the first secular textbook, a primer for teaching the alphabet. During the sixteenth century Russia published approximately fifty books, and during the seventeenth century almost seven hundred; these were largely religious works and a few textbooks.

In the seventeenth and eighteenth centuries absolutism became firmly established in Russia, and elements of capitalism emerged in the country's economy. Political, economic, social, and cultural problems that had become imminent by the end of the seventeenth century found their expression in the activities of Peter I (1672-1725), known as Peter the Great, who promoted the development of Russian culture and science, and established contacts with countries of Western Europe.

Educational, cultural, and library-related events that occurred during the reign of Peter the Great were numerous; many secular schools were established, the first Russian printed newspaper was issued in 1702, and a simpler typeface was introduced in 1708. Peter contributed to library development by founding in St. Petersburg in 1714 a large book collection which later became the core of the Library of the Academy of Sciences (now the Library of the Academy of Sciences of Leningrad), and finally the Academy of Sciences was created in 1724.

Various contributions to learning and bibliography were made by the polyhistorian, Mikhail V. Lomonosov, who lived from 1711 to 1765. His original research in linguistics, literature, and the physical sciences paralleled the work of Lomonosov's contemporaries in Europe, including the French chemist, Antoine Lavoisier. In 1755 Lomonosov founded the University of Moscow and established its library.

The imperial public library in St. Petersburg (now the Saltykov-Shchedrin State Public Library of Leningrad), was established in 1795 and opened to the public in 1814. In the late eighteenth century the first publicly supported libraries appeared in Russia. During the eighteenth century approximately 10,000 books were published. Between 1813 and 1821, V. S. Sopikov published his *Experience of Russian Bibliography*, a five-volume work.

The nineteenth century was characterized by social ferment in Russia. Political reaction against Czarist rule began in 1848, and by 1861 the serfdom was abolished. Although the country's economy and culture began to develop more rapidly, government oppression of the people contributed to increasing social conflict. By the turn of the century the struggle against czarist rule was led by the Russian working class and their political party, the Bolsheviks, with Vladimir Lenin (1870-1924) as their leader.

The late nineteenth and early twentieth centuries witnessed the accelerated development of librarianship in Russia, as evidenced by the establishment of public libraries in many towns. Particular mention should be made of the opening in Moscow in 1862 of the library of the Rumyantsev Museum, now the Lenin State Library. The growth and expansion of public and other types of libraries stimulated theoretical work of a number of Russian library science writers, including V. I. Sobolshchikov, N. A. Rubakin, and L. G. Khavkina, as well as the activities of the Russian bibliographers, V. I. Mezhov, G. I. Gennadi, and many others.

During the early twentieth century considerable acceleration of library activity, evidenced by the stirrings of professionalism, took place; for example, the Society of Library Science was formed in 1908, the professional journal, *Bibliotekar*, was published between 1910 and 1915, library courses were given in Moscow in 1913, and the *Knizhnaya Letopis'* (Book Chronicle) appeared in 1907.

Despite the best intentions of Russia's progressive forces to improve library service, such efforts were at first greatly thwarted by the grim social reality that was present in czarist Russia. At the turn of the century, it is estimated that 60 percent of its women in the 9 to 49 age group could neither read nor write. The social conditions varied throughout the country, and of course, from region to region. To mention an extreme example, in present-day Tajikistan illiteracy amounted to 98 percent, in Kirghizia it stood at 97 percent, and in Uzbekistan at 96 percent. More than forty nationalities had no written language of their own. By 1914, the country had a population of 160,000,000 with 76,000 libraries of which 60,000 were merely small collections located in parish schools. Only a limited number of readers was able to use the few large scientific libraries. Vast territories of the national outlying areas had no library service. In 1914, in the three previously mentioned republics of Central Asia and Turkmenia, not one public library existed, and in the territory of present-day Georgia, Azerbaijan, Lithuania, Moldavia, and Armenia, there were but a few.

In 1914 Lenin condemned barbarous measures imposed by the czarist government against libraries. He wrote with particular wrath that "rules which are a hundred times more restrictive are being issued against the public libraries!"[30]

The condition of libraries in czarist Russia was seriously affected by the economic dislocation of World War I, four years of foreign intervention and the subsequent civil war that ended in 1922.

When comparing the development of libraries in the Soviet Union with that of other countries, the reader should bear in mind the legacy that had come from czarist Russia. After the Great October Socialist Revolution of 1917, more commonly known in English-speaking countries as the Russian Revolution, the Soviets received a scanty heritage and had to start library construction anew throughout the greater part of the country with mainly the enthusiasm and support of the local people. Immediately after the revolution, Lenin issued directives intended to transform Soviet society through such measures as the eradication of illiteracy. To achieve such measures, all the major means of book production and dissemination were nationalized; for example, printing shops, paper factories, book storehouses, and shops were placed under government control. To assist in the development of libraries, Lenin issued a decree which envisaged the establishment of a common system, accessibility of all libraries, and a balanced book of collection.

In 1922 the Soviet republics of Russia, the Ukraine, Byelorussia, and others formed the Union of Soviet Socialist Republics. The ensuing years, until the country's entry into World War II in 1941, was a period of considerable progress in library development, marked by the following major events: (1) holding the first library congress of the RSFSR in 1924, (2) launching the journal *Bibliotekar* (Librarian) in the same year, (3) the reorganization of the library of the Moscow Rumyantsev Museum into the Lenin State Library of the USSR in 1925, (4) the Central Committee of the All-Union Communist Party (Bolshevik) issued its directive, "On the Improvement of Library Work," on October 30, 1929, (5) the first library school was established in Moscow in 1930, (6) the Decision of the Central Executive Committee of the USSR entitled, "On Librarianship in the USSR," was issued on March 27, 1934, (7) the All-Union library census was conducted also in 1934, (8) the All-Union conference on theoretical questions of librarianship and bibliography was held in 1936, and (9) the Decision of the ACP(B) Central Committee, "On Literary Criticism and Bibliography," was issued in 1940.

The late 1920s and the 1930s saw a rapid increase in the number of public libraries and the growth of their book stocks; also, the number of scientific libraries increased, and a network of technical libraries was established. By 1941, the USSR had 227,000 libraries of all kinds with a book stock exceeding 520 million items, whereas the readership had reached the 55 million mark. Particularly noteworthy were the achievements in librarianship in the Union Republics of Central Asia, Transcaucasus, the Ukraine, Byelorussia, the rural areas of Siberia, the Far East, and the Far North.

By that period, the following distinguishing features of librarianship in the socialist society had already emerged: (1) a profound concern for the satisfaction of user needs of all people, (2) the fastest possible cultural development of the formerly backward peoples and regions, (3) adherence to the established Party line, especially on the active use of libraries in the solutions of national problems, (4) the assistance rendered by libraries to the advanced part of the society—the Communist Party—in the socialist reconstruction of economy, technology, and culture, and (5) the molding of an advanced communist conscience among the masses of working people.

On June 22, 1941, Nazi Germany attacked the Soviet Union. This attack marked the entry on the side of the Allies of the Soviets into World War II, which ended in 1945 with the victory of the Allied powers, Great Britain, the United States, the Soviet Union, France, and China, with the Soviet Union playing a decisive role.

Hitler's invasion of the Soviet Union caused the country's people tremendous human suffering and material destruction. Libraries were either destroyed or badly damaged. The Nazis destroyed and plundered 43,000 public, 82,000 school, 334 high school and other libraries, including large scientific libraries in Kiev, Minsk, Odessa, and other cities. During that period Soviet librarians subordinated their entire labor to the fulfillment of the national aim of defending the country and destroying the aggressors. They conducted information-bibliographic work to aid the armed forces and the defense industry, and disseminated military-patriotic literature and publications about the joint struggle of the Allied forces against Hitler's Germany.

After the victory by the Allied forces and the defeat of Germany, Japan, and Italy, the Soviet Union began the massive work of rehabilitation and further development of the country's economy and culture. A great effort was made to restore the libraries damaged during the war. By 1951, the number of public libraries in the USSR surpassed the pre-World War II figure by 12 percent. The 1950s and the 1960s saw rapid development in the entire system of library service, especially in the development and expansion of the network of state public libraries. Within the period from 1953 to 1963, in an effort to create libraries needed in formerly backward republics and in rural areas, 32,000 state rural libraries were established in the USSR.

A noteworthy event in the postwar history of Soviet libraries was the directive of the CPSU Central Committee entitled, "On the State of Librarianship in the Country and Measures to Improve It," dated September 1959. This document envisaged large-scale construction of new libraries with new furniture, equipment, and books, the creation of standards for library equipment, and the training of increasing numbers of qualified librarians to extend library service. During the period from 1959 to 1974, these goals were on the whole fulfilled: the Soviet Union erected new buildings and designated space within new blocks for 50,000 additional libraries, including a number of large libraries. In summary, the 1959 decision of the CPSU Central Committee has been very effective in the development of Soviet libraries in the 1960s and the early 1970s: the supply of libraries with collections, reproduction facilities, and adequate furniture improved; redistribution of duplicates was effected; bibliographic work had expanded; and libraries had made better use of audiovisual materials. The training of qualified librarians at special higher and secondary educational establishments also expanded accordingly.

EUROPEAN SOCIALIST LIBRARIANSHIP: ITS BACKGROUND, EMERGENCE, AND DEVELOPMENT*

M. B. Nabatova

Library development in the socialist countries of Europe may be traced back at least to the seventh and eighth centuries when monastic libraries appeared in Germany. By the end of the first millennium libraries were also to be found in Czechia, the earliest belonging to the Prague episcopate. The second library, founded in 993, was located at the Benedictine Monastery in Brevnov, near Prague. In Hungary and Poland the first monastic libraries appeared in the late ninth century. The oldest Polish collection, that of the Capitulum in Gnezno, was founded in the eleventh century, and soon afterwards others were established in Plotsk and Cracow. In Bulgaria libraries appeared in the tenth century, at the czar's court and at several of the large churches and monasteries. In Rumania, in the Walachia and Moldavia principalities, libraries were created in monasteries. The largest of these were located in Transylvania in the towns of Brasov and Blagé.

The fourteenth century witnessed the foundation of a number of large universities in Europe and the creation of secular collections at the universities of Karlovy, in Prague in 1348, at Jagiello, in Cracow in 1364, and at a number of German universities.

Following the invention of a form of printing by use of interchangeable blocks by the Chinese in the eleventh century, Johann Gutenberg "reinvented" the process in Mainz, Germany in approximately 1455. Printing from movable type greatly simplified the printing of books in quantity and considerably expanded library holdings; consequently, during the first two centuries of printing in Europe, large private book collections were formed. Among these was the library belonging to the Hungarian King Mathias Corwin, known as "the Corviniana," one of the most celebrated private libraries of Europe. It once possessed hundreds of codices, in Greek and Latin, of which 168 have survived. One of the largest German scientific libraries, belonging to the court of Kurfürst Friedrich Wilhelm, was founded in 1659. The valuable collections of the representatives of the Polish gentry of the families of Radzivillow and Sapego, as well as the Library of King Sigismund I, in Wilno, also date back to this period.

---

*References provided by M. B. Nabatova have been deleted because they are to sources unavailable to the large majority of Western readers.

The first public library in Eastern Europe originated in Prague as early as the fifteenth century. During the eighteenth and early nineteenth centuries, the first libraries belonging to readers' societies appeared in Czechoslovakia and Germany. In Poland, at the beginning of the eighteenth century, the Zalusski brothers formed their famous collection, which passed to the state in 1771.

Large private libraries were formed in Transylvania, now called Rumania, in the eighteenth century. One such collection belonged to the governor of Transylvania, Bruckental, who accumulated books in many languages, including seventy-six incunabula and numerous rare manuscripts. This collection was located in Sibiu.

During the late eighteenth and early nineteenth centuries, the development of Czech science was promoted by the formation of numerous private libraries and by other collections belonging to various scientific, cultural, and educational societies. Czech readers' societies, which appeared in the 1830s and 1840s, loaned books not only to the members of the societies, but also to the local population as well. These libraries played an important role in the development of culture in the area. In the beginning of the nineteenth century, public libraries came into being in Czechia, and by the end of that century many cities and towns were proud possessors of readers' societies libraries. At first, these libraries were created on the initiative of cultural and educational societies, but, beginning in the 1890s, they were sponsored by city authorities. The first people's libraries were founded in Germany in the 1850s. In Poland public libraries were organized in the late 1800s. In Rumania during the same period, a number of small lending libraries were created. The first public reading room in Serbia was established in Belgrade in 1846. In the mid-nineteenth century similar facilities were opened in all of the large cities of Serbia, Croatia, Macedonia, and other parts of Yugoslavia.

City libraries were opened in Szeged in 1883, Prague in 1891, and Budapest in 1904. During the nineteenth century, cultural and educational institutions known as "reading houses" appeared in Bulgaria. While the main function of these organizations was to supply people with reading materials, there were also lectures and meetings of hobby groups, such as amateur theatricals, painting, folk singing, etc., as well as children's musical appreciation programs.

University and research collections, as well as public libraries, were organized in a number of Eastern European countries during the nineteenth century. The library of the University of Warsaw was opened in 1817. Others of this period included the libraries of the University of Bucharest, Jassy, Cluj, and universities centered in other cities in Rumania. In 1802, the private library of F. Szechenyi was acquired by the state of Hungary, and in later years it became the nucleus of the National Library.

During the latter part of the nineteenth century, in connection with the appearance of the first workers' organizations and the socialist-democratic parties, trade union libraries were set up in some of the countries of Eastern

Europe. The first of such libraries began functioning in Belgrade in 1895; by 1903, twenty-five such collections existed in Bulgaria. At the beginning of the twentieth century the first library legislation was enacted between 1898 and 1932, but it was largely without force. The total number of village libraries was about 2000, and their total holdings amounted to about 500,000 volumes, which averaged only about 1 book for each 24 inhabitants. Library users constituted only about 0.6 percent of the rural population.

In the years preceding World War II, networks of public libraries, national libraries, and large scientific collections functioned in Bulgaria, Hungary, Germany, Poland, Rumania, and Czechoslovakia; however, because financial support was insufficient, with the exception of Czechoslovakia, library service could not be extended to the entire population of these countries. Library use was complicated by the high illiteracy rate in some areas. During World War II, libraries suffered considerable damage. Afterwards, librarianship in the European socialist countries received support from the Communist and Workers' parties and government bodies. The resurgence of librarianship in the first years of the postwar period took place in conditions of tense struggle, and much was done in restoration and in the democratization of libraries and librarianship.

The Brno Congress of Czech and Slovakian libraries in 1948 was the first of many meetings at which representatives of all types of libraries participated. This congress denounced the indifferent attitude of some librarians to politics, and proclaimed the socialist program of library development in that country. During the 1950s similar meetings were held in all of the European socialist countries. This period was characterized by the rapid development of public library networks and the mass publication of books at moderate prices, two developments of the 1950s that continue to the present time.

LATIN AMERICAN LIBRARIANSHIP: ITS BACKGROUND, EMERGENCE, AND DEVELOPMENT
Gaston Litton and Richard Krzys

When Christopher Columbus landed in the New World on October 12, 1492, he first touched the Bahamas, probably on the island that is today called San Salvador. Believing that he had reached the Indies, Columbus called the inhabitants Indians. Anthropologists have theorized that these first Americans came to the New World from Asia via a land bridge that has long since disappeared but once connected what are now Siberia and Alaska. During their centuries-long migration to the tip of South America, the descendants of these Asiatic people evolved into the various tribes and nations of North American Indians as well as the indigenous people of Latin America, the Olmecs, Mayas, Aztecs, Toltecs, Chibchas, Quechuas, Incas, Araucanians, and other Indian nations.

Whether libraries existed among these indigenous people of pre-Columbian

America has been a topic of fascinating speculation among historians; for example, three Guatemalan librarians have collaborated to provide the following statement:

> Little is known about libraries during pre-Columbian times. Since few documents have been found and studied, there is so far no evidence of any organized collection even though the Mayan civilization had been one of the extraordinary ones of the world. The documents called *Codex* that have been found have been studied from the historical point of view, but not as part of any possible collection.[31]

This affirmation is in contrast with a comment by Rosa Zamora concerning pre-Columbian Mexico. Zamora makes an essential point concerning the indigenous population of Mexico which has a distinct bearing on librarianship in this area:

> Mexico's most ancient roots are Indian. In Meso-America, that is, the central and southern part including Yucatan plus what is now Guatemala, Belize, Honduras, El Salvador, Nicaragua, and Costa Rica, there were once highly developed cultures. . . . The acme of the Olmec Civilization took place at the beginning of our era; they developed a figurative writing and a calendar, highly valuable cultural elements that were used as patterns by the other Mesoamerican groups. The Mesoamerican cultures left a wealth of written material. In architectural monuments, sculptures, and paintings there are frequently inscriptions and numerical symbols, but there is still more valuable material: they wrote books that we now call *codices*. Only a few of these have been preserved, some of them in foreign museums. Unfortunately, the various modalities of writing used by the cultures of Mesoamerica have not been deciphered yet; consequently, there are large gaps in our knowledge of the pre-Columbian groups.[32]

As all students of Latin America are aware, and as Zamora recalls to mind in her area study, the natural development of the various Indian cultures was interrupted forever by the arrival of the Spanish conquerors who brought war, always a devastating influence on cultural affairs, and the evangelizing action of priests who strove to erase older cultures in order to introduce Christianity.

Lest this last comment appear to be an unfair judgment and condemnation of the really remarkable accomplishments of the various evangelizing religious orders in Colonial America, we reproduce the following clarifying statement by Zamora: "The same priests studied the American cultures and languages in trying to understand the Indian world they were evangelizing and they have left a great number of works that still are basic consulting texts for anyone interested in the American past."[33]

Zamora affirms that in Mexico libraries existed in the pre-Columbian period:

> Manuel Cruzado, based on Clavijero and Torquemada, tells us that upon their arrival in this country, the Spaniards found large collections of hieroglyphs

that narrated the artistic, scientific, religious, and war experiences of its inhabitants, as well as their travelling and the prosperity and magnificence of pre-Columbian Mexico. These collections were true libraries in which a large number of people were entrusted to copy, keep up, and arrange the manuscripts on amate paper or in strips of venison hide ten meters long or more, which were rolled or folded accordion-wise, putting a wood cover at each end so that they resembled books.[34]

Does this not recall the days of librarianship in medieval Europe before the secret of paper manufacture had travelled the long distance from China to Baghdad, and onward to Western Europe?

Zamora, reporting on these so-called pre-Columbian "libraries," disputed by others as being highly exaggerated or wholly imaginative, informs us that "the main collections were located at Texcoco and Tenochtitlan, and were kept in temples in the custody of priests. After the Spanish conquest these pre-Columbian 'libraries or archives' were lost, and although there are a few data left, we can assume that Mexicans understood at that time the usefulness and the need to preserve those manuscripts."[35]

The Roots of Latin American Librarianship

Zamora notes that "the colonial period yielded brilliant fruits in the fields of history, literature, architecture, and art."[36] This authority also notes the appearance of a non-European ingredient of its own, nourished in sources other than the basic Spanish.

Fortifying the foundation of a genuine Latin American culture were the appearance soon after colonization of printing, higher education, and libraries in various cities within colonial Latin America; for example, the basis for the rapid cultural development of colonial Mexico was laid at an early date. According to Zamora: "The first press (1539) and the first university (1563) in America were established in New Spain. Consequently, it is logical that the first library on this continent was also established in this country (1534)."[37]

Juan Iguíniz, one of Mexico's most productive and distinguished bibliographers, has written that colonial libraries were generally "religious institutions" with philosophy, theology, and related subjects predominating; but he notes that "during colonial times many private and educational monastic libraries thrived."[38]

The Pattern of Colonial Librarianship

Various book collections were developed in the convents and monasteries of Latin America during the colonial period for use in the missionary and educational activities of the Church; consequently, a pattern affecting the collections and personnel evolved. Because the users of libraries were mainly clergymen, the book collections that they assembled consisted predominantly of theological and philosophical writings. Usually the superior of a religious order assigned one member to act as custodian for the collection and to supervise its consultation. All libraries were merely reading rooms, and books were generally not circulated. As time passed, a younger member of the order was instructed in the simple functions and routines of the library. And thus it went, throughout three centuries of colonial rule, with the responsibility of the monastery library passing from monk to novice. When a monk was needed for other more pressing functions, a novice was trained to take over, and thus the pattern of colonial religious libraries was perpetuated.

In contrast to the near silence maintained within the monastery walls, civil disorder erupted in the streets in various regions in colonial Latin America; for example, during the early part of the colonial period, according to María Teresa Sanz, "the only concern of Chile was war. There were neither books nor schools, and there was such a shortage of paper that the poet Ercilla had to write many stanzas of his Chilean epic, *La Araucana*, on strips of leather."[39] Sanz notes that the most important libraries were those of the religious communities. At the time of the expulsion of the Jesuits in 1767, they possessed some 20,000 volumes which were distributed among their establishments in Chile. Sanz points out that "the majority of them were not, as one would believe, exclusively ecclesiastical books, but rather there were a great many dealing with science, philosophy, law, history and literature."[40]

During the eighteenth century private libraries were established by wealthy individuals in the Spanish, Portuguese, and French colonies; consequently, the character of book collections changed by the addition of secular works. Some of these private libraries resembled somewhat early public libraries in the British colonies of America that were later to form the United States; however, there was no movement within colonial Latin America to establish libraries comparable to those of New England.

Under the rule of Charles III of Spain, who reigned from 1759 to 1788, and Joseph of Portugal, who reigned from 1750 to 1777, various liberal reforms were instituted, for example, commerce among Spain and Portugal and their colonies began to develop. Despite these reforms, many individuals in Latin America believed that the liberal reforms of the enlightened monarchs did not go far enough; consequently, considerable unrest took place in the Latin American colonies. Wherever disorders occurred, they deterred the continuity of library development.

An interesting development in the face of civil disorder occurred in Argentina. Many of Argentina's founding fathers, as Josefa Sabor points out, "in spite of the exigencies of the war (of independence) and the difficulties surrounding an incipient political organization, demonstrated great interest in books and libraries.[41]

In the nineteenth century, according to Sabor, two events occurred which are of special interest in our discussion of background for Latin American librarianship. "The first was Domingo Faustino Sarmiento's activity in the development of education and libraries . . ., [and] the second was the development of bibliography."[42]

Juan Freudenthal commented on Sarmiento's role as follows:

> The Argentinian politician, pedagogue, and writer Domingo Faustino Sarmiento (1811-1888) was the first South American intellectual to fully grasp the potential of the public library as an instrument for the continuing education and self-development of the people. He was a man of strong convictions, and throughout his life he laid special stress on education, particularly while he was in charge of the Departamento de Escuelas del Estado de Buenos Aires (Department of Schools of the State of Buenos Aires) and later, as president of Argentina, 1868-1874. . . .
>
> During Sarmiento's presidency (1868-1874), Argentina became the site of some of the most innovative educational experiments in Hispanic America. He began the systematic distribution of reading materials to every corner of his country through the creation of nearly 2,000 libraries. He was convinced that no school should function without a library and that no social progress was possible without schools.
>
> Sarmiento stated as early as 1877 that: "It is not without reason that we place schools and libraries on the same footing, for the latter follow the former, and have developed simultaneously with the development of education. Thus the public library has become incorporated in the machinery and material of public education; for the first time, it forms part of the social organism, in the same way as the free and compulsory school."[43]

Toward the close of the nineteenth century, Latin America through external influences was beginning to shed its provincial outlook in favor of an awareness of its being part of a world community. When the First International agreement on the exchange of publications was held in 1886 in Brussels, Belgium—called the Brussels Convention for the International Exchange of Official Documents and Library Publications—Argentina, Brazil, and Chile were among the signatories.[44]

The Beginning of a New Era in Latin American Librarianship

From the colonial period to the wars of independence during the nineteenth century, librarianship in Latin America remained at the same phase of development, the custodial phase. No significant changes in library practice, such as attention to reader services, took place until the beginning of the twentieth century when library schools were created.

A little more than fifty years later, stimulated by various events which will be discussed shortly, a library education program of great hemispheric importance was established in 1956 in Medellín, Colombia. This was the Inter-American

Library School (Escuela Inter-Americana de Bibliotecología), a unit within the University of the state (departamento) of Antioquia. With initial financial support from the Rockefeller Foundation of New York and, in later years from the OAS, the Medellín school has been instrumental in setting standards and in the improvement of library education in other ways, generally in the hemisphere.

Meanwhile, of course, several library schools had been established in Argentina and Brazil. Single schools for the training of librarians had been created in various other countries of Latin America. The expansion of university education in the region and the creation of many professional schools, including those for library science, characterize the era immediately preceding and immediately following World War II.

The public library movement in the hemisphere received a strong stimulus from U.S. librarianship, beginning as early as 1927, with the opening in Buenos Aires of the first of what became an extensive worldwide series of binational centers, each with its up-to-date library, arranged according to the basic lines of American librarianship. Among the various features which they introduced were open stacks, liberal lending of books for home reading, a separate reference collection and at least a fundamental concept of reference service, the dictionary catalog, the Dewey Decimal Classification, and a wide variety of diverse cultural activities that promoted library use. These institutions, supported cooperatively by the United States and interested local residents, were extended eventually to each of the Latin American capitals and to many of the larger secondary cities as well.

Three larger institutions—model public libraries in the full sense of the word— were established by the American government, acting at first through the American Library Association, in three Latin American capitals. The first was opened in Mexico City (1942), the second in the Southern Hemisphere at Montevideo (1943), and soon afterwards in Central America the third at Managua, Nicaragua. The first of these libraries was named for Benjamin Franklin and the bases for its organization and operation were planned by no less important a figure in the profession than the former director of the New York Public Library, Harry M. Lydenberg. The Montevideo library was named for the presidents of Uruguay and the United States and was known as the Biblioteca Artigas-Washington, while the third installation honored Nicaragua's great poet, Rubén Darío.

The dedication of the Biblioteca Benjamin Franklin was considered so auspicious an occasion that the president of Mexico, Manuel Ávila Camacho, made the principal address, in which he stated:

> Because of its high purpose, its modern technical organization, the desire for intellectual relationship that inspired its founders—and even because of the illustrious name which it bears, in memory of one of the most celebrated personages of the New World—the library we are inaugurating today is a most valuable testimony of the friendship which links the people of Mexico and the United States.[45]

Until the binational centers and three American libraries made their appearance in Latin America, the prevailing concept of a library in the minds of many in the region was that resembling a medieval cloister, where a bibliophile or scholar or two worked in relative privacy over books and manuscripts which had been brought to them by an attendant who watched over the collection and kept out the curious.

Public libraries, long arrested in their development in Latin America by the custodial philosophy of librarianship, received further stimulus through the UNESCO-sponsored Conference on the Development of Public Library Service in Latin America, held in São Paulo, Brazil, in 1951. A direct result of that conference was the creation in 1954 of the Biblioteca Pública Piloto de Medellín (the Pilot Public Library of Medellín), a project sponsored in cooperation with the Colombian government.[46] This institution was the counterpart for the Western Hemisphere of a similar agency established in 1951 for the Eastern Hemisphere, in New Delhi, India. In both regions the purpose of the two institutions was the same: to demonstrate public library service to people who had never had such service available to them. Unfortunately, for a variety of reasons, including inadequate funding, an outdated book collection, and an unfinished and poorly situated building, the Pilot Public Library of Medellin has been regrettably slow in fulfilling its expectations.

The establishment in Bogotá, Colombia, by the Bank of the Republic, of a cultural institution known as the Biblioteca Luis-Angel Arango (Luis-Angel Arango Library), is another highlight in the public library movement in Latin America. With considerable financial support and the leadership of a single-minded, no-nonsense, would-be writer and lawyer, Jaime Duarte French, this institution has had a notable impact on the public consciousness of the unique contribution that a public library can make to the cultural sensibilities and esthetic awakening of the people.

Near the close of the 1950s the Cuban Revolution, which has had a profound impact on the entire American continent, has not left libraries untouched. Carmen Rovira, one of the considerable number of librarians who have been living and working in exile from Cuba for the past two decades, since the ascendancy of communism in the island, provides the following illuminating commentary: "The library situation in Cuba, like all other aspects of Cuban life, has changed radically since 1959. Information received abroad is fragmentary and not always reliable, but a general picture can be pieced together." Rovira continues her report: "In general, the post-1959 situation can be summarized thus: the disappearance of all privately-supported libraries whose contributions had been one of the main factors in Cuban library development; centralized state control of library services at all levels; increased coverage of geographical regions distant from the capital and of population sectors seldom reached before; decline of the influence of U.S. library techniques and methods, and greater dependence on East European sources, especially in information services."[47]

An appraisal of librarianship in individual countries could not be made. An especially lamentable omission is Brazil where numerous outstanding libraries exist and imaginative information services have become commonplace. The appearance of Brazilians on the international library scene came after World War II, with Rubens Borba de Moraes, who has since been followed by other outstanding Brazilian practitioners.

In addition, two significant steps were taken by some countries of the region to participate in pioneering efforts toward achieving bibliographic control. The first of these projects involved Latin American participation in the Machine Readable Cataloging project of the Library of Congress (MARC) and the cataloging data base of the Ohio College Library Center, in Columbus (OCLC). The second of these projects attempted to apply International Standard Bibliographical Description (ISBD) to Latin American national bibliographies.

THE UNITED STATES AND CANADA
H. C. Campbell and Gaston Litton

It seems highly improbable that any, except perhaps a very few librarians and library historians, attach any significance to the year 1876 in the development of North American librarianship. Yet, certain events occurred in that year which, as we shall see, had a far-reaching significance in the subsequent library progress of the two countries.

Following the founding of the earliest U.S. and Canadian settlements, nearly 200 years were to pass before there was much contact or communication between libraries and librarians of the New World. In this long period before 1876 certain elements were lacking which were necessary to unity, cohesion, direction, and singleness of purpose. The many isolated and unrelated happenings in librarianship on the American continent prior to 1876 do not, in themselves, appear especially impressive or distinctive. There is, in the reading about them, a certain monotony; it is a rather flavorless experience, which gives little or no hint that a period of greatness awaited Canadian and U.S. libraries in the post-1876 decades.

The Europeans who crossed the perilous North Atlantic in the seventeenth century to settle in the New World, to begin their life anew in a primitive, inhospitable wilderness, deserved better than they found.[48] As the inheritors of a European civilization that had developed a rich heritage of books and libraries, the cultural poverty of the New World during the first decades must have been almost overpowering for some of the colonists. Not all of those who were colonists of England and France in North America were literate by any means, but many among them were, and a select few deserve to be adjudged as belonging to the company of scholars. Who would rise to deny such a distinction to William Byrd, Increase and Cotton Mather, or Thomas Jefferson?

A few colonists brought with them their personal books when they came to

America. In time they acquired additional books from their distant fatherland, establishing the flow of knowledge to America with which they were identified forever thereafter. Eventually enterprising printers set up presses in the English and French colonies and were soon issuing books in small editions in the two languages. Personal libraries, while neither large in size nor especially numerous during the early part of the colonial period, were even more indispensable to their owners in America than they would have been in the Old World. Having left behind in Europe a rich, ancient culture and various cultural institutions, the creation of a personal library became as necessary to the lives of some of the colonists as shelter from the inclement weather and protection from hostile Indians were to all.

At an early date in this colonial experience modest libraries were also formed in the various institutions created in the New World wilderness by the religious orders, the government, the military, and even by fur traders. In each of these categories there were men of education who had been sent out by their countries to explore on the new continent, evangelize the Indians, set up a government for the protection of the new inhabitants, or to open trading posts and engage in commerce. These men not only collected and read books; they also contributed to the formation of libraries in institutions of learning and elsewhere.

Volumes bearing the ex libris of the library of the Jesuit mission in Canada, dating from 1632, are still in existence, as are also titles from the Jesuit College in Quebec, 1635, which is often cited as the first college library in North America. The battle that the colonists were waging in a vast, hostile wilderness was slowly won; it was also a victory for culture. By 1760, in New France, the number of books equalled the number of inhabitants—approximately 60,000.[49]

Such was the zeal for their books, that the British colonists in North America supported laws which were intended to dissuade any who might attempt to disperse collections that had been so laboriously formed. The practice of making private donations of books to institutions for public use began at an early date, and notable examples of generosity are found in the annals of Canadian and U.S. librarianship.[50]

It is at this point in the colonial library history of North America that one of the most interesting personalities of all times makes his brief, but decisive appearance, as a promoter of libraries. The life of this remarkable man was associated with many and varied activities—writing and publishing, statecraft and diplomacy, science and technology, invention and business. In all of these fields he made significant contributions. The library historian records with particular gratitude the contribution that young Benjamin Franklin made to the cause of reading when he founded a subscription library in Philadelphia in 1731. The subscribers to this library venture paid dues which entitled them to borrow books free of charge. The funds collected were used to buy books. The success of this enterprise, originated by Franklin and a few friends, led to the creation of other similar libraries elsewhere.

An innovation in the financial support of public library service was registered in the colony of Pennsylvania in 1742, with the chartering of a public subscription library which also pioneered in the printing of its catalog. Subscription-type public libraries appeared thereafter in various places. After the Revolution, when a national government had been established and there was tranquility once more in the land, new incentives appeared which resulted in the opening of libraries in the growing towns. There was experimentation too with various types of financing and organization, and the library annals of the period register not only examples of the aforementioned subscription libraries but also others which went by the name of "mercantile libraries," or were collections belonging to "mechanics institutes" or similar institutions.

Following the Constitutional Act of 1791, which created Upper and Lower Canada, the need for libraries to support the new legislatures resulted in provisions for the extension of library service to remote and hitherto isolated settlements in Canada. Official libraries were also established in the new states of the Union, an example of which was that of Massachusetts which was created in 1826.[51]

The private initiative which extended public library service to many communities was accompanied by a burgeoning of readers of all ages, who lent their moral support and enthusiasm to librarians eager to please and anxious to innovate. The result was the creation of a variety of types of library service designed to satisfy the increasing public demand for reading material and information.

Exploration of the West, the establishment of rail connections linking the Atlantic with the Pacific in both countries, and the growth of big cities following the American Civil War, are some of the factors which made for the rapid extension of library service in the two countries.

In this context let us cite several significant dates. To Montreal belongs the credit for being the first Canadian city to have a true public library, which dates from 1796; second place is usually given to the sister city of Niagara, Ontario, which first offered public library service in 1800. Boston, recipient of many accolades as a center of cultural activities, is generally accepted as being the first U.S. city to have a major public library; this agency opened its doors to readers in 1854. Little wonder that the Boston Public Library should become a leader in the field, since its destinies during the formative years were guided by two early library leaders—Charles Coffin Jewett and Justin Winsor. Many other notable librarians in the more recent period have also devoted their best talents to making this public library a notable example of librarianship in North America.

Many other U.S. and Canadian cities were soon to have public libraries. We will cite but three: Cincinnati, long considered "the intellectual center of the American West," opened its public library in 1856. Chicago, hub of U.S. and Canadian rail service when trains provided the principal means of massive and rapid transportation, rose to prominence as the nation's second city; a library was, of course, a pressing necessity and it was opened in 1873, with William Frederick Poole as librarian, who was also to make a notable contribution to the indexing of periodicals, as we shall see.[52] Chicago shared honors with a growing community in southern California, Los Angeles, which opened its public library also in 1873, beginning a national leadership in library service which continues to this day.

Not wishing to burden our brief survey with more names and dates, perhaps it will suffice to affirm simply that librarians of Canada and the United States had by now assumed an increasingly visible place in the promotion of libraries and in the development of the profession. Librarians began working with government officials, scholars, humanitarians and educators, and wealthy discriminating collectors who in the past had been the principal promoters of library service.

We now come to the chronological point in our essay when it is proper to comment on the library events of 1876.[53] While it is true that many innovations in librarianship were made in rapid succession in the post-1876 period, especially after 1900, the events we are now to describe were a prologue, as it were, to all that was to come in later years. The events of 1876, to which we now refer, were the following:

1. The 1876 U.S. Centennial year saw the founding of the American Library Association (ALA), which gave librarians of the United States and Canada a forum through which their varied library interests could be promoted. The founding of the ALA occurred at the end of a conference of librarians which was held on October 4-6, 1876, in Philadelphia. Justin Winsor was elected president of the new association with Melvil Dewey, now to make a grand entry on the world library scene, as the ALA's first secretary, a post he held for fourteen years, until his election to the presidency. ALA proved important for many reasons, but it is especially gratifying to report that this association has served for more than seventy years as the professional home to both Canadian and U.S. librarians. In 1946, with the steady growth of libraries in the two countries, and the number and variety of library positions in North America, Canadians satisfied their need for a national library organization of their own. During this long and uniquely close relationship of Canadian and U.S. librarians, professionals of the two countries worked together on many committees and divisions at the headquarters' office, as well as on the ALA council. The association held meetings in a number of Canada's most beautiful cities, which in itself constitutes an early and continuous contribution to international and comparative librarianship, twin subjects with which we are concerned in this study.

2. The Centennial year also marked the appearance of the first library periodical for the two countries, *American Library Journal*, which owes its existence to R. R. Bowker, founder of a publishing firm which has been especially attentive to the library profession for more than a century, and to a group of librarians of the day, which included Melvil Dewey, the periodical's first editor (1876-1880). Other library publications eventually made their appearance, some of which achieved great prominence in the two countries; but *Library Journal* has continued for over a hundred years as a vehicle for the ventilation by Canadian

and U.S. librarians of their ideas on professional questions of vital interest to both.

3. In the third initiative of 1876 Melvil Dewey was not an active participant, whereas in the two aforementioned initiatives, he was solely responsible. A person of many and varied interests besides his total absorption in librarianship (simplified spelling, shorthand, adoption of the metric systems, etc.), Melvil Dewey has been eulogized as "the most influential and effective librarian who has ever dwelt among us." The year 1876 marked the publication of the first edition of the Dewey Decimal Classification, issued in a little booklet forty-four pages. The original plan of the classification tables had been worked out by Dewey and used in the arrangement of the books at Amherst College Library, while he served as student-librarian. In the century which has followed upon publication of Dewey's Decimal Classification, his tables and relative index have passed through nineteen English language editions, growing and expanding with each. This continual growth of the work is in itself a testimony to the constant labor of Dewey and his loyal followers to update and expand the work, in response to its growing international acceptance and reflecting the expansion and multiplication of human knowledge. Soon after 1876, Dewey's classification scheme spread to libraries in other parts of the world and the demand for access to the tables in the vernacular led to the translation of Dewey's work in many modern languages.[54]

4. A fourth monumental work was also issued in this key year of 1876. We refer to Charles C. Cutter's "Rules for a Dictionary Catalog," which became a reference work for catalogers and teachers of cataloging everywhere. Much of the popularity of the dictionary catalog in libraries of all types in the United States and Canada may be attributed to the dissemination of Cutter's Rules which described a simple dictionary arrangement, familiar to all, as the basis for the organization of a library's catalog cards.

5. The first comprehensive study of libraries of the United States was published in 1876. Its wealth of detailed information about various types of libraries in the United States served as the basis for much constructive library development and planning. Its citation reads as follows:

> U.S. Bureau of Education. *Public Libraries in the United States of America: Their History, Condition and Management. Special Report: Part I.* Washington, D.C.: U.S. Government Printing Office, 1876.

Viewed in the light of their contribution to the formation of a certain unity of practices, these five accomplishments of librarianship in North America were decisive elements in the unity of Canadian and American librarianship. While we would be the first to admit to the necessity for specialization in librarianship, which provides sui generis solutions to complex problems, we cannot at the same time ignore the benefits that have accrued to librarianship in the United States and Canada from their possession of a common body of accepted theory and practice derived from the works and thought of Melvil Dewey, Charles Cutter, John Cotton Dana, Justin Winsor, and others of the post-1876 period.

Another major landmark in North American librarianship occurred not long after the eventful year 1876. We refer to the publication in 1882 of *Poole's Index to Periodical Literature*. This had its beginnings in an index prepared at Yale University by a student-librarian, John Edmands, in 1847. This was expanded and printed the following year by William Frederick Poole. The years passed and Poole, then head of the Chicago Public Library, resumed work on his index which was published in its comprehensive form in 1882 and carried forward in supplements to 1906. By that time the H. W. Wilson firm was ready to assume its leadership in the field of magazine indexing, bringing out the successor to Poole. This was the *Reader's Guide to Periodical Literature*, which indexes general periodicals to the present time. Periodicals belonging to special fields are indexed by other organizations which have been attracted to the growing field of periodical literature. A still later phase of this massive problem has been the application of computer techniques, from which have emerged great works like *Index Medicus* and *Chemical Abstracts*. These giant operations involve great numbers of specialized professionals and costly, complex electronic equipment. Indexing of periodical literature has in this century attained a high level of sophistication and comprehensiveness which makes the story of John Edmands and his one-man index for student users of the magazines at Yale University Library seem as remote in library history as Caesar's Commentaries.

Continuing the chronology of major advances in North American librarianship, the year 1887 marked the founding of the first library school to provide training for librarians at the university level. The place was New York City; the institution was Columbia College (now University). The initiator of this pioneering academic enterprise was—once again—Melvil Dewey. To this great innovator in librarianship the distaff side of the profession owes an especially great debt. Dewey not only respected women co-workers and treated them as equals throughout his career, he insisted from the very first that women should be admitted to the Columbia program. Thereby Dewey incurred the wrath of the board of trustees who held to the prevailing view of the times that a university education was the birthright primarily of males. Dewey also believed that the selection of candidates for the library science program should be based on factual information, and to that end he prepared a questionnaire. Utilization of a questionnaire was not then in general vogue in university admissions in the United States, and its use by Dewey for the new library program became another source of irritation to the aforementioned college trustees.

The training of librarians in universities developed slowly. For a number of decades numerous persons interested in a career in librarianship availed themselves of training programs offered by public libraries. These courses, emphasizing practical work, were of varying length and comprehensiveness. The best of them (such as those of the public libraries of Pittsburgh, Los Angeles,

Philadelphia, and other cities), in time, passed to universities where more attention could be given to the philosophical and theoretical considerations of librarianship. In this detail, as perhaps in others, North American librarianship was
merely following the pattern of development displayed in other disciplines.

Librarianship in the United States and Canada, by now, was moving forward
simultaneously in many directions, of which the following are examples:
(1) direct service to readers, including reference services, established at the
Worcester, Massachusetts Public Library; (2) the open-shelf basis for self-service,
originated at the Cleveland Public Library; (3) library service to children, administered in their own department, room, or corner by a librarian trained in story-
telling and other activities, originated by John Cotton Dana at the Denver
Public Library and soon to spread to libraries everywhere, east and west, north
and south of the Mile High City; (4) standardization in cataloging and classification, based on the works of Charles Cutter, Melvil Dewey, and many others;
(5) public taxation for library support, harking back to a New Hampshire law
of 1821.

The Library of Congress, founded in 1800, to provide bibliographic service
to the two national legislative bodies, had a spectacular growth in the second
half of the last century, as its usefulness to the various agencies of the federal
government became established. Then, in 1900, when Herbert Putnam assumed
the reins of this agency, the Library of Congress quickly extended its influence
beyond Washington, D.C., to all the states and territories, becoming the national
library in actuality, if not in name. Under Putnam's long brilliant administration,
totalling nearly forty years, the library of Congress, like the British Museum
under Anthony Panizzi in the previous century, became the innovator in the
development of many services and undertook an increasingly important participation in world librarianship.

Melvil Dewey, to whom librarianship is so greatly indebted, made yet another
major contribution to its development. Early in his career Dewey became a
firm believer in the need for "a means of testing, experimenting, cooperating on
supplies, methods, equipment, and standards." This led him to join with others
in establishing a commercial firm which was known as "Library Bureau." This
enterprise, of which Dewey served as president for twenty-five years, later
became a division of the Remington Rand Company and developed a line of
products of special interest to librarians, file clerks, archivists, and administrative personnel. The mass production of these items (catalog cards, guides,
filing equipment, library furniture, etc.) brought not only a high level of standardization, as well as lower costs, but also many improvements in service and
economies which in turn were passed on to the patrons of the U.S. and Canadian
libraries and archives, as well as to taxpayers of the two nations.

We come now to that point, in the unfolding of library history on the North
American continent, when we can comment on one of the greatest of all bene-
factors of libraries—Andrew Carnegie.[55] His contribution to the development
of public libraries in the English-speaking world is a remarkable achievement

which has often been told, but it especially bears repetition in our study. A Scottish immigrant to the United States when he was yet a boy, Carnegie adapted himself quickly to the special conditions of the expanding U.S. economy, advanced with extraordinary success, building a vast business enterprise dedicated to the production of steel. Reading was an important element in this success story, as Carnegie himself relates, giving ample credit to the generosity and guidance of a Colonel Anderson who loaned his books to studious lads. At an early age Carnegie became convinced that the rich should distribute their wealth during their lifetime. It was this conviction which motivated him to sell his properties and give away his money as systematically as he had developed his business. There was only one genuine remedy, so Carnegie believed, for the ills that beset the human race, and that is expressed in a simple word which Carnegie frequently used: enlightenment. Thus it was that, in 1880, Carnegie made an outright gift for the building of a public library in Pittsburgh, which was the scene of many of his business triumphs. This decisive gesture was the beginning of a series of gifts of money which he made to municipal authorities and others for the construction of public library buildings and other library-related projects. Between 1880 and 1919 Carnegie personally interested himself in the selection of the recipients of grants for the 2507 public library buildings he caused to be erected in the United States, Canada, and other parts of the English-speaking world. Appearing once before a special U.S. legislative commission studying working conditions, and doubtless recalling his profound faith in libraries as a source of enlightenment, to which his money had contributed so generously, Carnegie declared: "My chief business is to do as much good as I can in the world; I have no other business." As a working boy who had benefitted so much from the generosity of a certain Colonel Anderson and from the guidance of the gentle "library ladies," Carnegie, having achieved great financial success, devoted the last three decades of his life to library extension on an intercontinental plane, building public libraries and creating the Carnegie Foundation to carry on after his death other types of support to the enlightenment he believed depended upon reading and library assistance.

The beginning of a new century is often the occasion for the assessment of progress. By the beginning of the twentieth century the stage had been set for the development of libraries of all types throughout the North American continent. Not only has the number of public libraries multiplied enormously in the seven decades; also more and more branches have been established in residential sections far from the center of town, as cities have expanded. Bookmobile service, which became possible after 1900, with the development of motor transportation and paved streets, has expanded to serve greater numbers of people in rural and outlying districts.

By 1900 there was one library in the United States with over a million registered items. Eighty years later there were more than 100 major collections of that size.

By 1900 school and special libraries were appearing on the horizon of librarianship; in the succeeding decades these two types of institutions have developed services and installations of impressive quality, if not in numbers, in Canada and the United States.

By 1900 the federal governments in the two countries had numerous libraries serving the various official agencies; then, in the United States, beginning in the early 1930s, an extraordinary expansion of library service throughout the nation became possible through the appropriation of federal funds. By the 1970s it had become apparent that there was need for a National Commission on Libraries and Information Science, to study nationwide library programs and develop plans for a coordination of the nation's numerous information services.

Thus, when the United States celebrated its Bicentennial in 1976, a hundred years after librarianship in the two nations was said to have "come of age," library services had extended both horizontally and vertically. This expansion indicates the great strides that the profession has taken since those hearty, undaunted colonists braved untold hardship when they settled on the North American mainland in the early years of the seventeenth century.

Clearly visible during the early phases of North American librarianship, now extending over nearly four centuries of time, are the following four characteristics:

1. A marked missionary zeal exhibited by many library promoters
2. A compulsion to eradicate illiteracy in the population
3. A growing desire among first- and second-generation immigrants to attain security, comfort, and prestige as they work out their destiny in the New World
4. A clear business sense displayed by publishers and distributors of books and magazines, who regard libraries as their rightful market and exploit them to advertise their product

Across the vast North American continent — in every direction, east and west, north and south—the word "library" is a symbol of information. Wherever libraries exist, whatever their size, whichever category they represent, whoever their users, they epitomize free and uninhibited access to unlimited information. Libraries in the United States and Canada are synonymous with knowledge; they reflect the belief of the people of the two nations that information and knowledge are a source of power in an equalitarian society.

AUSTRALIAN, NEW ZEALAND, AND OCEANIAN LIBRARIANSHIP: THEIR BACKGROUND, EMERGENCE AND DEVELOPMENT
Dietrich H. Borchardt

Public libraries—but not library service—can be said to have started in Australia in 1827 when like-minded citizens of Sydney, New South Wales, organized a lending library on a subscription basis, though it was more than forty years before the Australian Subscription Library became the Free Public Library of Sydney. In New Zealand the first public library was established as part of the Mechanics' Institute set up in Port Nicholson (Wellington) in 1841, and this example was followed in other towns throughout the country.

The influx of British migrants brought with it demands for library services on a pattern similar to that developing in their country of origin; this pattern was that of the mechanics' institutes. Hundreds appear to have existed in Australia and New Zealand by the end of the nineteenth century. However, they did not propser like their British counterparts and failed to develop as a force in the cultural life of the colonies. Both in Australia and New Zealand the early settlers failed to recognize the importance of local government financing of mechanics' institutes and library services but were satisfied to accept and rely unduly on voluntary subscriptions and charity support. With the establishment of responsible government in Australia and New Zealand came financial dependence on central colonial government funds which has persisted to this day. The response to demand for such funds fluctuated according to the general financial state of each colony. It soon became evident that behind the unwillingness to establish sound local government there were tensions between town and country, between landed interests and individual works which could only be resolved by the central government. Even when municipal authorities were finally established in Australia and given some power to strike rates for general and specific purposes, library services had to wait until the twentieth century before they were at least partially supported by such rates.

The first Australian library open to every resident in the colony was the Melbourne Public Library which was founded in 1853, and commenced operations in 1856. The Free Public Library of Sydney was opened in 1889 and similar institutions were established in Hobart, Tasmania, in 1870; in Adelaide, South Australia, in 1884; in Perth, western Australia, in 1886; and in Brisbane, Queensland, in 1896. Though New Zealand introduced legislation in 1869 empowering local authorities to establish libraries provided that admission should be free, no libraries were immediately set up under this act. However, following the abolition of the provinces in 1876, responsibility for library services was partly accepted by the national government and financial assistance was granted to public libraries in the larger cities.

Although the modern concept of public library services was not seriously developed until the 1930s, a good deal of important groundwork was done early in the twentieth century. The records of the meetings of the Australasian Library Association and of the Libraries Association of New Zealand bear witness to the enthusiastic interest and foresight of the pioneers. The records of association meetings in Melbourne in 1909 published soon after the event[56] and in New Zealand between 1910 and 1912, as reported in McEldowney's *The New Zealand Library Association*,[57] contain references to the need for improved lending facilities in country areas (to be achieved, it was suggested, by means of loan collections made available from central library stocks), the establishment of good reference collections in all public libraries, better lending facilities to country-based students, closer cooperation between public libraries and educational institutions, travelling libraries, children's libraries, a national library, and the free issue of books.

Yet New Zealand did not fare too well with its public library services in the early days. Though the abolition of provincial governments placed the onus of public library support on the central authority, the awkwardly phrased Public Libraries Act of 1869, while ensuring free entrance to public libraries, permitted the levying of dues on books borrowed.

In Australia, the use of government funds for library services led to the development of reference libraries in the capital cities of each state, and somewhat later to the establishment of the National Library of Australia in Canberra. The term "state library" has been introduced only fairly recently to supplant the somewhat misleading name "public library" for the type of institution and service referred to. Some of the confusion was remedied as early as the turn of the century when the Melbourne Public Library and the Sydney Public Library became, respectively, the Public Library of Victoria and the Public Library of New South Wales. The other states soon followed suit, but in the 1960s the names were changed once more to reflect more accurately the scope and national character of these institutions; since then the term "state library" has been used in western Australia, southern Australia, Victoria, Tasmania, and New South Wales.

The state libraries of Victoria and New South Wales achieved, during the late nineteenth century, a leading role in Australia with regard to all aspects of library services: building development, book stock, and professional standards of librarianship. This preeminence they enjoyed unchallenged until after World War II, and none of the other state libraries has ever achieved comparable stan-' dards of service. However, postwar developments in the administration of library services in western Australia and Tasmania are of special interest and will be discussed in their context.

Municipal public libraries did not develop properly in Australia until after World War II; by contrast, New Zealand already had over 400 such libraries at the end of World War I.[58] In both areas the cornerstone for growth and expansion lay in the field of local authority finance. Suffice it here to say that Australian municipal public libraries are only now beginning to participate in the provision of book resources on a national scale and in the support of general cultural services.

A rudimentary public library service has existed in Fiji for some years, but in 1964 the Western Regional Library at Lautoke was opened and is now primarily responsible for the provision of a public library service in the domination. A public library service has existed in Papua, New Guinea since 1945. The attainment of independence in December 1973 is providing a particular stimulus to the development of library services which are recognized as being essential if democracy is to become a way of life.

Generally speaking, special libraries have as yet not developed on any serious level in Australia or New Zealand. There are noteworthy exceptions, such as the sophisticated conglomerate of special libraries that serve the Commonwealth Scientific and Industrial Research Organization (CSIRO) in Australia, and the smaller but well-integrated network of special libraries of the Department of Scientific and Industrial Research (DSIR) in New Zealand. Other government departments, both at state and commonwealth level, have also built up bibliographic resources and developed for the most part rudimentary information services. Not only lack of financial support, but more significantly lack of understanding on the part of users and want of properly trained staff, has prevented these library services from playing a constructive role in the Australian and New Zealand library systems.

Industrial undertakings have tended to be reluctant and often mean in their provision of library and information centers. This reflects inevitably the research interests of the companies concerned; because most of Australia's and New Zealand's large industrial enterprises form part of multinational concerns, research is usually carried out in the United States, the United Kingdom, or in Europe where head offices seem to believe that the Australian partner would be better employed carrying out instructions than trying to step out on his own.

The isolation of industrial and research groups in Fiji and in Papua, New Guinea has forced companies and organizations responsible for staff to create small special collections to support basic investigations as well as leisure reading. Some of them have over the years grown to quite sizeable collections and have been able to support general cultural activities. Into this category belong the medical collections in both countries and the libraries built up by firms like the Colonial Sugar Refining Company in Fiji.

Missions have of course also collected books for their educational and proselytizing purposes. These have been particularly important for the promotion of literacy among the young.

There is, however, one group of special libraries worth mentioning briefly in this overview. Together with its seven magnificent buildings to house the Australian legislature, there grew up equally magnificent gentlemen's libraries to educate and entertain the lawgivers. Though rarely called upon to provide legislative reference service in the first decades of their existence, these libraries enjoyed considerable financial support and were for many decades the most favored group of libraries in Australia.

In New Zealand, too, the library of the General Assembly grew up without much real purpose other than to be an ornament to that body. Thanks to differences in personalities and a more favorable climate of political opinion at a crucial period in the history of library development, the General Assembly Library was much more closely involved with the expansion and modernization of library services in New Zealand than was the case with its sister institutions in the Australian states.

Compulsory education was introduced early in Australia and New Zealand, and it inevitably brought in its wake the establishment of universities and other forms of tertiary education. To avoid confusion, it is stressed once more that in Australia, education is basically in the hands of the states, though the federal government has since World War II provided an increasing amount of financial assistance without demanding a great deal of influence in the state education programs.

In Australia the universities of Sydney and Melbourne were founded in the 1850s, and almost one and a quarter centuries later there are nineteen government-supported universities in Australia—one in the Capital Territory, six in New South Wales, four in Victoria, three in Queensland, two each in South Australia, and one in Tasmania.

New Zealand's first university was founded in 1869, and there are now six state-supported universities—one each in the four main centers and two in the country areas of North Island, at Hamilton and Palmerston North. An institute of agricultural research and teaching is attached to Canterbury University, Christchurch.

The University of Papua and New Guinea was established, in 1965, by the Australian government as an integral part of its policy of support for self-development in the Trust Territory. Thanks to its energetic and far-seeing first librarian, the library developed rapidly not only as a library service to the academic community, but also as a library with national responsibilities.

The Papua New Guinea University of Technology appointed its first librarian in 1969 after it had tried to manage without library services for several years. This slow start has prevented it from developing a useful collection until very recently. Staffing problems have forced the institute to play only a small part in the library scene of Papua, New Guinea.

To these postsecondary education centers has to be added the Administrative College in Port Moresby which was established in 1962 to provide courses for public servants ranging between two weeks and two years. Its library is a major resource center for government publications and books and serials on government and politics. Of special importance in this context is the college's library studies department.

The University of the South Pacific, in Fiji, is the latest major academic institution created by the European colonists in Oceania. Little can be said at this stage about its bibliographic resources and the impact it is going to make on library services in Fiji. It was founded in 1969, sponsored by the South Pacific Commission with the help of the British and New Zealand governments. In 1971 the University Library established a Pacific Collection which includes a legal deposit section for materials printed in Fiji and, by special arrangements, for material printed in the British Solomon Islands Protectorate. At last count the total collection had reached 40,000 volumes.

There are, also, a Derick Technical Institute of Suva and a Fiji School of Medicine, with small, basic library collections which do not as yet constitute an important bibliographic resource.

The University of Guam Library serves a student population of over 5000, one-twentieth of the total population of this island territory of the United States.

Of particular interest—both politically and academically—is the development of the colleges of advanced education in Australia. Conceived out of a recognition of the importance of vocational education and a certain disillusion with the educational performance of universities, the "c.a.e.s.", as they are commonly called, were meant to offer an "equal but different" approach to tertiary education. Until the report by the Australian government of the "Committee on the Future of Tertiary Education in Australia" in 1964/1965[59] little if any serious thought was given to these cinderellas of the state education systems. Then, suddenly, they became important and a good deal of attention had been paid to them ever since. Though still only of limited significance as bibliographic resources, their libraries are growing both in size and in quality. There is as yet no corresponding development in New Zealand, but in Papua, New Guinea the Australian concepts of education have left their influence and there exist vocational institutions which may well some day develop on the same lines as the Australian colleges of advanced education.

It is undeniable that Australian academic libraries have fared better than those in New Zealand, and in terms of bibliographic resources, the aggregate of volumes in the Australian university and college system far exceeds that of any other group of libraries in the area. Yet only Sydney University has established and developed library services on a level commensurate with that of universities in the United States, and none of the other Australian universities has a collection as rich or as significant for scholarly research. Nevertheless, each university library is larger than any municipal library in its region and the older institutions provide the most important bibliographic centers for their states.

Teachers' colleges in Australia and New Zealand, with some very recent exceptions, are administered directly by the State Education Department. In Victoria these colleges have been welded in 1973 into a multicampus university-like organization, called the State College of Victoria; in spite of its new title it is still strongly dominated by the State Education Department. Generally speaking, Australian and New Zealand teachers' college libraries are poorly stocked and inadequately financed. Only recently has there been a concerted effort in Australia to improve matters. Such improvements relate not only to library services in teachers' colleges but, more importantly, to the inclusion of courses on library use for teachers. In New Zealand the situation has not been quite as bad because teacher's colleges there have benefited from the zeal of the New Zealand Library Association and the good fortune of having had some outstanding librarians in the early postwar years.

In Papua, New Guinea teachers' college libraries are according to Linklater's

"Libraries and Librarians in Papua New Guinea"[60] better administered and relatively better stocked than many other institutions concerned with education. In addition to the government-controlled teachers' colleges, there are also several mission-run colleges engaged in teacher education, and most of these have a fairly high standard of library service. Five departmental training institutions cater to the education of future public servants. The best-run library among these is in the Administrative College, Port Moresby.

School libraries have lagged behind all other library services in Australia, and in New Zealand, too, their development has been very uneven. In spite of several expert reports on their shameful state, they were left to moulder as unwanted and intellectually rejected components of education in Australia until the early 1960s. Though the degree of neglect differed and in spite of token efforts made by some private schools, basic library services suffered because they were not regarded as essential to the educational process. However, in 1968 the concerted efforts of dedicated teacher librarians, notably L. H. McGrath, and of education experts concerned with teacher training such as Ernest Roe, and of some influential laymen like the late Dr. Andrew Fabinyi succeeded in persuading the Australian government to pump $27 million into secondary school libraries throughout the Commonwealth. This sum was available for the triennium 1969-1971, and a further grant was made for 1972-1974. Though the money available represented little more than a few thousand dollars each even for the larger schools, it stimulated state education departments to bestir themselves in the matter of library buildings, library staffing, and the coordination of library services. Indeed, the whole concept of school librarianship was reexamined in the context of the Australian UNESCO seminar on *The Role of Libraries in Secondary Education*.[61]

A significant recent achievement in school library services has been the introduction of centralized processing services which provide cataloging and shelf preparation of materials for school library collections. It is an attempt to combat the lack of skilled librarians available in the state education departments, and has been well-developed in southern Australia, Victoria, New South Wales, and Queensland. Similar services are available in Tasmania, western Australia, and the Australian Capital Territory.

In New Zealand school libraries received special attention as early as 1936 and in 1941 the New Zealand government instituted a scheme of supplying children's books to all schools. The School Library Service is part of the National Library activities, and close to two million books are supplied annually to schools. The service also offers assistance in the compilation of lists of books for purchasing by schools. However, lack of staff resources and resistance from teachers to the recognition of school librarianship as a distinct though integral part of the educational system prevented any further development.

In Papua, New Guinea school libraries have been fully recognized as fundamental resources in the struggle for literacy and democratic nationhood. Most teachers' colleges include in the curriculum some training in the use of books with children and a model school library has been established. The attainment of independence has focused attention on this aspect of librarianship; however, until individual school libraries receive more financial and administrative support their development is bound to be slow. Since 1975 a centralized processing serfice has been in operation and has greatly reduced the individual school's burden of purchasing, cataloging, and shelf-preparation.

School libraries in Fiji and in the Solomon Islands are not as yet a major concern of the government's educational program though lip service is paid to their importance and efforts are being made to have the bookstock widely used in the battle for literacy.

Mention must be made, at the end of this introductory note, of two factors that have singally contributed to the development of librarianship in Australia and New Zealand. The first is the visit in 1934 under the auspices of the Carnegie Corporation of New York, of Ralph Munn, director of the Carnegie Library of Pittsburgh, to New Zealand and Australia to examine and report on the library world of "down under." The two reports which sum up the rather depressing results of Munn's survey represent the great turning point before the outbreak of World War II. Known, respectively, as the Munn-Barr[62] and the Munn-Pitt[63] Reports, they contain a sharp critique of the neglect into which governments had allowed libraries to fall, of the apathy of the public at large, and of the shameful state of librarianship. The significance of these two reports was immediately fully appreciated, and there is now no text on libraries and library services in Australia and New Zealand that does not pay due praise to Ralph Munn and his two associates.

The other important factor which helped to develop librarianship in Australia and New Zealand was the establishment of graduate schools of librarianship. The New Zealand Library School was set up in 1946 as a branch of the National Library Service and was later incorporated as a division of the National Library. In Australia, almost fifteen more years had to pass before a school of librarianship was set up at the University of New South Wales, Sydney, in 1959, to supersede the librarianship training centers run by most of the state libraries in preparation for the examination of the Library Association of Australia.

NOTES

1. Edmund White, *The First Men* (New York: Time-Life Books, [c1973]), p. 18.
2. Robert Claiborne, *The Birth of Writing* (New York: Time-Life Books, [c1974]), p. 20.
3. Tom Prideaux, *Cro-Magnon Man* (New York: Time-Life Books, [c1973]), p. 93.

4. Claiborne, *The Birth of Writing*, p. 15.

5. Jesse H. Shera, *The Foundations of Education for Librarianship* (New York: Becker and Hayes, 1972), p. 103.

6. Elmer D. Johnson, *A History of Libraries in the Western World* (New York and London: Scarecrow Press, 1965), p. 21.

7. Ibid., p. 24.

8. Richard Krzys, "Library Historiography," *Encyclopedia of Library and Information Science*, ed. by A. Kent, H. Lancour, and J. E. Daily, Vol. 15 (New York: Marcel Dekker, 1975), p. 308.

9. Johnson, *A History of Libraries in the Western World*, p. 33.

10. Alfred Hessel, *A History of Libraries* (New Brunswick, New Jersey: Scarecrow Press, 1955), pp. 30-31.

11. K. T. Wu, "China, Libraries in the People's Republic of," *Encyclopedia of Library and Information Science*, ed. by A. Kent and H. Lancour, Vol. 4 (New York: Marcel Dekker, 1974), p. 627.

12. Pulin Baru, "Early Buddhist Monastic Libraries," *Indian Librarian* 27 (Sept. 1972), p. 72.

13. Kalpana Dasgupta, "How Learned Were the Mughals: Reflections on Muslim Libraries in India," *Journal of Library History* 10 (July 1975), pp. 241-254.

14. K. Navalani, "India, Libraries and Information Centres in: Public Libraries," *Encyclopedia of Library and Information Science*, ed. by A. Kent, H. Lancour, and J. E. Daily, Vol. 11 (New York: Marcel Dekker, 1974), p. 423.

15. Tilak Kultaratne, "History of Libraries in Sri Lanka," *Libraries and People: Colombo Public Library, 1925-1975. A Commemorative Volume,* ed. by Ishvari Corea (Colombo, 1975).

16. Paul Bixler, "Burma, Libraries in," *Encyclopedia of Library and Information Science*, ed. by A. Kent and H. Lancour, Vol. 3 (New York: Marcel Dekker, 1970), p. 498.

17. Ibid., p. 499.

18. Ibid., pp. 501-508.

19. Gertrude S. L. Koh, "Korea, Libraries in the Republic of," *Encyclopedia of Library and Information Science*, ed. by A. Kent, H. Lancour, and J. E. Daily, Vol. 13 (New York: Marcel Dekker, 1975), p. 462.

20. Hatsuo Nakamura, "Japan, Libraries and Information Centres in," *Encyclopedia of Library and Information Science*, ed. by A. Kent, H. Lancour, and J. E. Daily, Vol. 13 (New York: Marcel Dekker, 1975), p. 227.

21. Roland Oliver and J. D. Fage, *A Short History of Africa* (London: Penguin, 1975), p. 14.

22. Rita Pankhurst, "Libraries in Ethiopia," *Encyclopedia of Library and Information Science*, ed. by A. Kent and H. Lancour, Vol. 8 (New York: Marcel Dekker, 1972), p. 215.

23. Felix Dubois, *Timbuctu the Mysterious* (New York: Negro University Press, 1969), pp. 287-288.

24. Robert Munn, "Libraries in Kenya," *Encyclopedia of Library and Information Science*, ed. by A. Kent, H. Lancour, and J. E. Daily, Vol. 13 (New York: Marcel Dekker, 1975), p. 432.

25. Wilfred J. Plumbe, "Libraries in Africa," *Encyclopedia of Library and Information Science*, ed. by A. Kent and H. Lancour, Vol. 1 (New York: Marcel Dekker, 1968), p. 122.
26. *Libraries in the Union of South Africa, Rhodesia and Kenya Colony*. Memorandum submitted to the Carnegie Corporation of New York, 1929, p. 33.
27. John T. Strickland, "Patterns of Library Service in Africa," *Library Trends* 8 (October 1959), p. 178.
28. Wilfred Plumbe, "Libraries in Africa," pp. 124-125.
29. Ibid.
30. Vladimir I. Lenin, *Collected Works*, Vol. 41 (Moscow: Progress Publishers, 1961), pp. 323-324.
31. Raquel Flores, Rosario Dominguez, and Eva de Sagastume, "Guatemala, Libraries in," *Encyclopedia of Library and Information Science*, ed. by A. Kent, H. Lancour, and J. E. Daily, Vol. 10 (New York: Marcel Dekker, [c1973]), pp. 238-239.
32. Rosa Ma F. de Zamora, "Mexico, Libraries in," *Encyclopedia of Library and Information Science*, ed. by A. Kent, H. Lancour, and J. E. Daily, Vol. 18 (New York: Marcel Dekker, [c1976]), p. 1.
33. Ibid., p. 2.
34. Ibid., p. 4.
35. Ibid.
36. Ibid., p. 2.
37. Ibid., p. 4.
38. Ibid., p. 5.
39. Maria T. Sanz B.-M., "Chile, Libraries in," *Encyclopedia of Library and Information Science*, ed. by A. Kent and H. Lancour, Vol. 4 (New York: Marcel Dekker, [c1970]), p. 615.
40. Ibid.
41. Josefa E. Sabor, "Argentina, Libraries in," *Encyclopedia of Library and Information Science*, ed. by A. Kent and H. Lancour, Vol. 1 (New York: Marcel Dekker, [c1968]), p. 522.
42. Ibid.
43. Juan R. Freudenthal, "Public Libraries, International: Contemporary Libraries in Latin America," *Encyclopedia of Library and Information Science*, ed. by A. Kent, H. Lancour, and J. E. Daily, Vol. 24 (New York: Marcel Dekker, [c1978]), p. 429.
44. Ibid.
45. Gloria Johnson, "Cultural Centers and their Libraries in Latin American Countries," (M.L.S. thesis, Carnegie Library School, 1951), p. 25.
46. Richard Krzys and Gaston Litton, *A History of Education for Librarianship in Colombia* (Metuchen, New Jersey: Scarecrow Press, 1969), p. 154.
47. Carmen Rovira, "Cuba, Libraries in," *Encyclopedia of Library and Information Science*, ed. by A. Kent and H. Lancour, Vol. 6 (New York: Marcel Dekker, [c1971]), pp. 328-331.
48. Louis B. Wright, *The Cultural Life of the American Colonists* (New York: Harper, 1957).

49. National Library of Canada, *The First Canadian Library, 1632-1800* (Ottawa: 1972), p. 15.

50. "Library," *World Book*, Vol. 12 (Chicago: Worldbook-Childcraft International, 1980), pp. 210 passim.

51. Elizabeth Homer Morton, "Canada, Libraries in," *Encyclopedia of Library and Information Science*, ed. by A. Kent and H. Lancour, Vol. 4 (New York: Marcel Dekker, [c1970]), pp. 71-157.

52. J. M. Smith, *A Chronology of Librarianship* (Metuchen, New Jersey: Scarecrow Press, 1968), p. 111.

53. See the articles on libraries in the following encyclopedias: *Americana, Compton, World Book.*

54. Winifred B. Linderman, "Dewey, Melvil," *Encyclopedia of Library and Information Science*, ed. by A. Kent and H. Lancour, Vol. 7 (New York: Marcel Dekker, [c1972]), pp. 142-160.

55. Stanton Belfour, "Carnegie, Andrew," *Encyclopedia of Library and Information Science*, ed. by A. Kent and H. Lancour, Vol. 4 (New York: Marcel Dekker, [c1970]), pp. 192-200.

56. Library Association of Australia, 2nd General Meeting, Adelaide, October 9-12, 1900, *Transactions and Proceedings* (Adelaide: Government Printer, (1901).

57. W. J. McEldowney, *The New Zealand Library Association, 1910-1960 and Its Part in New Zealand Library Development* (Wellington: New Zealand Library Association, 1962).

58. New Zealand. Department of Statistics, *Census of Libraries, 1969* (Wellington: Government Printer, 1971).

59. Australia. Committee on the Future of Tertiary Education in Australia, *Tertiary Education in Australia; report . . .* (Canberra: Government Printer, 1964-1965), 3 vols.

60. W. Linklater, in Library Association of Australia, *Proceedings of the 16th Biennial Conference Held in Sydney, August, 1971: Progress and Poverty* (Sydney: LAA, 1972), pp. 81-98.

61. *The Role of Libraries in Secondary Education* (Canberra: Australian Government Publishing Service, 1972).

62. R. Munn and J. Barr, *New Zealand Libraries; a Survey of Conditions and Suggestions for Their Improvement . . .* (Christchurch: Libraries Association of New Zealand, 1934).

63. R. Munn and E. R. Pitt, *Australian Libraries; a Survey of Conditions and Suggestions for their Improvement . . .* (Melbourne: Australian Council for Educational Research, 1935), Reprinted Adelaide: Libraries Board of South Australia, 1967.

5

Analysis: Worldwide Perspective on the Profession

Richard Krzys, Gaston Litton,
and Area Research Associates

MIDDLE EAST
Richard Krzys

To begin to comprehend Middle Eastern librarianship, one might compare it to a unique coin. Its shiny observe shows the deeply etched designs of library buildings of the most up-to-date architecture; its dull reverse, seemingly struck by a medieval mint, reveals faint worn outlines of library buildings of the Middle Ages. This juxtaposition is symbolic of Middle Eastern librarianship; its practices appear on the surface to be contemporary, but under scrutiny they reveal a foundation of medieval customs and traditions.

To understand this combination of tendencies, one must be au courant with our profession's state of the art; to comprehend its underlying customs and traditions, one must assimilate the *Koran* and the nature of Islamic cultural institutions dating back to the Middle Ages. Specifically, one should be familiar with the great mosque and university libraries tracing back to the fabulous period of the caliph Harun al-Rashid.

Characteristics

Middle Eastern library development:

1. A high esteem exists for learning and the book.
2. Its centuries-old tradition of library development tends to delay modernization of services, technology, and techniques.

3. Its philosophy of librarianship traditionally favored library use by royalty, as well as religious and political leaders, and the elite classes, but current philosophy is beginning to move toward providing service to the ever-increasing educated masses.
4. Lack of understanding exists among government officials of the necessary role of libraries within educational and technological advancement.
5. The level of library consciousness among government officials is more influential than the enormous wealth of the area in causing progressive change in library development.[1]

CENTRAL, SOUTH, EAST, AND SOUTHEAST ASIA
Richard Krzys

Anyone who acquaints himself with the vast Asian continent is impressed, if not bewildered, by the seemingly infinite variety of the patterns assumed by the area's history, politics, economics, and social conditions.

The history of Asia began millennia ago in three river valleys, the Tigris-Euphrates in Southwest Asia, the Indus in South Asia, and the Yellow River in East Asia. Within these areas may be found today three significant types of library development, that of the Middle East, those of Pakistan and India, as well as that of the People's Republic of China.

As we view the political interaction of the areas, we note various political tendencies and their implications for librarianship; for example, the late assertion of the political nationalism of the nineteenth century that had already manifested itself in Italy, Germany, the United States, and France. Prior to the feelings of nationalism that were not to be felt in Asia until the twentieth century, Asian librarianship was still a continuation of the ancient tradition; however, the dramatic changes that occurred in Asian politics beginning with the twentieth century saw their parallels in shifts in our professional practice that became evident in China, India, and Japan: In 1912 Dr. Sun Yat-sen overthrew the Manchu dynasty in China and established a republic that was continued by Chiang Kai-Shek and then overthrown once more in 1949 by Mao Tse-Tung; within India the rise to power of the charismatic leader Mohandes K. Gandhi began in the 1920s and culminated in 1947, when India was granted independence from British rule; excessive nationalism within Japan during the 1930s and early 1940s pushed the country first into military supremacy in Southeast Asia and then to the brink of disaster in 1945, when Japan suffered total defeat by the United States and allied forces. In each case—within China, India, and Japan—the political changes that ensued following the growth of nationalism as well as the growth in the information needs of government, industry, and education gradually shifted the countries from an ancient to a modern library tradition.

Today Asian countries are riding waves of nationalism that find expression in significant progress in manufacturing and programs of social welfare. Many Asian peoples, most notably the Japanese, Koreans, and Taiwanese, have been attempting through their newly achieved prosperity to assure adequate employment, food, clothing, shelter, and medical care for their swelling populations. Fortunately, Asian government officials are beginning to comprehend that education and good library service are concomitants of successful programs of social welfare.

Prior to the post-World War II period, the economic situation in most Asian countries suffered from having a one-crop economy. When the rice, corn, or rubber crop was good, the countries thrived economically, and libraries had possibility of receiving financial support; however, during lean years caused by crop failures, the economies of Asian countries suffered greatly and libraries received little or no financial support. The Asian economy also suffered prior to World War II from exploitation by foreign industries that extracted Asia's precious resources—coal, tungsten, and iron ore—shipped them to Europe and the United States, and returned them to Asia as costly manufactured goods for resale to Asians at high prices. With the increase in scientific farming methods and local control of their mining operations, Asian countries within recent years are experiencing more stable economies, which have resulted in improved financial support for libraries.

Asia's complex social composition, representing people of diverse languages, customs, and religions—evident even within a single country, for example, India or Pakistan—has complicated the task of providing library service. The difficulties become obvious when one focuses on the problems of providing single components of library service like collections development. Building uniform collections for various ethnic groups within a community is made extremely difficult or impossible in countries whose populations speak more than one language. India, for example, has fourteen major languages and hundreds of dialects, but fortunately has English as its second official language. (Hindi is the other official language.) To further complicate the picture, many of the minor languages have no publishing industry to support them. Diversities of custom and religion have also created problems, especially in maintaining uniform standards for library service. In some Islamic countries, for example, where the separation of sexes is required on religious grounds, offering equal library services for men and women remains an unsolved problem.

Characteristics

Asian librarianship, like the continent itself, has bewildering differences of development; for example, outstanding examples of national and academic libraries are outweighed by the inadequacy, or in some cases, the nonexistence of public and school libraries. Despite these disparaities, some similarities within the continent have produced common characteristics within Asian librarianship. David Kaser summarized them as follows:

1. Perhaps the key trait affecting libraries is a widely held esteem for books and learning.
2. Low levels of literacy and per capita income have tended to keep books out of the hands of most of the populace.
3. Books have been thought of as passive carriers of gentility and culture, with little true relevance to current major problems of society, rather than as dynamic instruments of educational, technical, economic, and social change.
4. Libraries have most often been looked upon as priestly or princely things, appropriate to pagodas and palaces but not to the marketplace.[2]

Within the countries of the Middle East, school libraries are still in their developing stages, for example, the Library of the Al-Khalil Bin Ahmad Middle School for Boys in Kuwait. (Courtesy of Dr. Mohammed Aman, University of Wisconsin, Milwaukee, Wisconsin.)

In some Islamic countries of the Middle East, male and female children have separate library facilities, as shown in this secondary school for girls in Kuwait. (Courtesy of Dr. Mohammed Aman, University of Wisconsin, Milwaukee, Wisconsin.)

Exterior of the main building of the National Library of Beijing reveals its ancient tradition. (Courtesy of National Library of P.R.C.)

Interior of the National Library of Beijing shows a mixture of Chinese and Western library practices. (Courtesy of National Library of P.R.C.)

Reference Room of the National Library of Beijing and library users with American Cultural Attaché John Thomson in the foreground. (Courtesy of Donald Hausrath.)

Historic opening session of the China Society of Library Science in Beijing in 1979. (Courtesy of National Library of P.R.C.)

A new and used book and scroll store in Beijing sells books in the ancient and contemporary formats. (Courtesy of Donald Hausrath.)

Elementary school children enthusiastically use a school library in the Philippines. (Courtesy of International Federation of Library Associations.)

The Executive Board of the International Federation of Library Associations (IFLA) visits a library in Japan. (Courtesy of International Federation of Library Associations.)

An adult user examines a display in the Central Adult Section of the National Library of Singapore. (Courtesy of Mrs. Hedwig Anuar, National Library, Singapore.)

A children's book club in session at the National Library of Malaysia. (Courtesy of Halijah Othman, National Library of Malaysia.)

The National Library of Malaysia visits children in a hospital. (Courtesy of Halijah Othman, National Library of Malaysia.)

Part of the Reading Room of the Public Lending Unit, National Library of Malaysia. (Courtesy of Halijah Othman, National Library of Malaysia.)

Teachers reading in the Hong Kong Teachers' Association Library. (Courtesy of International Federation of Library Associations.)

Japan's National Diet Library was opened to the public on June 5, 1948. (From H. Suzuki, in *Encyclopedia of Library and Information Science*, ed. A. Kent, H. Lancour, and J. E. Daily (New York: Marcel Dekker, 1975), 13:251.)

AFRICA
Harry Kibirige

The African continent contains a variety of libraries at various levels of development. Over the centuries, the continent has experienced vicissitudes of cultural and social mobility. Civilizations, like the ancient Hellenic civilization in Egypt, the medieval Afro-Arab culture in West Africa, and the medieval civilization of Timbuktu and other cities on the East African coast, had flourishing libraries. Such libraries as the Great Alexandrian or Sankore Library at Timbuktu flourished concurrently with the periods which nourished them. What reversed this trend?

Centuries of slave trade and pillage are to a marked extent responsible for the dearth of societal progress. At the threshold of modern times, Africa emerged as a browbeaten and culturally stagnant region of the world. Libraries, museums, and art gallaries are symbols of cultural tranquility and progress. It is thus no surprise that until the twentieth century, library and information services development on the continent had been lagging far behind that in Europe and North America. Today, the relative situation is gradually changing, for some of the African nations have laid firm foundations for consistent development. For instance, in the university library sector, some of the best organized libraries in Africa compare very well with libraries in Europe.

In spite of constant UNESCO encouragement, library legislation is still lacking in several African countries. Not only general, but legal deposit laws have not been enacted. It may be argued that there is very little publishing activity in most countries and legal deposit laws would not result in significant publications accumulation. It should, however, be noted that absence of such laws precludes making a start and the little that may be on the market is lost forever. Coupled with this problem is the lack of active government support. It is a truism that laws are made by the government. Thus lack of government enthusiasm and active support leads to lack of response in this direction. African librarians and information specialists have to work very hard to improve public relations. Sam Ifidon's conclusion was most pertinent when he said, "Thus the African librarian has the problem of both the ignorance of, and the need to educate politicians, civil servants and educationalists about the place of libraries in a country's infrastructure."[3]

As indicated earlier, bibliographic services in Africa are underdeveloped, except in Nigeria and South Africa. Since they are prerequisites for consistent and national bibliographic programs, legal depository laws must be enacted throughout the African continent.

Librarianship as a profession is still very traditional in that manual systems predominate, with very rare cases of automation in Nigeria and the Republic of South Africa. While associations exist in several countries, they have not been effective in influencing the trend of library development. Hopefully, as the

The National Free Library of Rhodesia moved into this modern building in 1962. (Courtesy of the National Free Library of Rhodesia.)

The Kennedy Memorial Library of Haile Sellasie I University was given by the United States Agency for International Development in 1970. (From R. Pankhurst, in *Encyclopedia of Library and Information Science*, ed. A. Kent and H. Lancour (New York: Marcel Dekker, 1972), 8:222.)

number of professionals on the market increases, these associations will be much more influential than they are today. Judging by the rate of production from the available library schools, it will take a long time to develop a sufficient number of dynamic professionals. In the meantime, the present generation of librarians should lay the groundwork on which posterity will continue to build viable library and information services.

At first glance, the picture painted here may appear grim. On closer examination, however, one should realize that more libraries and library services have been established within the last fifty years than in the whole of the nineteenth century. As the desire for economic and social advancement intensifies, library and information services will increasingly be seen as vital components of development programs. Glenn Sitzman's comment was timely when he said, "It is my belief that so far as one can predict the future, the future of librarianship in . . . Africa is to be read in the development of the past ten or twelve years. The prospects are not gloomy. Despite the struggle for more improvement in working conditions, salaries, book budgets, etc."[4] In short, the next decade or two are likely to have a higher rate of progress than the previous ones.

Characteristics

Dorothy G. Collings characterized the library development of Africa as follows:

1. The Arab states of Northern Africa have a centuries-old library legacy, which sometimes impedes efforts at modernization.
2. Within French-speaking Middle Africa, continental library traditions are reflected.
3. Within English-speaking Middle Africa, British and American library influences are predominant.
4. Southern Africa's Angola and Mozambique have little library development. Zimbabwe is somewhat more advanced. By world standards, South Africa provides full-scale library services of high quality for the small white minority but only limited, racially-segregated services for the rest of the population.[5]

WESTERN EUROPE
Jean-Pierre Clavel

The origin of Western European civilization is to be found in the Graeco-Latin culture transmitted principally by the Church during the Middle Ages. All other influences are secondary. Western European culture had its roots in the Graeco-Latin world and was nourished by the Renaissance which dominated Western Europe in the fourteenth century, spreading northward from Italy. However, the intellectual movement which preceded the establishment of the first universities and cultural centers antedates the Renaissance. Universities had begun to appear at the end of the twelfth century, each bishopric being made responsible for the creation of its own "high school." By the end of the fifteenth century universities had become numerous in Western Europe. The Reformation in the sixteenth century accentuated the tendency toward higher education. Other universities appeared after the French Revolution, and still others arose towards the end of the nineteenth century. This trend has been renewed since the end of World War II.

At the present time in Western Europe there are more than 250 universities, plus a great many national or regional academies. There are also numerous learned societies, each university sponsoring its group for medicine, natural science, history, philosophy, the arts, theology, law, and other fields.

As to the history of printing from moveable type in Western Euope, it had a rapid development during the fifteenth century in the Rhineland, from which sector of Germany it spread to the neighboring states, very rapidly to Italy, Switzerland, France, and the rest of the continent.

Since the fifteenth century when approximately 40,000 titles were issued, the number of books printed annually has grown very rapidly from year to year; also, the number of imprints of any one book increased considerably during the sixteenth century. A very considerable number of books dating from that period is to be found today in Western European libraries. It is not uncommon to find a library of only average importance, situated in a university town, a bishopric, the home of an enlightened prince, or any other center having a tradition of culture, which numbers among its holdings several thousand books printed before 1600. In spite of the destruction of libraries which occurred during the numerous religious conflicts, the Thirty Years' War, the Napoleonic campaigns, and World Wars I and II which partially or wholly destroyed numerous libraries, one can still estimate the holdings of Western European libraries at nearly one milliard (one thousand million books).

The development of printing has paralleled the growth of culture in Western Europe, and is directly proportional to the population. It was in the more populous regions that printing first took root in the fifteenth century, this being a zone stretching from the Rhineland to Rome, which was already the axis for a great commercial and cultural exchange. It was in the populated regions of Western Euope that culture, represented by books, spread most rapidly. Other more sparsely inhabited areas of Western Europe did not witness the appearance of printing until quite late in the seventeenth and eighteenth centuries, and, in some regions, at an even later date.

One can thus affirm that printing, which developed from the need to multiply less expensive texts destined for the masses, is the product of urban civilization. On the other hand, rural zones for a much longer period were without the benefits of printing and still remained illiterate.

Population

Especially revealing are the rate of urbanization and living standards, which are two strong motivating forces for the development of libraries. Tables 5.1 and 5.2 illuminate this subject.

Table 5.1 Population Characteristics of Western European Countries

Country	Population (000) (1981)	Inhabitants per square kilometer	Rate of urbaniza- tion	Median of educational attainment
Austria	7,523	89	52	3.2
Belgium	9,870	322	87	?
Denmark	5,130	119	65	?
Finland	4,800	15.6	51	4.1
France	53,950	96	70	5.0
Germany	61,832	249	79	?
Great Britain	55,962	229	90	9.7
Greece	9,700	66.5	?	6.1
Ireland	3,460	44	57	8.9
Italy	57,150	185	48	4.0
Netherlands	14,250	413	78	4.7
Norway	4,150	12.6	43	5.5
Portugal	10,000	95	?	2.9
Spain	37,750	70	43	3.9
Sweden	8,330	20	81	12.7
Switzerland	6,403	155	78	5.5

Note: Considerable illiteracy is still to be found in Greece, Spain, Italy, and Portugal.

From an examination of the table of population density in Western Europe, one may easily conclude that the development of libraries does not bear a direct relation to the population. Sparsely populated countries such as Norway, Sweden, or Finland possess excellent libraries, whereas Italy is less well endowed. The rate of urbanization most assuredly is favorable to library development. However, the various demographic phenomena (density, urbanization) are only one factor; other causes elude a purely quantitative analysis.

The political element is of a very real significance in this discussion. Libraries have developed most in those countries whose political regime possessed the following characteristics: stability, parliamentary democracy, and a concern for social progress. As for political parties, those which have been leaders in library development in recent years have been of the socialist tendency (the Northern countries and Germany). Dictatorial regimes have never encouraged library progress since traditionally libraries have philosophically favored the free flow of information. Whether the motives have been religious or political, the censor has always been an obstacle to the unlimited growth of libraries.

Table 3.2 Standard of Living in Western European Countries

Country	Per capita income in dollars (1979)	Standard of living: private consumption per inhabitant in dollars (1978)	Number of private cars (000) (1977)	Number of television sets (000) (1976)	Number of kilometers covered by train (1978)
Austria	$ 6,739	$ 6,739	$ 1,870	$ 1,770	7.31 bln
Belgium	10,800 [1980]	9,025	2,810	2,600	7.14 bln
Denmark	8,470	9,869	1,380	1,640	3.08 bln
Finalnd	5,814	6,090	1,080	1,710	2.99 bln
France	8,619	7,908	3,620 [1978]	14,500	53.51 bln
Germany	9,507	9,278	20,020	19,230	19.23 bln
Greece	2,881	3,209	839,341 [1978]	1,170	1.57 bln
Ireland	3,533	2,711	682,960 [1979]	665	964.8 bln
Italy	4,191	3,076	1,640	12,380	39.2 bln
Netherlands	7,754	8,509	3,850	3,770	8.1 bln
Norway	8,762	7,949	1,110	1,090	2.71 bln
Portugal	1,754 [1974]	1,509	1,030 [1976]	723	5.51 bln
Spain	2,830 [1974]	3,625	5,940	6,640	16.76 bln
Sweden	10,071	9,274	2,880	2,980	5.56 bln
Switzerland	9,439	12,408	1,930	1,810	9.3 bln
United Kingdom	4,972	4,955	14,920 [1979]	18,270	30.7 bln

The financial structure of a country is also an important factor in library progress. Large countries which allot resources through regional authorities, and small countries which by their very size constitute groups with regional characteristics, have favored the growth of libraries. The librarian who is personally acquainted with the decision-makers in his country has a better prospect of seeing his projects realized than his colleague in a larger nation who must channel his requests through an anonymous administrative system.

A quite different element, which may also be a determinant, is the climate and the number of hours of darkness. In a pleasant climate the growth of libraries is possibly less accentuated than in those countries where because of severly low temperatures the public must spend long evenings by the hearth.

In this discussion we must not overlook the importance of private initiative as displayed by a disinterested populace having some influence upon their local authorities. A sense of civic responsibility is not without importance to library development. A similar initiative in favor of public works, especially of a cultural nature, is found more often in rich countries than in poor ones. In this sense Table 5.2 showing the living standards of the countries of Western Europe is revealing. Those countries having a high standard, almost without exception display the best developed libraries, the richest bibliographic collections, the most advanced services to the public, and the best trained and most numerous staff.

The linguistic element does not seem to have played a decisive part in the growth of libraries in Western Europe. However, the multiplicity of languages spoken on the continent does complicate work methods, cataloging rules, and the computer entry format. Research libraries acquire books in what are called the "accessible" languages: English, German, French, Italian, Spanish; on the other hand, the Nordic tongues, Dutch, and Greek are considered outside their respective areas to be languages of "difficult access." Thus, certain languages have only a very limited diffusion (in a single country or in one area of a given country), and their literature when published in the original language makes less of a cultural impact than when it is translated into one of the widely diffused languages. Consequently, the libraries of those countries whose language is of limited diffusion must accept this reality and plan their acquisitions accordingly.

Religion has played a part, and still does exercise an important influence, on library development in Western Europe. It is clear that countries which adopted Protestantism in the sixteenth century developed libraries more boldly, saw their industries flourish, and printing advance remarkably.

Education

The percentage of illiterate Western Europeans is low. Of a total population of more than 360 million inhabitants, not more than 2.5 percent are illiterates, of whom nearly all are natives of the Mediterranean countries or Portugal.

On the other hand, the number of students in Western Europe is high. In 1975 there were 14.5 million. Of necessity, students are assiduous frequenters of libraries, and after the conclusion of their studies they generally continue to use libraries.

Many countries have organized higher education along the lines of the so-called "open universities" which attract adults lacking the necessary academic qualifications but possessing an inquiring mind. These enterprises may be quite modest, but they also generate library use among their students.

Culture

In every cultural field Western Europe has been preeminent, but especially so in painting, sculpture, drawing, and engraving (the latter often occupying a choice place among the holdings of the very large libraries). For centuries Italy, the Germanic countries, France, and Spain have produced a great number of artists whose works today adorn the walls of European and American galleries. The illuminated manuscripts of the Middle Ages, which are on permanent display in the richest libraries of the world, are another example of the cultural wealth of Western Europe.

Italy and Germany share the highest laurels for their contribution to the development of music. The largest libraries of these countries possess immense collections of musical scores, there being more than 200,000 musical works alone in the Staatsbibliothek Preussischer Kultur Besitz in Berlin. The numerous phonograph record libraries are yet another indication of public appreciation of music. It is difficult to estimate the number of symphonic orchestras in Western Europe, since an agreement on the definition of what constitutes an acceptable orchestra is difficult due to the varying levels of performance and a severe competition among the many performing groups. Each city of more than 500,000 inhabitants possesses what is generally accepted as a good symphonic orchestra. The radio stations have greatly encouraged such musical ensembles. In some regions the number and quality of symphonic orchestras is greater than in others. For example, Geneva and Lausanne together have scarcely 400,000 inhabitants, yet they possess the Orchestre de la Suisse Romande which is world-renowned and the Orchestre de Chambre de Lausanne, which is a notable ensemble devoted especially to the performance of contemporary music. Besides these professional ensembles, there are also numerous groups of semiprofessionals and amateurs, conservatory orchestras, ancient music ensembles, and such.

The number of museums in Western Europe exceeds 5000. All large cities possess a museum. Certainly, the Louvre and the British Museum are the two most famous in the world. But tiny localities of less than 2000 inhabitants often possess a museum. In general, it may be said that all cities of 50,000 inhabitants or more possess a theater. On the other hand, only the very largest communities have an opera, the upkeep of which constitutes a heavy drain on any city's budget. The municipal authorities subsidize shows, travelling troupes, concerts, and the like. Sometimes this is done admittedly for tourist purposes but more often, perhaps, it is done openly for prestige. This practice is prejudicial to libraries whose services are considered to be less glamorous.

Economy

With regard to the national revenue of each of the Western European countries, we should add that it is very diversified within each country. Certain countries producing a high gross national product have regions which are inexplicably deserted (e.g., the center of France). One must, therefore, use these figures for comparative purposes with prudence. The development of libraries represents a heavy financial outlay which has a direct relationship to the wealth of the country (a nation with a positive balance of payments and a high gross national product), the rate of urbanization, and the degree of industrialization (for the agricultural laborer and the urban worker read relatively little).

These elements explain the sustained development of libraries in Western Europe. The Nordic, Germanic, Flemish, and Anglo-Saxon countries are the most advanced; on the other hand, the less-developed countries spend correspondingly less money on their libraries.

Transport

The question of transport affects only those libraries which engage in interlibrary lending services. Public transport, especially the postal service, is of great importance to libraries. Although in certain countries the circulation of books is facilitated through libraries paying lower fees than the general public, in country after country this privilege is slowly being abolished. A decline in the quality of the postal service must also be registered. In certain nations the libraries themselves have organized privately the transport of books from one institution to another. Public transport is also important to the library user. Generally this service is well organized. This is all the more necessary since public and research libraries have usually been situated in the center of town. Now because of traffic congestion, it is no longer possible for a library user to park his private car in the vicinity of these centrally located libraries. This same situation becomes equally burdensome for the library staff.

Communication

Books There are many successful book clubs in Western Europe whose enormous diffusion of reading material is due to the very advantageous prices which they offer to their subscribers. Large editions of 50,000 or more copies make it possible to offer really competitive prices; a 250- to 300-page volume bound in imitation leather, when produced in a large edition, may sell for as little as $3.00. This presentation has been one of the reasons for the success of these editions, since many book club members build personal libraries inexpensively with these acquisitions. By creating series of 20 to 30 volumes, and by choosing popular authors such as Arthur Conan Doyle and Georges Simenon, book clubs have been able to capture an important hold on the book market. This action of the book clubs has probably been more beneficial to culture in the long run than formal literary prizes and similar activities. Except for a few important prizes (such as the Goncourt or the Renaudot in France), these literary contests appear to have had little effect on the diffusion of books. Book fairs such as those held in Frankfort or Brussels are useful to publishers who need to contact agents, locate clients for translation and other work, or for carrying out other activities related more directly to the diffusion of new books soon to be published. In these activities the commercial aspect is of great importance. Rarely do libraries associate themselves directly with these enterprises, as it is difficult for them to participate in them and derive any financial advantage from them. Because of the publicity surrounding the book fairs, whatever their aim may be, these events do encourage the diffusion and reading of books, and contribute indirectly also to the development of libraries. Indeed, Western European librarians consider it advantageous to their libraries to cooperate with the sponsors of book fairs and with bookmen generally, even if the benefits to their libraries may not be immediately apparent.

Other Information and Documentation Services As IFLA and FID have collaborated regularly for many years, the various services which make up these organizations also work together. As mentioned above, rarely do the national libraries of western Europe maintain a scientific and technical documentation service. The organizations which are responsible for this task—such as the Centre de la Recherche Scientifique in France—operate independently of national libraries. However, they provide information services to the research libraries of their respective countries, and sometimes furnish this service to institutions abroad. These documentation centers also publish current bibliographies relative to science and technology.

Radio and Television The appearance in the world of communication of these two media, each separated from the other in time corresponding roughly to one generation, has certainly been detrimental to the expansion of reading. As a result of both, there has been a general decline in the circulation statistics of public libraries, with even the disappearance of some small libraries. In certain countries the total number of libraries has declined considerably since the beginning of the century, a phenomenon having two related causes: on the one hand, an exodus of the rural population from their farms and their migrations to towns and cities, and on the other, a steady multiplication of radio sets. The spread of television has had a similar negative effect on reading, but this decline has been less marked due partly to the high price of the sets, which has placed them beyond the reach of certain sectors of the population, and also in part to the mediocrity of the programs, and partly because of the aforementioned rural exodus which had already taken place. The decline in borrowing statistics of public libraries, which occurred immediately after the introduction of television, was short lived and less marked than that resulting from the radio.

Characteristics

The following characteristics of Western European librarianship have been revealed through our study.

1. Librarianship has developed old traditions and institutions, for example centuries-old legislation supporting legal deposit of library materials.
2. Library development tends to be more advanced in the North than in the South, corresponding to the levels of financial support given by the countries in the two regions.
3. The status of librarians is in direct relation to the regard in which the profession is held by the public
4. The multiplicity of languages complicates methods, rules, and computer formats.
5. International cooperation is common among European library agencies.[6]

An attractive reading room in the Cantonal and University Library of Lausanne, Switzerland. (Courtesy of Jean-Pierre Clavel, Head Librarian, Canton and University Library of Lausanne, Switzerland.)

The Töölö Branch of the Helsinki City Library was opened in 1970 and was designed by architect Aarne Ervi. (From H. M. Kauppi, in *Encyclopedia of Library and Information Science*, ed. A. Kent and H. Lancour (New York: Marcel Dekker, 1972), 8:479.

The Reference Room in the Töölö Branch of the Helsinki City Library is spacious. (From R. Sievanen-Allen, in *Encyclopedia of Library and Information Science*, ed. A. Kent and H. Lancour (New York: Marcel Dekker, 1972), 8:480.)

The Catalog Hall of Helsinki University Library includes this aesthetically beautiful interior. (From R. Sievanen-Allen, in *Encyclopedia of Library and Information Science*, ed. A. Kent and H. Lancour (New York: Marcel Dekker, 1972), 8:486.)

Opening session of the 45th Congress of the International Federation of Library Associations in Tivoli, Copenhagen in August 1979. (Courtesy of International Federation of Library Associations.)

The Swedish Library Association held its 1978 meeting in Gothenburg, Sweden. (Courtesy of Jan Nyberg, Swedish Library Association.)

SOVIET UNION
B. P. Kanevsky

In each society the library is a social agency closely connected with the prevailing culture and fulfilling, apart from information functions, those of an ideological nature. In this sense, the work of any library in the Soviet Union, like any literary work or like the work of publishing houses, bookshops, and printing shops in the country, is based on Communist party principles, on which Vladimir I. Lenin wrote in the early 1900s.

Soviet Libraries and those of other socialist countries are libraries of a new, socialist society; they differ radically from all other libraries not only in the composition of their collections but also in the makeup of their readers and in the entire social nature of their work, including the nature of relationships among libraries, society, and the Soviet state. From the very first days of its existence, the socialist state has assumed the responsibility for the country's cultural development, including the library service of the entire population. In the context of a socialist society, the library changes from a passive keeper and, at best, an intermediary between the book and the user, into a propagandist of the book, and, above all, of the one which is most relevant for the solution of crucial economic, social, political, cultural, and moral problems vital to society.

The work of the libraries of the Soviet Union should be considered against the background of the entire socioeconomic system of the country, in close connection with the huge and very complex economic and cultural organization which the Soviet Union embodies at the present time. The size of the country, its multinational composition, rapidly developing social processes—all these leave an imprint on librarianship in the USSR; of course, the development of Soviet libraries cannot be understood correctly, nor can any comparison be made, without taking these socioeconomic factors into account.

As of 1982, the population of the USSR was 268 million (annually it increases at the rate of 4.5 million). With regard to the size of its population, the Soviet Union ranks third in the world after the People's Republic of China and India.

The division of the Soviet population by sex is uneven: men constitute 46.5 percent and women 53.5 percent. This ratio is still the echo of the tragic years of World War II, in which the country lost millions of its citizens, largely young men. The majority of the Soviet population lives now in towns (166 million or 62 percent), and the minority in the country (101 million or 38 percent). The country has over 470 towns with populations over 50,000 each. Moscow, the capital of the Soviet Union, has approximately 8 million inhabitants. These figures show a shift to urban living, reflecting vast social changes in the Soviet people: before 1917, only a small part, actually 18 percent, lived in towns; socialist industrialization, mechanization of agriculture, and a number of other factors promoted large-scale migration of the populations from the country to the town. This change required a larger number of town libraries and an increase in their holdings; however, library service of the rural population constantly requires special attention; for example, the changes in the educational level of the rural population (the increase in the number of village dwellers with higher and secondary specialized education) necessitates the raising of library service of the rural population to that of city dwellers.

According to the census conducted at the end of the nineteenth century, exactly twenty years before the Russian revolution of 1917, a mere 28.4 percent of the people were literate; in 1970 the literacy level amounted to 99.7 percent. In 1976, as many as 121 million people, including 77 percent of all the people engaged in the national economy, had attained a secondary (including incomplete secondary) education. The USSR has at present some 1.3 million scientific workers; in addition, there are 4.9 million students enrolled in higher education establishments, an average of 190 students per 10,000 of the population. Complete secondary education is obligatory in the Soviet Union. This wide range of educational activity and its large number of students create a strong demand for books which directly affects the work of the country's libraries.

Their activities are also affected in many ways by the multinational composition of Soviet society. This relationship is reflected both in the nature of the librarians' work, as Soviet librarians are active propagandists of the best books of all national literatures of the Soviet Union. A large number of translations of books from national languages are made into Russian, which is the language of intranational communication of all peoples of the USSR. Within the Soviet Union, there are over 100 nations and nationalities, and books are published in 89 of these languages. Of the people of the USSR, the most numerous are the 144 million Russians, followed by 45 million Ukranians, 11 million Uzbeks, 11 million Byelorussians, 6 million Tartars, and 5.3 million Kazakhs; another 14 nations and nationalities total up to 1 million.

Each of these preserves and develops the best traditions and national forms of their own culture, enriching them with new socialist content and with ideas of socialist humanism and proletarian internationalism, thus promoting cordial relations among Soviet socialist nations. The building of a developed socialist· society, the process of rapprochement and unity of nations and nationalities in the USSR have led to the emergence of a new historical community of people —the Soviet people.

Lastly, libraries being cultural agencies, their work should be regarded as part of the state system of cultural and educational agencies: in the USSR there are over 135,000 clubs (over 20,000 in cities and about 115,000 in rural areas), over 154,000 cinemas (over 25,000 in cities and about 129,000 in rural areas), 570 theaters, about 1300 museums, and 214 concert organizations. Also, the Soviet people have 122.5 million radios and over 60 million television sets.

The interaction of the book and mass media is complex and ambiguous; in the Soviet Union this interaction proceeds in one direction. Despite the wide diffusion of the cinema, radio, and television, the demand for books in the

Soviet Union continues to be enormous. For this reason, the statement of the General Secretary of the CDSU Central Committee, Leonid I. Brezhnev, "It is rightly regarded that the Soviet people read more books than any other nation in the world" is well-supported by the facts of Soviet librarianship.

The Soviet library is a dynamic system closely linked with its social environment, with the life and concerns of the country as a whole; it has prestige with the people and renders effective assistance to the Communist party of the Soviet Union both in educating a well-developed and socially active person—a citizen of the developed socialist society—and in solving state economic, political, and cultural tasks. This is the feature that distinguishes libraries of the Soviet Union and other socialist countries from their counterparts in the rest of the world.

Characteristics

Soviet librarianship—occupying a huge area of the surface of Europe and Asia, and serving hundreds of millions of people of different nationalities—has certain common characteristics.

1. Soviet library practice is based on Communist party principles devised by Vladimir I. Lenin (1870-1924).
2. These principles reflect the Communist party spirit in all library activities, and state the concept of freedom of access to libraries and the planned character of library development.
3. The socialist socioeconomic system, based on the social ownership of the means of production and the goal of a balanced development of the national economy, includes library development.
4. The main task of Soviet libraries is to carry on active propaganda of the policy pursued by the Communist party and the Soviet state.
5. Underlying the planning of Soviet libraries is the assumption that they will expand and play an increasingly active role in the national economy and culture.
6. In the USSR librarianship is considered a profession that enjoys widespread prestige.
7. Activities, collections, and the nature of the librarians' work within Soviet libraries are affected by the multinational composition of Soviet society.
8. The plans of library development in the Union Republics take into account the local conditions and national characteristics, as well as approved state five-year plans and the allocation for the development of cultural and educational institutions for which these plans provide.[7]

EASTERN EUROPE

M. B. Nabatova

Interlibrary cooperation impressively contributes to the development of librarianship in the socialist countries of Europe. This takes many forms, including seminars, conferences of directors of library development in the ministries of culture of each of the countries, meetings of the directors of national libraries, managers of methodological centers, chiefs of business missions, the loan of specialists, the exchange of materials, and, finally, the implementation of joint research projects.

In the socialist countries of Europe thorough study is made of the Soviet library experience. The professional press informs practitioners regularly about the most important events in the Soviet library world and about publications on library science in Russia.

The librarians of socialist countries participate in numerous international conferences and seminars. Bilateral seminars are also devoted to the summary of aspects of library development, urgent problems in librarianship and library science, as well as the improvement of the profession in the socialist countries. This form of cooperation originated in 1965, the first meeting being held in Moscow, a later one in Prague, with binational seminars devoted to librarianship being sponsored subsequently with great frequency. A number of conferences of specialists from the European socialist countries have been held in recent years, being devoted to research in reading, acquisition problems of the national libraries, international book exchange, the problems of scientific libraries (classification, subject cataloging, union catalogs, research in library science, bibliography, and other subjects).

The conference of the chiefs of centers of library science and methodological activities of the libraries of the socialist countries have become a regular form of cooperation. The first such meeting was held in Berlin in 1962. Similar conferences have been scheduled frequently in subsequent years.

As it was emphasized in Bucharest in 1974, the major problems of socialist library science include unified systems of library services, interlibrary cooperation, collaboration with the information system, library management and methodical guidance, and centralization of activities within the library networks.

Because the Communist and Workers' parties and the governments of the socialist countries are permanently concerned with librarianship, the profession has reached a high level of development. That evolution seems assured because conditions favorable to progress have been created.

Library laws have been approved and plans have been implemented in the European socialist countries for the expansion and improvement of the public library networks which involve the construction of new library buildings, the consolidation of the material base of libraries, and the equipment of large scientific libraries with the best of modern techniques.

Libraries have become truly popular centers for the dissemination of socially useful knowledge and active educators of the working people, in the spirit of Marxism-Leninism. In all socialist countries, the bulk of the urban population, all young people, and a considerable part of the rural population, now have access to library service.

Books have been brought within the reach of broad sections of the public; the quantitative indices of the activities of libraries have grown impressively and qualitative changes are constantly taking place. Readers' demands for political, scientific, and popular science literature constantly increase. Libraries now play an important role in educating the working people towards a spirit of internationalism and appreciation of the achievement of the various fraternal socialist countries.

National libraries are not only the most important keepers of stocks of national literature but centers of national bibliography, methodological and scientific activities in librarianship, the history of bookprinting, the sociology of reading, international book exchange, book hygiene, and restoration. The role of national libraries in the library systems of the socialist countries continues to grow, especially as they are centers for the coordination and cooperation with public and scientific libraries of the country.

National libraries, more actively than ever before, contribute to the development of the overall state information system, as they expand their own informational functions. At the present-day level of development of librarianship in the socialist countries, the expansion of cooperation and the strengthening of of ties between the libraries have become the most efficient means for meeting readers' demands for literature in different subject fields. In a number of the socialist countries cooperation between local libraries is expanding into cooperation between aggregates of libraries and library systems.

The ideology of Marxism-Leninism, common to all socialist countries, the growing cooperation of the countries of the socialist community in all fields (economics, politics, science, and culture), create conditions favorable to further expansion of the relations between the libraries of the socialist countries.

Libraries, in their capacity as mass ideological institutions which function in every populated area and in all spheres of social life, play a highly important role in the development of socialist culture, science, and economics. Through active propaganda and through the dissemination of the works of the founders of Marxism-Leninism, party documents, progressive fiction and special literature, libraries contribute to the many-sided education of the working people. At the same time they also contribute to the raising of cultural standards and to the professional education of the people.

Characteristics

Because of its close alliance with the Soviet Union, Eastern Europe has developed a librarianship that resembles its Soviet counterpart in various respects. The characteristics of Eastern European librarianship are as follow:

1. The leading principles in the work of all libraries in socialist countries are the Communist party spirit in all of their activities, the concept of freedom of access to everyone, and the planned character of library development, formulated by Lenin.
2. Librarianship in East European socialist countries is characterized by participation of the libraries in the implementation of the complex construction program of a developed socialist society, laid down by the congresses of Communist Workers' parties of 1975 and 1976.
3. All European socialist countries implement Lenin's instructions concerning the role, function, and organization of a uniform and planned library system.
4. In all European socialist countries librarianship is being developed along planned lines. Five-year and even longer-term plans are being carried out.[8]

General Reading Hall of the Lenin State Library of the USSR. (Courtesy of O.A. Diakonova, Department Chief, Department of Foreign Librarianship and International Library Relations.)

Social Sciences Reading Hall in the Lenin State Library of the USSR. (Courtesy of O. A. Diakonova, Department Chief, Department of Foreign Librarianship and International Library Relations.)

LATIN AMERICA
Gaston Litton and Richard Krzys

People and Society in Latin America

To gain an insight into librarianship in this vast and complex region, one should take note of certain important social factors, such as its ethnic composition, as well as the diverse cultural, social, and economic stratifications of its people. Above all, one should be aware that illiteracy has continued to handicap sizeable percentages of the population, in spite of the sporadic and sometimes spectacular efforts that have been made in various regions and cities to eliminate it.

In an earlier publication, we provided the following comment on the Latin American people and society, giving a clue to the complexity of their ethnic composition: "The Spaniards, Portuguese, and French who settled in the New World brought with them the European traditions with which they were familiar and which they, in turn, attempted to superimpose upon the cultures of the indigenous people whom they subjugated; namely, the Aztecs, Toltecs, Mayas, Chibchas, and Incas."[9]

Nowhere is this assimilation process more evident than in Mexico where the people proudly proclaim their roots in many ways, such as on a colorful tile in a Mexico City restaurant: "Christian by the grace of God; gentlemen thanks to our Spanish descent; noble lords from our Indian ancestry—we are, then, the Mexicans."[10]

Add African stock to the mixture already described and one becomes aware of the even greater racial complexity that exists in some countries of Latin America.

> Coupled with the pattern of life known to the African slaves who were brought to the Americas, the racial composition of the Latin American people of today has resulted from a free and uninhibited mingling and mixture of indigenous, European and African elements. Although these factors contribute to the formation of a Latin American people, subtle and sometimes not so subtle differences appeared which separated the people of one region from those of another. Central America, Paraguay, and Peru have a strong indigenous influence, while Haiti's people are a blend of French and African racial stocks, while Argentina, Chile and Uruguay reflect, on the other hand, the strongest European influence resulting from a heavy immigration during the nineteenth century. Brazil, meanwhile, is a racial potpourri, with a more recent immigration from the Orient and Europe, as a complement to its traditional dominant strains originating in Portugal and Africa. These mixtures have produced an extreme social and economic stratification, reflected in a small upper class, a small but growing middle class, and a large number of people occupying the lowest rungs of the social and economic ladder.[11]

In this free blending of diverse social elements, librarianship has not remained untouched. One of the most retarding effects upon the development of library services has resulted from the high rate of illiteracy. Something of the seriousness of this problem is indicated in the following passage: "Although an accurate assessment of the illiteracy is an impossibility due to the present paucity of statistical studies within the various countries of Latin America, it can safely be affirmed that of the 240,000,000* inhabitants of Latin America, approximately one-half of the adult population has had no opportunity to learn to read. This unfortunately high rate of illiteracy should be considered as adversely affecting the most significant aspects of Latin American librarianship."[12]

Latin America Inherits a Romantic Tradition

For any understanding of present-day Latin Americans, one should be aware of the romantic tradition prevalent even today, which was brought to the shores of the New World by the Spanish and Portuguese who sailed the caravels that plied the waves between the Iberian peninsula, the Caribbean isles, and the

*Latin America had over 349,000,000 inhabitants in a 1978 estimate.

American mainland. The seeds of this tradition were implanted in American soil by the explorers who mapped the new territories for their far-off Catholic kings, and by the missionaries whose goal was nothing less than the conversion to Christianity of every inhabitant of the new lands.

> A pattern of thought and administrative procedures was successfully transferred to the New World colonies of Spain and Portugal, superimposed upon the simple way of life of the indigenous people, and permitted to flourish during more than three centuries of colonial status. Native-born revolutionaries successfully ended this colonial status during the nineteenth century, but they did not greatly disturb or modify the uniformity of customs, religion, architecture, or the general way of life which, now more than 150 years later, are visibly apparent to anyone who travels south of the Rio Grande. This romantic tradition and the unquestionable uniformity of thought have left a heavy imprint of individualism on all activity of Latin America, including its library practice.[13]

Bases of Disunity

A closer examination of the countries of Latin America should make it abundantly clear that, as there is unity on some matters, in other aspects there is a very marked disunity among its people.

One of these causes of disunity is the large number of languages spoken by the people. Spanish is the dominant language of those countries which originated from Spain's extensive penetration of America. Portuguese, in a similar manner, is the language of Brazil which was colonized by Portugal. France, on the other hand, had a decisive part in settling Haiti where French is spoken.

On the subject of the language barrier, which impedes the free flow of library materials, information, and ideas, mention should be made of the linguistic situation existing today in Mexico and Central America where large segments of the population speak only, or primarily, an indigenous tongue and find effective communication in Spanish to be difficult or impossible. To understand the situation more fully, one should be aware of the large numbers of people in the interior of South America who speak only Guarani, Tupi, Quechua, Aymara, and other indigenous languages.

There are other bases of disunity, created by the Latin Americans themselves, which take the form of tariff bariers and customs restrictions. At certain times and places these are so oppressive and vexatious that any advantages for the international book trade or international library cooperation among Latin American countries are considerably lessened.

"It would be wrong," according to Miguel Angel Piñeiro, "to consider Latin America as a single cultural, social and economic unit. The contrasts are striking, and it is absurd to talk about a specifically Latin American man, trait of character or temperament. In librarianship, too, Latin America is far from being homogeneous. Libraries are the product of their environment, and where the environment lacks homogeneity they simply reflect its defects, lack of foresight on the part of the authorities, failure to appreciate the library's role in education, lack of money, absence of the necessary legislation. Yet in Latin America there is a long history of libraries."[14]

A State of Dependency

As we pointed out on another occasion, "The economy of Latin America during its first 300 years could best be described as 'semifeudal', by which term is meant the ownership of immense tracts of land by a few landowners who held near illiterate laborers in virtual serfdom and general backwardness, to cultivate their land. This situation fostered a dependence of most of the nations of Latin America on the world's major industrial powers for the majority of their manufactured necessities. There existed, too, what has often been described as a one-crop economy; in other words, the dominance of a single crop or mineral as the principal source of income for a given country."[15]

There has undoubtedly been some alleviation in the economic situation in recent years, especially through the efforts of the Alliance for Progress and similar programs, some of which originated in the United States, while others derived from generating forces within Latin America itself. Even so, the total economic picture remains far from optimistic. "Century-old traditions of the virtual enslavement of the masses, a dependence upon foreign markets, and a one-crop economy, as well as an inordinate interference by bureaucratic functionaries, have contributed directly to an unfavorable climate for the general development of these nations."[16]

What has been the effect upon library development of this economic dependency of the Latin American nations? "Librarianship has not escaped this reality; there has been perpetuated among many Latin Americans a pessimistic attitude or an indifference toward reading, study, and investigation as the basis for rapid personal advancement and steady national progress. There has been a continual reliance on more advanced nations for their concepts of librarianship, instead of facing up to the local situation and the careful planning of solutions in accordance with national needs and commensurate with the means, financial and professional, at their disposal."[17]

Political Instability

To gain a clearer understanding and appraisal of the situation of librarianship in Latin America, the observer should take into account the widespread, critical, and endemic political unrest and instability, and a general lack of continuity in almost all phases of public administration in the Latin American republics. It is well to remember that "the colonial educational pattern and civic mores left the people of Latin America poorly prepared for self-government; consequently, their history has been bloodied by turmoil, border disputes, and an almost continuous feuding between the principal political parties."[18]

Fortunately, some stability in Latin American government has been achieved during this century, but even this modicum of success must be discounted because of the profound political disturbances which have occurred in various countries in very recent times. As might be expected, "This political unrest has taken a heavy toll of progress generally but especially so in the cultural field, causing severe setbacks for libraries, physical damage to buildings and collections, discontinuity in their administration, the dislocation of personnel, and a painful draining of meager budgets."[19]

It would be difficult to find a clearer example of this depressing situation as it affected librarianship than the massive exodus of Cuban librarians, after 1959, which resulted in the general weakening of the human resources available for the professional development of that country's libraries. At the same time, world librarianship, and particularly librarianship in the United States, improved its situation considerably by the contributions of Cuban librarians who fled the Castro Communist regime.

Characteristics

Permeating Latin American librarianship are the following characteristics:

1. A pessimistic attitude or an indifference exists among many Latin Americans toward reading, study, and investigation as the basis for rapid personal advancement and steady national progress.
2. Books and libraries have only recently come to be regarded as essential elements in the education process in Latin America.
3. There has been a continual reliance on more advanced nations for their concepts of librarianship, instead of devising solutions in accordance with national needs and means, financial and professional, available.
4. The unstable nature of the book trade in Latin America adversely affects bibliographic control.
5. The most serious obstacle to professional status of librarians is the predominantly custodial function exercised by most Latin American librarians.
6. Latin American librarianship has shifted from being a local phenomenon toward international involvement of various nations of the Americas.[20]

THE UNITED STATES AND CANADA
H. C. Campbell

Historical Background

Among the historical factors which are constantly at work in determining the future direction for various aspects of the North American way of life are the 300-year-old patterns of settlement, the ethnic and linguistic background of a multicultural population, and the differing physical settings and climates of each of the various regions of the vast continent. Even if the transportation and communication facilities of the twentieth century have to some extent, under the most favorable conditions, removed the complete isolation of one region from another, there are still many completely separate and distinct regional differences within North America that must be taken into account in organizing and planning library services.

Such matters as the linguistic and religious background of the Spanish and Caribbean South, the French heritage of Quebec, the German and Lutheran influence in the Mid-west United States and Canadian prairies are all important. The literary productions of the various regions, from Newfoundland to California, also continue to play an important part and reflect the different aspirations of a wide range of people.

Libraries have a continuing role to play in conserving the history of each part of the continent, and in making it possible for each generation to appreciate its historical past. Much of the strength of local libraries, whether university and college, school, public or governmental, is in this function to conserve and preserve local history, biography, literature, architecture, technology, etc. In this, these libraries are following the patterns of libraries abroad, and providing the focus for community appreciation of historical antecedents.

Geography

The ten regions outlined in Table 5.3 represent one convenient method of dividing the North American continental land mass on a functional geographical basis. In this division the current boundary between the United States and Canada is ignored. Each region is made up of several states of the United States and provinces of Canada. The library and information services that have developed within each region have been influenced by many geographical factors, as well as political and historical ones.

Within each of the ten regions in Table 5.3 can be found many forms of cooperative library activities. In most cases there are stronger library activities within certain parts of the region than between the regions. Urban settlement within each region and its growth in the twentieth century has most often determined the basis for library resource sharing patterns and the creation of the various functional library networks which exist. In some cases the existing national boundary in regions that embrace parts of the United States and Canada can be considered for certain purposes to be nonexistent, wiped out by the periodical press, radio, television, and the telephone.

Population

It was noted earlier that ten distinct geographical regions could be deliniated in North America, each one with a population ranging from less than a million to

Table 5.3 Geographical Divisions of the North American Continental Land Mass

Region	Composition	Population (1980)
Southwest	Arizona, Colorado, New Mexico, Texas, Nevada, Utah	23 million
South	Mississippi, Louisiana, Alabama, Missouri, Arkansas	18 million
Southeast	Georgia, Florida, North Carolina, South Carolina, Tennessee, West Virginia, Virginia, District of Columbia	39 million
Pacific[a]	Hawaii, California, Oregon, Washington, British Columbia	34 million
West[a]	Kansas, Nebraska, North Dakota, South Dakota, Wyoming, Oklahoma, Montana, Idaho, Alberta, Saskatchewan	13 million
Midwest[a]	Iowa, Illinois, Indiana, Michigan, Minnesota, Manitoba, Ohio, Wisconsin	50 million
North[a]	Alaska, Yukon, Northwest Territories	471,000
Central and French Canada	Ontario, Quebec	13 million
New England and the Atlantic Provinces[a]	Massachusetts, Rhode Island, New Hampshire, Maine, Vermont, Nova Scotia, New Brunswick, Prince Edward Island, Newfoundland, Labrador	12 million
Metropolitan Atlantic Seaboard	New York, New Jersey, Maryland, Delaware, Pennsylvania, Connecticut	45 million

[a]Combining parts of the United States and Canada.

more than 50 million. This population is becoming increasingly urban, rather than rural, with important consequences for libraries.

For the past fifty years, since the mid-1930s the growth of urban metropolitan population centers in all parts of North America has been studied and commented upon. What has been seen was the appearance of first one "megalopolis" after another, beginning on the Atlantic seaboard, then in California, and finally in Texas. There was an attendant dropping of population in rural areas. Now the financial pressures on the megalopolis to survive are beginning to reverse this trend, and the next forty years may see a different concentration of population and settlement. While the Fort Lauderdale metropolitan area in Florida may continue to record a 19 percent population increase from 1970-1973, and Santa Ana in California shows an increase of 11 percent, metropolitan areas such as New York and Cleveland declined 3 percent and Pittsburgh, Los Angeles, and St. Louis showed declines of from 3 to 19 percent in the same three-year period. Between the 1970 and 1980 census the metropolitan area of New York declined 13.8 percent, Cleveland 28.8 percent, Los Angeles showed an increase of 2.4 percent, while St. Louis registered a decline of 31.7 percent during the decade between the 1970 and 1980 censuses.

The states of New York, Rhode Island, and the District of Columbia showed a net decline in metropolitan area population from 1970 to 1975, while all others had increases and a share in the 5 percent overall metropolitan area growth of the period. Yet regional differences in population growth were significant, and metropolitan areas in Alaska, Arizona, Colorado, Florida, Hawaii, Idaho, Nevada, New Mexico, Utah, and Wyoming all registered increases between 12 and 25 percent in the five-year period.[21]

In Canada, metropolitan centers have not yet started to decline, but continue to follow the growth and development trends laid down in earlier years in the United States. However, the metropolitan urban population growth change in Alberta and formerly rural Ontario is comparable to that in Colorado and Utah, showing the same tendency toward leaving the already large centers to struggle with their inherited problems.

Education

The annual expenditures of the state governments of the United States and the provincial governments of Canada, which have the basic responsibility for education at all its levels, except for the armed services, showed a continuous rise in costs for education and increasing number of persons of all ages in attendance at educational institutions over the past decades.

Since the year 1950, one notes that there has also been a dramatic rise in the United States and Canada in the level of school attainment by persons of age twenty-five and over. The data in Table 5.4 are the figures for the United States from 1950 to 1980.[22]

Libraries and information services thus must be equipped for a more literate user and a larger number of users. The regional differences in various parts of the continent in educational attainment are marked, and the drive to equalize this has had important consequences for libraries in both countries.

Table 5.4 Level of School Attainment for Persons over Twenty-five Years of Age in the United States

Level of school completed	April 1950	April 1960	March 1970	March 1980
Less than five years of elementary school (%):				
White	8.7	6.7	4.2	2.6
Nonwhite	31.4	13.5	14.7	9.1
Four or more years of high school (%):				
White	13.5	43.2	57.4	70.7
Nonwhite	13.4	21.7	36.1	54.0
Four or more years of college (%):				
White	6.4	8.1	11.6	17.9
Nonwhite	2.2	3.5	6.1	10.7

Culture

The North American cultural impact on the world is carried out largely through the creation, production, and distribution of a wide range of cultural materials, including those in the fields of music and film, as well as print. North American libraries are just as much a recipient of the impact of North American culture as libraries in foreign countries. It is therefore important in looking at the place of the library in the cultural scene in North America to realize that it must be selective and protect itself from being overburdened by the immense cultural output around it. Most libraries select only those items that they consider needed. This has been one of the historic determinants of library specialization and one which is being continued. At a time when there was general acceptance of a fixed standard of selection for cultural materials in North American life, the library championed the reading of the "best material" for the ordinary person as well as the acquisition of worthwhile technical information and practical knowledge required by young and old. At the present stage of North American popular culture, when the exploitation of emotion and sensation is occupying a larger and larger share of the interest of the publishing and distribution industries, the library, whether college, school, university, or public, has found that it must make room for popular and transient material, as well as try to continue to serve earlier standards of usage.

In 1980, U.S. advertising agencies spent $54.7 billion, which was an increase of 9 percent over the previous year. There is no doubt that the mass distribution of advertising messages has come to occupy a very large portion of the publishing and distribution services in North America. Libraries and their users have had to adjust to this fact.

Transportation

In 1979 the state of California recorded having 15 million motor vehicles out of the 149 million in the entire country. In the whole of Britain there were only 16.5 million vehicles. California also spent $17.6 billion in airport construction, and Texas $13.6 billion.

The U.S. major trunk-line air passenger carriers, who in 1974 carried approximately 40 percent of the world's scheduled traffic, seemed to have reached their peak of passengers in the early 1970s, and are showing declines. Canadians continue to expand air and motor vehicle use, and to expand construction of both domestic and international airline terminals. Canada's airline use by passengers is the same as that of France, with only half the population.

The North American continent is thus highly oriented to the use of air and automobile transportation facilities, and to the cost of maintaining and expanding these. Such a policy has transformed the North American life-style in less than two decades, and all indications point to continuing emphasis on the role that transportation will play in daily life.

Government

The form of national government of the United States and Canada is a federal one. One country has a president, the other is a constitutional monarchy having a prime minister. Both governments are alike, however, in containing national political parties which provide the means of representing differing views of citizens on important issues. The rights of citizens to express their views fully, and to have a vote in political decision-making, is guaranteed by legislation.

In recent years, libraries in North America have had more and more interaction with the forces of both government and politics. The reason for this is largely because citizens and students, the main users of libraries, have decided that if they wish to make changes and improvements in library services, they should employ political processes in order to do so. More and more students and citizens have become involved in the management and control of library services, and have confronted administrators of libraries with their demands. For the most part libraries have responded quickly to such requests and have generally taken account of the needs of their users. In some cases, particularly where the libraries are attached to institutions which themselves are under wider attack, as in the field of postsecondary and secondary education, there have been protracted wrangling.

On the federal level in both Canada and the United States there has been lengthy action to try to secure federal government support for strengthening and maintaining existing library activities. Much of the effort has been led by library organizations themselves, and in this they have utilized the same tactics and strategies that citizen movements and other reform bodies have employed.

The whole area of government interaction in library and information services is a crucial one, now that to a large extent all library functions, except those supported by private business, are financed by public funds. With something over $3 billion a year being expended in the United States and over $350 million in Canada for libraries, it is clear that government's responsibility will always be of paramount interest, and the development of government policies will always be a subject in which library debate and action are foremost.

Communication

It was a Canadian, Marshal McLuhan, who evolved the concept of the "global village" with its citizens' lives transformed by their sharing in all of the means of communication available to them. The practical demonstration of the impact of print, television, telephone, and photography have been on hand in North America for three distinct generations. Each generation has had to make use of expanded communication resources, and each generation of library practitioners have had to revise their appreciation of the impact of communication media on their profession. The graphic arts and computer technologies are now dominant, where linear print once held sway. These new communication methods are radically changing North American librarianship, and there is every apparent expectation that further and equally revolutionary communications methods lie in the not too distant future.

The introduction of the computer microprocessor into general application in the United States and Canada in 1975 meant that North Americans are being offered them in such devices as point-of-sale terminals in department stores; automatic money dispensers in banks; and television-like parlor games in hotel lobbies, barrooms, and the home. A microprocessor from Texas Instruments, Inc. was introduced which could process four information "bits" at once and was five times as fast as earlier versions, with circuits only half the size of previous models. France, Great Britain, and Japan also have similar equipment, and the new generation of electronic computing services is being prepared for library and information service use, as well as for the home.

What this means for libraries is that many of the clerical tasks that are still associated with library operations can be transferred for machine-based manipulation. The advent of automated circulation systems, machine-readable reference services, and machine-assisted catalog and index production is at hand.

The function of the CRT operator is being integrated into the library clerical and subprofessional work force, as well as the positions of system analysts, computer programmers, and video and audio technicians.

Economy

With the United States accounting for well over one-third of the manufacturing output of the world, not counting that of the USSR and Eastern Europe, the impact of the U.S. economy outside of its borders is enormous. U.S. manufacturing output goes through a cyclical series of increases and decreases, and in the latter half of the twentieth century has been relatively stable. This has allowed the United States to maintain a dominant position in the world. Periodic economic industrial recessions have not been so acute in Canada, which is less dependent on its industrial productivity since it depends on that of the United States and relies more on its position as a supplier of raw materials, iron ore, pulp and paper, wheat, nickle, etc. as a basis for its income.

Thus, the United States, with the highest per capita standard of living in the world, and Canada, with the fifth highest, are in key positions to show what the benefits of investment in libraries and information services can provide. It is clear that much of the success of North American industry and business has been brought about because information is used as a resource, and is managed and organized with the same economic rules as other commodities. Libraries and information services are accordingly a part of the basic structure which supports the total economy of the continent, and in fact are one of the linking forces which provide for this economy to grow. Libraries as much as television and radio have made Canada an integrated part of the U.S. economy.

As such, the position of Canada is unlike that of most other countries. Canada is linked directly to the United States by ties of communication, language, basic capital investment in raw materials, and as a market and supplier of essential materials to provide the support needed by the United States.

Characteristics

Our study has revealed the following characteristics regarding librarianship in North America:

1. The librarianship of the United States and Canada is built on European library traditions from England, France, and Spain.
2. "The library" has been regarded as a symbol of access to information and knowledge in an equalitarian society.
3. Rationalization of the bibliographic record has been tied into international efforts.
4. The strength of libraries in the United States and Canada has been derived from their close relationship to both education and to industry.
5. American librarianship has attempted to modify, expand, or discard every facet of librarianship.
6. In North America, excluding Mexico, the influence of the librarian, and more recently the information worker, has become increasingly widespread.
7. There exists a growing trend to automation of many information activities.
8. Women have played a significant role in the development of the library and information professions.

9. North American library service achieved international recognition through its dedication to opening the doors of knowledge to all types and conditions of persons.

10. The task of North American libraries has been characterized by providing access for its citizens mainly to local book production.

11. The advent of computer-based reference and information services has continued the trend toward reliance on North American-produced information, and particularly in English.

12. Future U.S. and Canadian library planning will probably pay greater attention to international guidelines for world library and information science cooperation.[23]

The Library of the United Nations in New York City provides delegates with materials on international law, economic and social affairs, and other fields in which the United Nations is involved. (Courtesy of World Book-Childcraft.)

The National Library of Canada, whose present building dates from 1967, is one of the outstanding national libraries of the world. (Courtesy of Public Archives of Canada.)

The beautiful Canadian Library of Parliament located in the Parliament Building in Ottawa, houses half a million volumes and serves Canada's legislators. (Courtesy of Canadian Government Travel Bureau.)

The congestion and activity at the 1979 ALA Annual Conference in Dallas was typical of the conferences of the American Library Association. (Courtesy of American Library Association.)

The ALA Professional Exhibit during the 1976 Centennial Conference reminded librarians that their professional association, the American Library Association, was a century old. (Courtesy of American Library Association.)

Storefront libraries enable users to obtain library materials in their own neighborhoods. (Courtesy of World Book-Childcraft.)

The present building of the Biblioteca Nacional, Asunción, Paraguay was not designed to be a library. (From Y. M. de Freundorfer, in *Encyclopedia of Library and Information Science*, ed. A. Kent, H. Lancour, and J. E. Daily (New York: Marcel Dekker, 1977), 21:413.)

Hospital libraries bring enjoyable reading directly to the patient's bedside. (Courtesy of World Book-Childcraft.)

Within school libraries children are provided with realia, for example, birds' nests, to examine for study purposes. (Courtesy of World Book-Childcraft.)

Bookmobiles, or "libraries on wheels," deliver books and other materials to people in areas unable to provide a permanent library. (Courtesy of World Book-Childcraft.)

Public libraries bring a variety of resources from all over the world to communities throughout the United States. (Courtesy of World Book-Childcraft.)

This children's section of a public library is designed especially for young patrons and includes colorful posters, a gingerbread playhouse, and furniture made for children. (Courtesy of World Book-Childcraft.)

A skillful storyteller not only entertains but also encourages young children to read. (Courtesy of World Book-Childcraft.)

Mrs. Kaye Zimmerer, Senior Library Assistant, involves a group of children in reading following a story hour. (Courtesy of Long Branch (New Jersey) Public Library.)

Mrs. Muriel Scoles, Supervising Library Assistant, displays a reproduction of a painting that is available for home borrowing. (Courtesy of Long Branch (New Jersey) Public Library.)

A child selects her own book in the Topping Library for Children. (Courtesy of Long Branch (New Jersey) Public Library.)

Ann Hewitt, Director, shows a large print book read by users with vision problems. (Courtesy of Long Branch (New Jersey) Public Library.)

AUSTRALIA, NEW ZEALAND, AND OCEANIA
Dietrich H. Borchardt

The dominant feature of Australia and New Zealand is the sparsity of population and the relative youth of urban settlement. Important characteristics are the firm adherence to principles of egalitarian democracy formulated and evolved in the nineteenth century, and the relative homogeneity of the population—a feature more dominant in New Zealand than in Australia which has had a tremendous influx of non-Anglo-Saxon migrants since 1946. Though Australia and New Zealand are loyal members of the British Commonwealth of Nations and recognize the British monarch as the head of government, they are entitled to, and do exercise the right of, wholly independent political decision-making. They are not in any sense dependent on Whitehall or any other government outside their own frontiers. It is also of some significance that Australia, New Zealand, and the smaller nation states of Oceania (with the exception of Papua, New Guinea, which has a common border with Indonesia) do not share a land frontier with any other nation.

Details of population statistics and related data are published annually in the *Official Yearbook of the Commonwealth of Australia* and in the *New Zealand Official Yearbook*; the *Pacific Islands Yearbook*, which by contrast is published by a commercial firm, appears less frequently, and lacks the authority of the Australian and New Zealand publications which are prepared by the respective government statisticians. However, both Fiji and Papua, New Guinea are also issuing official statistics, and other national governments in Oceania, whether wholly or partly independent, maintain and publish from time to time, details of political and economic data. There is no need, therefore, to cite such data here.

Since the density of population in Australia, New Zealand, and Oceania necessarily affects library services, attention is drawn to the rather uneven distribution of the population. The respective density of settlement in the areas discussed in this chapter is approximately as follows:

Australia	1.8 per km^2
New Zealand	11.6
Fiji	31
Papua, New Guinea	8.4

With the exception of literacy, no other factor has the same influence on library services as density of population. Though Australia's cities range in terms of inhabitants from 20,000 to over 3,474,000, New Zealand's largest urban center, Auckland, has only a population of about 900,000.

Disparities in Papua, New Guinea are very great indeed; the metropolitan area of Port Moresby had a population of about 113,449 in 1979, but there are innumerable small villages in the highlands, some of which have not yet been visited by Europeans. Fiji, an independent dominion since 1970, comprises over

300 islands of different sizes, but less than a third are permanently inhabited. The total population amounts to about 625,000 (1981), of whom 42 percent are Fijian; 50 percent Indian; and 9 percent Chinese, Europeans, Pacific Islanders, etc. Suva, the capital, also has about 66,018 inhabitants (1978).

Within Australia and New Zealand there are sizeable groups descended from the original inhabitants. These groups differ greatly. The Maoris of New Zealand represent about 9 percent of the total population of New Zealand. A long tradition of government-sponsored assimilation has enabled the Maori population to avail itself of all the educational facilities the country has to offer. The compulsory provisions of the Education Act apply to all children in New Zealand. There are some rural areas with a dominant Maori population, but there exists no racial discrimination, though personal prejudice is by no means fully eradicated. The Maoris are represented in the New Zealand Parliament by four members elected on a separate vote by those who are no less than half-blooded Maori.

The Aborigines of Australia number about 116,000 and represent only 0.8 percent of the total population. Basically nomadic, they have found it more difficult than the Maoris to come to terms with the exotic European style of life. Literacy among the Aborigines is still relatively low, but the increasing trend toward urbanization forces them to acquire more European skills. The first senator of Aboriginal descent entered Parliament in 1971.

The rediscovery of Rousseauic ameliorism by those who consider themselves twentieth century political men par excellence has brought in its train a new reverence for the "Noble Savage," an abhorrence of paternalism, of aggressive Europeans, and above all, of an economic view of society. (Such contradictions as happen to occur between this philosophy and the facts of life do not exist, by decree.) Consequently, attention is being paid to real and imaginary disadvantages suffered by indigenous populations at the hand of European land grabbers, developers, financiers, and economically motivated politicians. Sadly one reads in an article by Coleman, "Library Service to the Urban Aboriginal," that the library

> . . . is an agency of European culture and like other agencies it could be, and often is, patronizing toward and/or uninterested in Aborigines. The buildings themselves are usually not very attractive, they are formal and lack warmth —many people, not only Aborigines—do not feel welcome in a library. It seems an institution like other bureaucratic institutions made up of rules and cold lack of interest.[24]

But it is admitted elsewhere in the same article that reading "though not historically part of the Aboriginal society . . . is not an activity shunned by Aborigines." The insuperable problem is that practically all books available are of little interest to the Aborigines and are superficial in relation to their background and realms of experience. The answer, a simpleton might suggest, is that books are written by those who know for whom they are writing.

Concern with the recently discovered or rediscovered "elitist character of libraries" was expressed by the Labor governments of Australia and of New Zealand when first elected in December 1972. The notion has since been rather lost in the ever-changing game of political point-scoring. Whether justified or not, it is another aspect of the difficulties arising from the uneven distribution of population in the areas here discussed, as well as the greatly divergent cultural background of population groups in Australia, Oceania, and to some lesser degree in New Zealand.

Both Australia and New Zealand have one further problem caused by certain population characteristics. The postwar influx of migrants without adequate knowledge of English has created pockets of foreign-born people who until recently received very little, if any, consideration in municipal public libraries. The reason for this neglect was not xenophobia—a trait mercifully rare in Australia and New Zealand—but lack of concern and, indirectly, the ignorance of all languages other than English among the basically Anglo-Saxon Australians and New Zealanders. Attempts are now under way to remedy this situation, but it will take some time to bring practical relief to non-English-speaking migrants.

Real as this problem is in the Australian and New Zealand context, there might nevertheless be some overestimate of the awareness of library services among migrants. Perhaps this question warrants more detailed investigation, and particularly comparative study by some future researcher.

In a society where egalitarianism dictates that all shall have equal opportunities and where strong trade unions successfully argue for shorter working weeks, leisure and the use of leisure time becomes automatically a matter of interest and concern. There is practically no illiteracy in Australia or New Zealand; but there is a good deal of limited functional literacy as distinct from full literacy, though this is difficult to measure statistically.

Education in Australia and New Zealand is free, secular, and compulsory for children from six to fifteen years of age. In 1971/1972 each country spent about 4.7 percent of its gross national product on education, and in 1976/1977 this figure rose to over 6 percent. Higher or tertiary education is free in Australia (since January 1974) and relatively inexpensive in New Zealand. As a result, a fairly high proportion of the population attends universities and colleges. Besides, adult education classes cater to a great variety of vocational and general interests. In New Zealand much of the adult education work is centered on the universities and tends to tie in with their academic objectives. In Australia, some universities have developed extensive adult education programs, but the several Adult Education Boards, or Councils, of the states concern themselves with the broader aspects of nonvocational education. State and municipal libraries are expected to provide supporting literature for such courses, but there exists no formal arrangement to assure efficient cooperation. The Australian Adult Education authorities maintain some libraries to support their classes. As leisure becomes a more significant part of everyday life the demand for adult education classes and university extension courses is likely to grow, with a concomitant demand for public library services.

Communications and mass media play a significant part in Australia, New Zealand, and Oceania and help to overcome the isolation of communities due to the sparsity of the rural population and the great distances between urban centers. Radio and press are free from blatant political interference, but Australian state governments in particular tend to adopt a prurient stance on moral issues. Severe censorship restrictions affect books, magazines, films, and radio and television broadcasting. In addition to the control of imports through the Australian government, there exist diverse and strict state controls of printing and publishing. In the vast majority of instances, the regulations are applied to deal with matters relating to sex and violence. There is no record of recent instances of political censorship, but there have been such cases under the guise of libel suits.

The daily press in Australia and New Zealand is traditionally conservative in its political leanings, but the standard of reporting is reasonably fair; some of the leading newspapers are over 100 years old.

Broadcasting and television emanate from government-controlled and commercial stations in Australia and New Zealand. However, the commercial services in Australia are much bigger and better developed than those in New Zealand. Approximately 85 percent of New Zealand and 92 percent of Australian homes have television sets. New Zealand has had color television since the end of 1973, Australia since 1975.

Both Australia and New Zealand provide special radio programs for Oceania. Virtually all national territories maintain radio networks for educational and entertainment purposes. However, television services are rare as yet. Now Caledonia and Tahiti have television for normal entertainment purposes, and American Samoa has it for educational purposes only.

In Australia and New Zealand, as elsewhere in the world, there is no evidence that radio and television have affected the reading of books and serious journals.

Librarianship in Australia, New Zealand, and Oceania has been shown to fall into two distinct categories. One is characteristic of the state of affairs commonly associated with recently emergent nations; the other is representative of librarianship in industrially developed countries. It reflects, therefore, what had been emphasized at the beginning of this chapter: The geographical region here considered is far from uniform as regards culture, civilization, economic standards, and political development.

In Oceania, where writing and literacy do not form an integral part of the native traditions, there has been no need until now for libraries or librarians. But the lessons learned in the nineteenth and twentieth centuries when the island people became acquainted with European cultural achievements and when colonizing, commercializing, and proselytizing influences made them aware of the power of a civilization based on written records, they recognized the need to emulate what appeared to be the source of success, including the preservation of such records.

It is still a long way before any of the island nations of Oceania will have a library service to meet the requirements of industry and commerce in their twentieth century form. It may indeed be questionable whether they will have to go through the same stages of library development as Europe and North America have done. Some of the pains and mistakes might be prevented if understanding advisers help pave the way.

The most important requirement for librarianship in Oceania is a rapid increase in the professional library staff native to the several nations of the area. Whether or not English becomes the official language of the region—and the demands for economic development would support such a trend, however strong the claims for national identity as expressed through a national idiom—the librarians working in Oceania during the next twenty-five years will have to know several of the indigenous languages in order to be able to help with the social readjustments required by the effects of the politically determined industrialization. The picture is typical and has been the subject of the writer's survey, "Library Services in Underdeveloped Areas; a Critique of issues."[25]

If Australia is short of experienced and qualified library staff, this is largely due to the demands made by enormous distances and the concentration of most of the population in less than a dozen large cities. Distance and sparsity of medium-sized urban centers are making demands on library services which cannot be met by the qualified staff presently available.

The situation is aggravated by the fact that the present population of 15 million cannot raise enough financial support to apply mechanized processes on a scale that would seriously mitigate the problems of distance and of staff shortages. As the population increases, and as the government's decentralization policies become more effective, library services will inevitably spread. The challenge before the profession in Australia is to prepare itself for the application of more sophisticated solutions to technical services so that as the requisite hardware becomes less costly to install, readers' services can be more fully developed. There is no shortage of talent, and the profession is very well acquainted with world trends in librarianship. The better Australian professional journals are widely read abroad and are cited in the literature.

In New Zealand the problem is akin to that in Australia, but the solution requires a different emphasis. The smaller scale of operations, compared with Australia, and the higher density of population offer great opportunities for regional approaches to library services. The profession is more than ready to tackle the problems but until local authorities change their attitude toward library cooperation, little will be achieved. Librarianship in New Zealand tends to be inward-looking and is more homespun than its Australian counterpart. Large-scale programs are not contemplated for want of national financial resources, and for the present, professional efforts are concentrated on consolidation.

Lastly, there is the question of international standing of the Australian and New Zealand library profession. It is satisfying to record that librarians of both countries have played significant roles in the library work of UNESCO. Acting as advisers or as seconded officers to run library services in developing countries for a year or two (and sometimes longer), both Australian and New Zealand librarians have done well by their hosts and ensured the good reputation of their own country.

Characteristics

The common traits of librarianship in Australia, New Zealand, and Oceania are as follows:

1. Australia, New Zealand, and Oceania have little in common with regard to the development of their librarianship.
2. Within Oceania the native culture, although sophisticated in many important respects, was originally based on oral tradition.
3. Libraries and library services in Australia and New Zealand have reached an entirely different level of achievement from those in the various national communities that make up Oceania.
4. Both Australia and New Zealand are essentially European in their traditions, culture, social and political structure, while non-European elements dominate the life and civilization of Oceania.

The National Library of Australia has improved reference service and developed new services for its users. (From H. L. White and F. J. Balnaves, in *Encyclopedia of Library and Information Science*, ed. A. Kent and H. Lancour (New York: Marcel Dekker, 1969), 2:118.)

5. As a profession, librarianship is now well established in Australia and New Zealand. Yet even in Australia and New Zealand librarianship has only a tenuous hold on professional status.

6. Librarianship in Australia, New Zealand, and Oceania has been shown to fall into two distinct categories: One is characteristic of the state of affairs commonly associated with recently emergent nations, and the other is representative of librarianship in industrially developed countries.[26]

NOTES

1. The characteristics of Middle Eastern librarianship were formulated by Richard Krzys from data provided by Mohammed M. Aman.

2. David Kaser, "Library Development in Asia," in the article, "Library," in *The Encyclopedia Americana*, Vol. 17 (New York: Americana Corporation, 1977), p. 324.

3. Sam E. Ifidon, "Special Problems Facing African Librarians: The West African Experience," *Libri* 24, no. 4 (1974), p. 311.

4. Glen L. Sitzman, "African Librarianship, an Overview," *Africa Report* (September-October 1975).

5. Dorothy G. Collings, "Library Development in Africa," in the article, "Library," in *The Encyclopedia Americana*, Vol. 17 (New York: Americana Corporation, 1977), pp. 320-321.

6. The characteristics of Western European librarianship were formulated by Richard Krzys from data provided by researcher Jean-Pierre Clavel.

7. The characteristics of Soviet librarianship were formulated by Richard Krzys from data provided by researcher B. P. Kanevsky.

8. The characteristics of Eastern European librarianship were formulated by Richard Krzys from data provided by researcher M. B. Nabatova.

9. Richard Krzys and Gaston Litton, "Latin American Librarianship," *Encyclopedia of Library and Information Science*, ed. by A. Kent, H. Lancour, and J. E. Daily, Vol. 14 (New York: Marcel Dekker, 1975), p. 53.

10. Antonio Montes de Oca, "Mexico," *Lands and Peoples*, ed. by Jay Bennett et al., Vol. 5 (n.p.: Lexicon Publications, c1977), p. 317.

11. Krzys and Litton, "Latin American Librarianship," p. 53.

12. Ibid., pp. 53-54.

13. Ibid., p. 52.

14. Miguel Angel Piñeiro, "UNESCO and Library Services in Latin America," *UNESCO Bulletin for Libraries*, 20, no. 5 (Sept.-Oct. 1966), p. 245.

15. Krzys and Litton, "Latin American Librarianship," p. 52.

16. Ibid., p. 53.

17. Ibid.

18. Ibid., p. 52.

19. Ibid.

20. The characteristics of Latin American librarianship were prepared by Richard Krzys and Gaston Litton.

21. U.S. Department of Commerce, Bureau of the Census, *Current Population Report* (Washington, D.C.: Government Printing Office, 1976).
22. U.S. Department of Health, Education, and Welfare, Office of Education, *Digest of Educational Statistics* (Washington, D.C.: Government Printing Office, 1981).
23. The characteristics of U.S.-Canadian librarianship were formulated by Richard Krzys from data provided by researcher H. C. Campbell.
24. R. Coleman, *Australian Library Journal*, 22, no. 10 (November 1973), pp. 391-400.
25. D. H. Borchardt, *Journal of Education for Librarianship*, 9, no. 2 (Fall 1968), pp. 123-137.
26. The characteristics of Australian, New Zealand, and Oceanian librarianship were formulated by Richard Krzys from data provided by researcher Dietrich H. Borchardt.

6

Juxtaposition: Consideration of the Profession's Variants

Richard Krzys and Gaston Litton

Throughout this study we have examined eleven aspects of world librarianship: (1) bibliographic control, (2) legislation, (3) financial support, (4) the profession, (5) practitioners, (6) associations, (7) educational agencies, (8) literature, (9) service agencies, (10) services, and (11) planning. Our study has already examined these aspects through the process of analysis. Now, through juxtaposition, we arrange side by side the variants of the aspects that may occur in the nine geographical areas of the world: (1) Middle East, (2) Central, East, South, and Southeast Asia, (3) Africa, (4) Western Europe, (5) Soviet Union, (6) European Socialist Republics, (7) Latin America, (8) United States and Canada, and (9) Australia, New Zealand, and Oceania. Subsequently, in Chapter 7, we present our comparison.

Here, however, we employ juxtaposition for the purpose of hypothesizing, that is, proposing tentative explanations for the similarities and differences evident in the variants, leading to the formulation of concepts of *metalibrarianship*—a term we devised to denote the philosophy and theory of world librarianship—in terms of hypotheses, theories, and laws. Limitations of our data restrict us to concentrate on *elements* of the topic, in other words a preliminary statement of a body of knowledge that when refined through further tests of validity may become the philosophy and theory of our profession worldwide.

BIBLIOGRAPHIC CONTROL

As we consider the state of bibliographic control throughout all nine areas of the world, we discover that universal bibliographic control (UBC) is still an unrealized goal of world librarianship. Within the Middle East, Asia, Africa, Latin America, and Oceania, bibliographic control is yet to be achieved in the majority of their nations; however, in Europe, the United States and Canada, as well as in Australia and New Zealand, bibliographic control has been achieved and ranges from good to excellent.

Generalizing from what we have observed thus far, we can hypothesize that bibliographic control is a characteristic of developed countries and that its achievement to any satisfactory degree is dependent on the presence in each country of the following six elements: (1) a copyright law, (2) a depository law, (3) enforcement of the depository law, (4) knowledge of the auxiliary discipline of bibliography, (5) a national library, and (6) a national bibliography; furthermore, we hypothesize that the index of bibliographic control increases in direct proportion to the degree of the enforcement of the depository law.

LEGISLATION

Juxtaposing the legislation to be found throughout the world, we find considerable unevenness as to its history, type, and scope; for example, within the Middle East only the most elementary form of legislation—the depository law—is to be found, and it is a post-World War II development.

Asia, in contrast, has a long history of legislation, the oldest dating as far back in China as 1122 B.C.?, and taking the form of depository laws and censorship restrictions. Throughout the rest of Asia, deposit and censorship laws have tended to precede other forms of library legislation, and they were introduced and enforced by colonial powers. Among the Asian countries without a colonial past, Japan has legal deposit laws dating from 1878, and Thailand's comparable law dates from 1941. Considerable activity regarding introduction and revision of library legislation took place following World War II in Asia.

Within the African continent lack of library legislation has been cited as an obstacle to permanent library development. In northern Africa, for example, only Egypt has copyright laws, and they are as recent as 1955; in eastern Africa, Kenya, Uganda, and Tanzania have elaborate library legislation, including provisions for public library services, while Ethiopia and Somalia have no such legislation. Within southern Africa, South Africa and Namibia have library legislation providing for depository and public library services. Regarding central Africa, only Zambia has library legislation. Finally, as for western Africa, legislation is to be found only in Nigeria, Ghana, and Sierra Leone.

Throughout Europe—Western and Eastern—library legislation providing for depository and guaranteeing the right to read or access to public libraries is to be found.

As for the Americas, a considerable body of library legislation exists in Latin America, but because of lack of enforcement, the legislation is either ineffective or ignored entirely. Although there is no reference to library legislation regarding bibliographic and library services in the constitutions of the United States and Canada, such legislation does exist within the countries' states and provinces, and it may be described in a word as being "effective."

Regarding library legislation "down under," Australia and New Zealand have appropriate legislation, with New Zealand taking the lead in enactment of public library legislation in 1869; Australia's comparable legislation began in 1939 with the state of New South Wales leading the way. Within Oceania, only Papua, New Guinea has a copyright act dating from 1978 and a statutory depository act of 1979. Throughout the rest of Oceania, library service has been provided by the governments under whose authority the various islands have been governed.

We hypothesize that library legislation is dependent upon the library consciousness of a country's politicians and legislators; the greater their understanding of the nature, purposes, and needs of libraries and librarianship, the more adequate is the library legislation enacted by these officials.

FINANCIAL SUPPORT

Regarding financial support for libraries in the Middle East, we are unable to provide data because such costs are included within educational expenditures; however, judging from the evidence available to us from the continuous building programs in Saudi Arabia and Kuwait, the financial support for libraries must be limited only by its ability to be assimilated into the economy.

When attempting to determine such support in Asia, one must distinguish between public and school libraries on one hand and academic and special libraries on the other. The former category usually receives reduced support because it often is considered "frills" when the economy falters; however, special and academic libraries tend to be financed in accordance with their needs.

Concerning financial support for libraries in Africa, one may accurately generalize that a shortage of capital funds, reflecting the poor economic infrastructure for most African countries, tends to plague libraries as well. Libraries in Africa may be said to function with inadequate funding. How severe the problem is may be judged from the situation regarding national libraries; largely because of financial difficulties many African countries do not have national libraries.

Within an area study describing Western Europe, Jean-Pierre Clavel stated:

> The amount of financing devoted to libraries may be hypothesized to be in direct proportion to the determination of the public authorities to promote reading and culture. Viewed in this light, the attitude of the Nordic countries is exemplary. A preliminary examination of the subject leads to three

conclusions: (1) the Northern countries spend, relatively speaking, more money on their libraries than the southern nations of Western Europe, (2) the Protestant nations are more generous to their libraries than the predominantly Catholic countries, and (3) the industrial societies support their libraries more than their agrarian counterparts.[1]

Stating that the same generalization does not apply to financial support for public libraries, Clavel adds:

. . . the financial support allotted by public authorities to libraries accounts for only a part of the general expenditures made by, or on behalf of, the reading public. The private contribution of readers themselves to providing their own reading matter varies greatly from one country to another. This initiative seems to be the more important; however, in the countries of central Europe than in the South, or even in the North.[2]

Clavel concludes his remarks by stating:

. . . everywhere libraries are requesting even greater financial support, and that in the past their hopes of securing this assistance have been fulfilled more frequently and adequately in the North than in the South of Europe.[3]

Financial support for libraries in the Soviet Union and Eastern Europe is an unknown quantity. In report after report relating to library development in Eastern Europe, one sees in the expenditures columns the letters "N.A.," indicating not available. That the Soviets and their satellite countries expend a realistic amount for library development cannot be denied, especially when one realizes the significant role that libraries play in socialist economies.

Within the Americas considerable contrast is provided by the financial support for libraries given by Latin American countries and that given by the United States and Canada. To place such support in proper perspective, one should bear in mind that Latin America is constituted by a group of developing countries; whereas, the United States and Canada are developed countries. In general, regarding Latin America, it may be said that only special libraries receive financial support commensurate with their needs. Even in cases like the Pilot Public Library in Medellin, Colombia, an agency partly supported by UNESCO, has financial support been inadequate in terms of stated objectives.

In order to gain proper perspective on financial support for libraries in the United States and Canada, we must view such support from both its world and intranational settings. From their earliest colonial history both countries have held a high regard for books and information, and correspondingly have given adequate-to-generous support broadly to their various types of libraries; in fact, when such support is converted into the values for foreign currencies, librarians from abroad have pondered the figures with near disbelief, as if they were considering astronomical distances. Intranationally, that is, within the United States and Canada, library support shows unevenness from region to region; for example, the U.S. Atlantic Seaboard and Canada's Maritime provinces have public library support per capita that are approximately twice as great as such support in the Western prairie states and provinces. Support for public libraries in the Atlantic Seaboard of the United States is more than three times per capita the support that is given in the South of the United States.

Unfortunately, the data regarding financial support for libraries in Australia, New Zealand, and Oceania are inadequate for comparative purposes.

Our information regarding financial support for libraries throughout most of the world suggests that certain characteristics must be present: it must be adequate, continuous, and have a legal basis. Concerning adequacy, the financial support should be sufficient to carry out the objectives of library service as agreed upon by the library's governing body; this support must continue annually and not be subject to erratic fluctuations; and, finally, the support must have a legal basis to ensure its adequacy and continuity.

THE PROFESSION

To assess the professionalism of library activity throughout the world, we applied the six elements that are generally believed to constitute a profession: (1) a systematic theory which delineates and supports the skills that characterize the profession, (2) a level of authority which comes from extensive education in the profession's systematic theory, (3) community sanction and approval of this authority as expressed in the conferring on the profession of such powers as accreditation, formulation of standards of performance, and establishment of rules for admission into the profession, (4) a code of ethics which regulates relations of professional persons with clients and colleagues, (5) a professional culture sustained by formal associations, consisting of its values, norms, and symbols and having at its center the career concept, and (6) service orientation.

Bearing in mind the criteria for the evaluation of a profession in relation to the findings of our research study, we conclude that when measured by its peaks of performances—for example, within Egypt, Japan, the Republic of South Africa, the northern countries of Western Europe, Great Britain, the Soviet Union, and within the Americas, including Canada, the United States, and Brazil, as well as Australia and New Zealand—world librarianship is a profession. That is not to say, however, that our profession is without weaknesses. Certainly, its inadequacies are more obvious in the profession's philosophical and theoretical base.

One of the most frequently voiced criticisms of the philosophy of librarianship is that it is a field that has a title but little or no content. Surely, the field appears to be sparse if the practitioner considers only the philosophical precepts operating within his/her own country or cultural area; for example, the librarians from the United States are so imbued with their philosophical beliefs that they hardly recognize them as such; and the philosophy of Canadian librarianship is so similar to its United States counterpart that the practitioners hardly perceive the subtle differences between them; however, if the librarians from either of these countries were to compare their professional philosophies with those of practitioners in the Soviet Union or some countries of the Middle East, the differences between their professional philosophies would become readily apparent.

Those countries of the Middle East that practice strict adherence to the Islamic religion believe that both sexes—male and female—should not utilize library facilities at the same time, which leads to separate facilities or separate hours of service for both sexes. Within many countries of Asia, Africa, the Soviet Union, the socialist republics of Eastern Europe, and Latin America, censorship of books exists either at the publisher or within libraries. Countries of Western Europe, the United States and Canada, Australia, New Zealand, and Oceania attempt to include materials on various beliefs of controversial issues; within the socialist countries, including the Soviet Union, the People's Republic of China, the socialist republics of Eastern Europe, and Cuba, authorities consider the book as a device for propagandizing the state's official beliefs to the masses, and the librarians of those countries are considered propagandists for the state.

We hypothesize that the growth of librarianship is a response to the growth of knowledge and humanity's need for information; as knowledge increases, and as humanity's need for information increases, so too will librarianship continue to develop. Also, the growth of librarianship is dependent on the service orientation of its practitioners. Within the English-speaking countries, where the tradition of serving one's fellow man is considered an honorable pursuit, librarianship has flourished; in regions or countries of the world where service is considered demeaning—for example, in the Iberian Peninsula and in Latin America—librarianship has experienced a difficult development.

PRACTITIONERS

Although practitioners have existed as long as our civilizations have had libraries, the professionalization of the librarian did not begin until Melvil Dewey established the first library school in the world in New York as the School of Library Economy at Columbia College in 1887. Practitioners may be categorized in terms of their level and function, with the level corresponding to their educational attainment and their function corresponding to the essential activity they perform. The following five levels may be observed: (1) the library technician, (2) the paraprofessional, (3) the librarian I, (4) the librarian II, and (5) the library administrator.

ASSOCIATIONS

Associations exist within the Middle East, although—with the exception of the Egyptian Library Association, which traces its origin to 1945—they are relatively recent phenomena dating generally from the 1960s; most Asian countries have associations dating from after World War II, although—similar to the situation in the Middle East—Japan has an earlier association dating from 1892. The situation in Africa differs from region to region; for example, within northern Africa, except for Egypt, no countries have associations; within eastern Africa, active associations are to be found in Ethiopia, Kenya, Uganda, and Tanzania; in southern Africa, except for the Republic of South Africa, associations are still in the planning stages; and, it may be generalized that within western Africa, Anglophone countries have more active associations than Francophone ones. Since the close of the nineteenth century, all European countries, Western and Eastern, including the Soviet Union, have had associations, with the first being the Library Association of the United Kingdom founded in 1877. Within the Americas we see widely differing patterns of development among their associations: The United States has been the world leader in the establishment and activity of its American Library Association founded in 1876, and since 1946 the Canadian Library Association has addressed itself to professional problems with ever-increasing vigor, culminating in significant achievements in the nation's librarianship, for example, involvement in improving bibliographic and library services, as well as creating a vital national library. In contrast, the numerous Latin American associations, existing in most countries, tend to be ineffective in their activities and erratic in their existence. Both Australia and New Zealand have active associations, with the New Zealand association dating from 1910, and being the first in the area. Associations in Oceania are recent, dating from the 1970s.

We hypothesize that the continuity of existence of an association is usually directly proportionate to the strength of the personal ambitions of its members, whereas the effectiveness of an association is directly related to the intensity of professional interest of the association's members.

EDUCATIONAL AGENCIES

Educational agencies of various types and levels are to be found throughout the world. The Middle Eastern countries, for example, offer the most comprehensive library education in Egypt at Cairo University in a program dating back to the 1949 library training that was first offered by the Cairo Library Association. Today, the program at Cairo University is offered at the bachelor's, master's, and doctoral level. Since 1960, Iraq has offered short courses taught by UNESCO experts. Lebanon offers programs at the secondary and undergraduate levels. In addition to providing undergraduate library education, Kuwait and Saudi Arabia offer graduate education. Israel's program is provided at the graduate level. Asia has a scarcity of library schools; bachelor's level courses are more common than master's level programs; and few library schools offer the Ph.D. Africa also has a scarcity of schools. Egypt's program, leading to the B.A., M.A., and Ph.D. is the most advanced in northern Africa and throughout the continent. Among countries of eastern Africa, only Ethiopia and Uganda have programs of library education. Uganda's programs offer a two-year undergraduate course, a one-year postgraduate course, and a certificate program. Ethiopia offers an undergraduate program. Within southern Africa, education for librarianship is offered only in the Republic of South Africa, where programs range from the paraprofessional to the doctoral level. Central Africa has only one school offering undergraduate training at the University of Zambia; western Africa, on the other hand, has eight schools: five in Nigeria, and one each in Ghana, Liberia, and Senegal which offer programs from the paraprofessional to the doctoral level. Western European programs may be divided into three groups: (1) Great Britain and the Nordic countries emphasize public services; (2) Germany, Austria, Switzerland, the Netherlands, Belgium, and France emphasize cataloging; and (3) Italy, Spain, and Portugal emphasize cultural and humanistic studies in their programs. Practicum also forms a part of library education in all three of the groups of Western European countries. Within the Soviet Union and all the Union Republics, there exist centers for educating practitioners. Librarians of the junior and middle grades are trained at technical centers established at the college level; in addition, higher level education is offered at universities. Institutes provide specialized training in a particular area of librarianship, for example, scientific and technical information. In the socialist republics of Eastern Europe, training aimed at preparing various levels of practitioners is available from the undergraduate to specialist levels. Within the Americas, training is offered in Latin America mostly at the undergraduate level; inasmuch as the programs in Canada and the United States at the master's level are accredited by the American Library Association, they tend to be similar in content, although a small number of the programs in these countries are of two-years rather than one-year duration. In addition, both countries offer instruction at the undergraduate and doctoral levels. Within Australia, New Zealand, and Oceania, Australia offers the largest variety of library training from the undergraduate to the Ph.D. level; New Zealand's program is being restructured and will offer graduate level courses. As for Oceania, its island groups depend on Australia and New Zealand for their professional level courses, although short courses have been offered from time to time in various areas of Oceania.

Educational agencies interact with the variable of need for practitioners. As the need increases for practitioners, the number of educational agencies tends to increase. The contrary of this hypothesis also holds.

LITERATURE

Consideration of the literature written by our professional colleagues throughout the world inclines us to believe that the following nations have produced original vital contributions: (1) India, (2) Great Britain, (3) France, (4) Germany, (5) the Soviet Union, and (6) the United States. All other countries have library literature that depends heavily on the countries identified. Until each country produces a library literature that is expressed in its native language or languages and based on its culture or cultures, such literatures are considered to be imitative of more vital counterparts from other countries.

SERVICE AGENCIES

Within the Middle East, the mosque library is characteristic of the area and numerically is in greatest abundance. Also, a large number of academic agencies are either in existence or under construction. If we were to exclude the United Nations libraries, which are *sui generis*, and the national libraries, which are by definition limited in number within a country, the school library has probably the smallest number of examples, although the extensive educational planning in the Middle East and the changing attitudes of politicians toward the role of libraries in education should increase the number of school libraries significantly within the next decade.

Asia, Africa, and Europe have seen a marked increase in the growth of academic and special libraries since World War II. The next decade should see comparative increases in public and school libraries because of the emphasis on eradicating illiteracy.

Within the developing countries of Latin America, there should be a large increase in school and public libraries; however, in the rest of the Americas, including Canada and the United States, a sizeable increase will take place in the use of computerized data bases, especially in microcomputers for public libraries and home use.

Australia and New Zealand will eventually experience a similar increase in computerized data bases. Also, they will witness a marked increase in the number of school libraries.

We hypothesize that service agencies are predominantly urban phenomenon, and they tend to increase in number as population density increases. Also, service agencies tend to develop more fully in predominantly industrialized rather than agricultural nations.

SERVICES

Within the countries of the Middle East, Asia, Africa, and Latin America, technical services tend to be emphasized over user services; whereas, within Northern and Eastern Europe, Canada and the United States, Australia, and New Zealand, public services are viewed as the *raison d'être* for library services and are emphasized.

PLANNING

Planning in the Middle East has experienced both intranational and international activity. Within the oil-rich nations of Saudi Arabia, Kuwait, Oman, Qatar, and the United Arab Emirates, planning has occurred as reflected in the various five-year plans of these countries. Internationally, the Middle East has benefitted from the services of the Arab League Educational, Cultural and Scientific Organization (ALECSO), which since 1970 has aided library planning in the area through the conducting of seminars devoted to book production and distribution as they relate to library development.

Asian countries have often benefitted from planning that has been the work of local authorities, professional associations, and individual librarians. Centralized planning for library services on a national basis has been carried out by the People's Republic of China, the Socialist Republic of Vietnam, the Central Asian Republic of the USSR, as well as Ceylon. In most Asian countries, the Ministry of Education is responsible for the development of school and academic libraries; however, some countries—India, for example—place library planning under the local control of states. Outside sources of planning have been UNESCO, the Ford Foundation, the Asia Foundation, the Colombo Plan, and the British Council.

Our information about library planning in Africa is inadequate to make conclusive generalizations. However, we can state that within most African countries planning is a function of the national governments through their ministries of education. Furthermore, it may also be observed that those African nations which were once colonies of European countries have often received personal assistance in planning from librarians from the colonizing countries; thus Nigeria has been aided in this regard by Great Britain, etc. However, language has also played a role in assistance in planning in that Nigeria, being an English-speaking country, has also benefitted from the services of library planners from the United States.

Within European countries, including Western Europe, the Soviet Union, and Eastern Europe, planning has largely been the province of national governments; foremost in this regard have been France, the Soviet Union, and the socialist republics of Eastern Europe.

Planning within the Americas is not advanced, and this observation applies equally to the United States as well as its lesser developed neighbors. Within Latin America this condition can be explained through the professional isolationism that has characterized most Latin American countries, the exceptions being in some Central American countries and Colombia where the OAS, various foundations, and individual experts have assisted in library planning. Until the 1960s, Canada and the United States were without planning on the national level. The impetus for national planning by these countries came from a UNESCO initiative in 1974, when both countries, through the acquiescense of their leaders, accepted the recommendations for national planning formulated by UNESCO in its Paris meeting of 1974 devoted to the planning of national documentation, and library and archive infrastructures. The United States has experienced tardy development in national library planning; not until the 1979 White House Conference on Library and Information Services has there been any library planning on the national level within the United States.

Within Australia and New Zealand, the tendency to foster cooperative enterprises, at least in principle, has acted as a stimulant to national library planning. Through the efforts of the Australian Advisory Council on Bibliographical Services (AACOBS), library planning on the national level has been more successful in Australia than in New Zealand.

Our worldwide consideration of national library planning indicates that such activity represents a degree of sophistication in a country's library development. Also, we observe that the success of national library planning tends to be higher in countries where centralized governments exist—for example, in France, the Soviet Union, and the European socialist republics.

NOTES

1. Jean-Pierre Clavel, "Western Europe," (ms. written by Mr. Clavel to provide the data for this comparative study).
2. Ibid.
3. Ibid.

7

Comparison: Metalibrarianship—The Philosophy and Theory of World Librarianship

Richard Krzys and Gaston Litton

We present here our comparison in terms of the hypotheses of Chapter 6. Here we endeavor, wherever possible, to assemble the valid definitions and hypotheses into philosophy and theory. Additionally, we identify any of the field's interacting variables and formulate what we call "lessons of world librarianship." To accomplish these operations, we examined the aspects of librarianship in light of seven characteristics: (1) nature, (2) purpose(s), (3) origin, (4) categories, (5) the interacting variable(s), (6) development, and (7) demise. Finally we verbalize the laws of world librarianship that our total analysis has revealed.

RESEARCH IN WORLD LIBRARIANSHIP

Before leaving this world-wide examination of the profession, we wish to make some further observations regarding its research. We believe that one serious defect exists in the conception of research held by many of our profession's researchers throughout the world. It is their failure to investigate problems in librarianship on a worldwide basis. As we have affirmed in this research study, librarianship is a profession practiced *throughout the world*; therefore, to formulate a philosophical and theoretical body of knowledge regarding the phenomenon, it is necessary to design research studies drawing data from the world population rather than samples from circumscribed areas of the world. Unless the researcher is specifically interested in investigating, let us say, reference practice in Saudi

Arabia, it will be necessary for the researcher attempting to formulate a theory of reference to design a research study investigating the world population of reference service.

Regarding the nature of our profession, although librarianship is a world profession, its practice is always influenced by local determinants, for example, the area's history, culture, economy, etc. Therefore, although we can speak of library science as being universal and "nonnational," or unaffected by determinants of a local nature, librarianship, because it represents a response to human needs and arises within a cultural context, is a cultural or national phenomenon. To restate our belief, as long as various cultures exist throughout the world, and as long as legislation and mores differ from country to country, librarianship will differ from region to region and country to country. Therefore, although library science applies universally to the problems of selection, acquisition, and use of graphic records throughout the world, it is both possible and proper to speak of a Middle Eastern or Canadian librarianship.

SUGGESTIONS TO RESEARCHERS

Students and researchers of world librarianship searching for topics for future investigation are urged to read thoughtfully the new knowledge formulated in *World Librarianship*. The sections that should be read with special care are (1) hypotheses, (2) theories, (3) interacting variables, and (4) laws. New knowledge identified there can serve as the critical bases for future studies or for topics whose research can be replicated for additional tests of validity.

BIBLIOGRAPHIC CONTROL

Earlier we hypothesized that bibliographic control is a characteristic of developed countries and that its achievement to any satisfactory degree is dependent on the presence in each country of the following six elements: (1) a copyright law, (2) a depository law, (3) enforcement of the depository law, (4) knowledge of the auxiliary discipline of bibliography, (5) a national bibliography, and (6) a national library. Furthermore, we hypothesized that the index of bibliographic control increases in direct proportion to the degree of enforcement of the depository law.

Our hypotheses and theory of bibliographic control have proved valid with exceptions relating to its purpose and requirements. Although enactment of a copyright law is generally a requisite element to the achievement of bibliographic control, the law is sometimes not passed for that reason. Rather, it is enacted for the purpose of exercising censorship by a government over its nation's authors. What is the exception to our requisites for bibliographic control? Switzerland has achieved bibliographic control without a depository law. The function of deposit is achieved in Switzerland through a "gentlemen's agreement" that exists among the country's publishers and its national library. We may explain this exception to our hypothesis by stating that in the case of Switzerland, the social mores take on the force of law and substitute for the nonexistent depository law.

Universal Bibliographic Control (UBC) remains, at this writing, an unrealized goal of world librarianship,[1] but rather than state pessimistically that UBC will remain unrealized, we can affirm optimistically that UBC can be achieved; however, in accordance with the lessons that librarians have learned in attempting to realize their goal thus far, it will require rigorous application of the principles of International Standard Bibliographic Description (ISBD). A first step to realization of ISBD, however, will be the universal transliteration of all languages, non-Romanized as well as Romanized, into formats employing Latin alphabets.

Our theory of bibliographic control, interacting variables, and phases of development have also been validated.

LEGISLATION

Concerning the purposes of library legislation, Frank M. Gardner stated that "only legislation can empower the appropriate authorities to provide and ensure adequate financial support and efficient administration according to a national standard. Only legislation can define the functions of the providing authority, create the conditions in which it may fulfill those functions, and ensure development."[2] Gardner's statement added that "the purpose of library legislation is to provide service for the entire population in some form or other," and also, that legislation or professional standards "should embrace every shade of opinion, without prejudice to anyone."[3] Gardner concluded that "the national scheme in all its parts should aim at free service."[4]

Library legislation is composed of those statutes and laws which define, establish, facilitate, or support librarianship, its agencies, activies, processes, or services.

The development of our profession's legislation follows a pattern throughout the world. Enactment of copyright law is usually the first step, followed by passage of a depository law. Legislation providing for the creation of some type of library then follows. Involved in the demise of our profession's legislation is first its less frequent enforcement, followed by its total disregard.

Earlier we hypothesized that library legislation is dependent upon the library consciousness of a country's politicians and legislators; the greater their understanding of the nature, purposes, and needs of librarianship, the more adequate is the library legislation enacted by these officials.

We know of no exceptions to this hypothesis; in fact, we may attribute the enlightened library legislation that has been enacted in Great Britain, France, Germany, the United States, Canada, Australia, and New Zealand to the library consciousness of their politicians.

Unfortunately, the contrary form of this hypothesis is also valid. In many countries of the Middle East, Asia, Africa, and Latin America, where legislation that is counterproductive to the development of librarianship is to be found, it is a commentary on the lack of library consciousness on the part of the countries' politicians. We refer specifically to three unfavorable types of legislation: (1) that requiring fiscal accountability of the librarian, (2) the type demanding an excessive number of depository copies from publishers for a country's official bibliographic agency, usually the national library, and (3) legislation imposing a tax on bibliographic records.

Laws of fiscal accountability require the librarian to pay for any items missing from the annual inventory of the collections. This legislation not only imposes a financial burden on the practitioner, it also fosters unfavorable attitudes of service among librarians. Aware that his annual salary will be reduced through deductions for losses from the collection, the librarian may react paranoidly that each user is a potential thief and may assume an overly custodial philosophy of librarianship, resulting in "protecting" the collection from the very public the collection was intended to benefit.

Unfortunately, fiscal accountability laws are not the only legal obstacles to service. If a country's depository law requires more than the minimum number of copies of a book or other graphic record than is needed for purposes of providing bibliographic and physical access to the item within the national library, the country is not providing the requisite access; it is imposing a tax on publishers. That such injustices usually occur in underdeveloped countries having small unstable publishing industries only intensifies the smallness and instability of such publishing industries.

Finally, we have encountered legislation that attempts to tax reading through the imposing of a fee to be paid by the library or the reader each time a book is used within a library. The revenues thus derived are to be paid to the authors. Theoretically, the principle of the legislation may appear beneficial because it rewards the author for his services; however, practice shows that such legislation has the long-range effect of discouraging reading. Since librarians are expected to promote reading and library services, they should discourage any legislation that diminishes the growth of reading or library services.

FINANCIAL SUPPORT

This term refers to the provision of the monetary base essential for the establishment, maintenance, and development of libraries or the library profession.

Our experience with financial support for libraries throughout the Americas and our deductions based on the area studies presented here suggest that certain characteristics must be present in the financial support given to our profession's agencies: it must be adequate, continuous, and have a legal basis. Concerning adequacy, the financial support should be adequate to carry out the objectives of library service as agreed upon by the library's governing body; this support must continue annually and not be subject to erratic fluctuations; and, finally, the support must have a legal basis to insure the adequacy and continuity of the support.

The origin of financial support for libraries is the legislation that authorizes governmental units to vote taxes and/or utilize public funds for the support of libraries. For agencies that are supported by public funds, the legislation takes the form of statutes; for agencies that are private or special libraries not supported by public funds, the legislation takes the form of corporate or institutional policies and/or private grants.

Concerning the variables that have been observed to interact with financial support, they may be said to be the following: (1) the economic situation of the country, (2) its source of income, (3) the degree of development of the country, (4) religion, (5) climate, and (6) the degree of library consciousness among government officials. A country's economic situation appears to be directly proportionate to the country's financial support for libraries; those nations with high gross national products (GNP) and a high per capita income tend to give greater support per capita than countries with low per capita incomes and low GNPs. Nations that have a larger urban than rural population, and a predominantly industrial society, tend to give greater financial support to libraries. Regarding a nation's degree of development, it has been observed that the developed countries of the world tend to provide higher per capita financial support for libraries than countries that are developing or underdeveloped nations. Religions can also affect financial support; for example, nations where Protestantism is the dominant religion tend to provide more financial support for libraries than countries where Roman Catholicism is dominant. A similar relationship may exist between Judaism and Islam, as well as Hinduism and Buddhism, although our research has no data to validate or invalidate the financial support/religion hypothesis outside of the contexts of Protestantism and Roman Catholicism. Climate may also affect support. Generally, those countries found in the cooler zone of each hemisphere tend to provide greater financial support than those nations in the warmer parts of the same hemisphere. Finally, the last interacting variable has been discovered to be library consciousness among government officials. Where library consciousness is strong among government officials, the degree of financial support for libraries is greater than in countries where officials have low levels of library consciousness. This situation holds true even in countries, for example, the Middle East, where financial resources available within a country may be extremely high per capita.

Regarding the variables that have been posited to interact with financial support, "sources of income" bears further comment. Financial support tends to be better in countries that have a diversified economy rather than one dependent on a few commodities. Financial support is highly vulnerable to fluctuation in countries that have a "one crop economy." The developing countries of Asia, Africa, and Latin America usually fall into this category, often having coffee, bananas, sugar, etc., as their single crop. However, equally vulnerable is the financial support of countries whose one "crop" is among the extractive commodities of copper, silver, gold, diamonds, and even oil. Income derived from these precious commodities can falter badly if a disruptive element, for example, a natural disaster or a strike, disturbs the equilibrium of that commodity. The disturbance may affect all elements of a nation's development, including library development. The astute library observer can usually detect such periods of instability through their telltale signs—broken runs of periodicals, interruptions in continuations, and inadequate numbers of acquisitions in the library collection.

The variable relating to library consciousness of public officials and financial support is of profound significance, and its implications and "cure" should be understood as a "lesson of world librarianship."

If librarians are confronted by situations of inadequate financial support, they should analyze the situation to determine its causality. If lack of library consciousness among public officials is the cause, the librarian should consider the following approach to coping with the problem: an orientation program for government officials, explaining the nature, missions, and services of libraries, may enlighten some uninformed politicians.

Or sometimes a simpler, less formal approach may prove advantageous, for example, as was the case with one librarian from the American Virgin Islands who was troubled by an inadequate budgetary allocation for periodicals. Not having the time for more formal communication, the librarian telephoned the government official and asked directly why she had been given the inadequate allocation. The official replied, "Why should I give you more money for periodicals when all you do is throw them into the trash?" Hearing this question, the librarian requested a brief but immediate appointment to see the official. Upon reaching the government office, the librarian invited the official into her car and drove her to the library. The librarian then showed the official row upon row of the orderly Princeton files filled with periodicals and explained that the retrospective runs of periodicals were used for study and research. After this demonstration of the information potential of periodicals, the government official not only granted the librarian the requested budgetary allocation, but she became an enthusiastic supporter of the library.[5]

THE PROFESSION

Since the nineteenth century the literature of librarianship has frequently addressed one question: "Is librarianship a profession?" According to Landau, the profession of librarianship denotes" . . . the collection, preservation, organization and use of recommended communications."[6]

Gates has indicated six elements that she believes constitute a profession: (1) a systematic theory which delineates and supports the skills that characterize the profession, (2) a level of authority which comes from extensive education in the systematic theory, (3) community sanction and approval of this authority as expressed in the conferring on the profession of such powers as accreditation, formulation of standards of performance, and establishment of rules for admission into the profession, (4) a code of ethics which regulates relations of professional persons with clients and colleagues, (5) a professional culture sustained by formal associations, consisting of its values, norms, and symbols and having at its center the career concept, and (6) a service orientation.[7]

Of the elements that Gates enumerated as essential to a profession, we have found that five are universally considered to be essential. However, criterion number three regarding "community sanction and approval of this authority" involves an attribute which is demanded of professions within the North American culture but is not considered essential by all cultures throughout the world; for example, the process of accreditation is replaced in one culture by the creation of a library education program by the country's ministry of education, thus granting immediate approval. Within another culture, rather than accrediting an educational program, the aspirant to the profession is examined by the country's library association.

Admittedly, the philosophy of librarianship remains today an undeveloped area of this discipline. It is proper to point out, however, that a literature of library philosophy does exist, and statements that are philosophical in nature regarding our profession can be traced to antiquity.

Not until we arrive at the seventeenth century and encounter Gabriel Naudé's *Avis pour Dresser une Bibliothèque*, however, do we arrive at a writing in librarianship of a truly philosophical nature. Rather than rules, regulations, or procedures, we find concepts relating to the origin, nature, and purposes of libraries in this treatise associated with the library of Cardinal Mazarin.

A radical departure from previous statements of library philosophy was made in the early twentieth century by the Russian government headed by Vladimir Lenin following the Russian Revolution of 1917. Commenting on the philosophy underlying Soviet library practice, Natalia I. Tyulina stated:

> Socialist library science discloses the social role and special characteristics of a socialist library; the principles and methods of subordinating library work to the political, economic, and cultural goals of the country; the organizational forms, ways of differentiation, and methods of serving the people by means of books with the purpose of attracting the basic mass of the population to systematic reading and to the use of libraries.[8]

Two years prior to the Russian Revolution a kind of "intellectual revolution" was developing within U.S. librarianship. In 1915 Alvin S. Johnson made a study of American librarianship. Two important results of this survey were immediately forthcoming. One was the C. C. Williamson Report on training for library services, published in 1923, and the establishment five years later of the Graduate Library School of the University of Chicago (GLS). It is not germane to our discussion of the philosophy of librarianship to describe either of these important landmarks of library development in the United States. It will suffice merely to state that the GLS was responsible for various publications, among which was a philosophical treatise entitled *An Introduction to Library Science*, by Pierce Butler, one of the several outstanding faculty members of the school. Butler affirmed in his work, published in 1933, that: "Unlike his colleagues in other fields of social activity, the librarian is strangely uninterested in the theoretical aspects of his profession. . . . The librarian apparently stands alone in the simplicity of his pragmatism: a rationalization of each immediate technical process by itself comes to satisfy his intellectual interest." Butler predicted that "an organic body of scientific knowledge will be built up to account for the complex activities of this social agency also. The librarian in the future will have at his service precise information where now he has only ad hoc hypotheses formulated from the peculiar conditions of his individual experience."[9]

How was the librarian to transform the ad hoc hypotheses to precise information? Butler believed that by applying scientific method to problems of librarianship a body of scientific knowledge would be formulated. Now, almost half a century after Butler's treatise, we would appear to be still in the beginning stages of developing a library science.

In the 1950s librarians began to hear of documentation, and somewhat later, of information science. These developments exerted a significant impact on librarianship, forcing the formulation of its philosophy and theory:

> Because of the emerging science of information, librarianship is, for the first time in its long history, compelled to formulate, self-consciously, its role in society, to examine critically its intellectual foundations, and to view itself holistically—as an integrated system that serves man, both as an individual and as a member of society, throughout life. Despite the relationship of librarianship to its coeval culture, the library has been recognized as a sociological entity only within the last half-century.[10]

Having discussed the nature of librarianship, we shall now turn to discussion of its purpose, origin, categories, interacting variables, and development. The purpose of librarianship is to serve mankind in its search for information, knowledge, and truth through the instrumentality of the graphic record. We may identify the origin of librarianship in man's desire to serve his fellow man through the provision of graphic records. Categorically, librarianship may be divided into four areas, predicated on the basis of the clientele served: (1) public, (2) school, (3) academic, and (4) special. At least two variables have been identified as interacting with the profession, namely the growth of knowledge and the intensity of the service orientation of a people. Regarding its development, librarianship may be observed to experience five phases: (1) collecting, (2) selecting, (3) organizing, and (4) interpreting of materials, followed by the (5) administrative phase. Will there be a demise of librarianship? Being a service profession, librarianship will survive as long as it provides a unique service to humanity; when librarianship ceases to respond to the changing needs of humanity or when the service it provides is no longer unique, that is to say, when the service is provided as effectively or better through some other profession or vocation, then we shall see the demise of our profession.

PRACTITIONERS

As defined here, practitioners are individuals involved in the essential activities of librarianship, regardless of whether or not these persons hold the professional library degree.

Although practitioners have existed as long as our civilizations have had their libraries, it was not until 1887 that the professionalization of the librarian began. In that year Melvil Dewey established the first library school in the world, the School of Library Economy at Columbia College, in New York.

Certain generalizations can be made about librarians throughout the world. Evident to the researcher and obvious even to the casual observer is the preponderance of women within the profession. Some qualifications of this generalization are necessary to set the record straight: (1) Since the beginning of library history, librarians were predominantly men; (2) historically, feminization of the profession is a recent phenomenon; (3) today most librarians in the Middle East are men; (4) in Western European countries men are numerically dominant in one type of library, while women are the majority in the remaining types of service agencies; and, (5) women have made significant contributions to the advancement of the profession.

As an elaboration of the generalizations just stated, we should begin by affirming that from the earliest history of librarianship, its practitioners have been predominantly men, and scholarly men, we should add. From the librarians in the Alexandrian Library of antiquity—Demetrios of Phaleron, Zenodotus of Ephesus, Callimachus of Cyrene, etc.—to the medieval, Renaissance, and Enlightenment librarians, our profession's practitioners were men. Other noteworthy examples were Magnus Aurelius Cassiodorus, Nicholas Clement, Gottfried Wilhelm von Leibniz, and also the notorious Giovanni Giacomo Casanova. Yes, all were scholars and librarians, and Casanova was also a lover of books.

To explain the feminization of the profession, we should be aware that women did not enter the profession in large numbers until the nineteenth century. Sidney L. Jackson explained the phenomenon as follows:

Women had long been employed on farms, in textile mills, and even in mines. The Crimean and Civil Wars precipitated women into the rapidly enlarging field of nursing, and they soon afterward became predominant in school teaching. Their entry into librarianship followed as the night the day the rise of the library supported from public funds, especially in the United Kingdom and the United States, and the ease of paying women less than men for any given task.[11]

To explain the preponderance of male practitioners throughout the Middle East we must recall that Islamic society is male-oriented and, for the most part, male-dominated. Presently, the thrust of library development in that area is in academic agencies, and male librarians are in the majority; however, if within a generation or two, the emphasis shifts to public library development, a larger work force will be required, and educated women may be permitted to fill that need.

In Western European countries the predominance of female librarians holds true with one significant exception. Men tend to work in academic libraries, and gravitate toward scholarly positions more than women librarians, who predominate in public libraries.

As to the contributions of women to librarianship, undoubtedly they have been significant. These contributions range from library educators like the pioneering Mary Wright Plummer, director of both Pratt Institute Free Library and its library-training class, to various outstanding practitioners and library educators throughout the world in recent years.

Unfortunately, the contributions of women librarians have not apparently been rewarded professionally throughout the world. Although women hold the majority of jobs in world librarianship, women do not occupy a corresponding proportion of administrative positions throughout the world. Our research study indicates that explanations underlying this phenomenon differ from culture to culture.

Our study and the literature examined indicate the ironic fact that women who contributed so greatly to the library profession generally have not been rewarded promotion-wise for their efforts. Although the clue to this situation has been involved with the social and economic situations in which women work, the key to future advancement of women librarians may lie more with their subject preparation than with social conditions.

In attempting to draw a profile of practitioners, one additional characteristic has surfaced: Librarians generally are resistant to changes in their professional practice. Although this characteristic is evident today, it can also be shown historically. Librarians, since early in their profession's history, showed a preference for papyrus as a writing material, even when parchment was beginning to be used more widely. Another example of librarians' resistance to change has been the preference for manuscript books after Gutenberg's invention had demonstrated the economic advantage of the printed book over its handwritten predecessor.

Other examples of this characteristic may be drawn from closer to the present day; for example, during the late nineteenth century when typewriters were beginning to be used over the "library hand," many librarians clung tenaciously to the handwritten catalog card. Not only the typewriter but the telephone had a difficult time gaining access into the library. Many librarians thought that the noisy jangle of the telephone was not suitable for the librarian's quiet world; some still do. When audiovisual software first threatened the bookish domain of the library, many librarians considered the library no place for phonograph records, films, and various types of microforms. The librarians' resistance to such software may be shown by their separatist treatment of media. First, phonograph records were granted a corner, if not a place, in the library; in other words, phonograph records were first segregated into one place in the library until it was decided that they should be placed, as all other library materials, in their correct subject area. Then phonograph records of readings of literature were placed with literature, and music phonograph records were placed in the music area of the library. It was quite a while before media, which were given separatist treatment in the collection, were fully integrated in the main card catalog. Further examples of resistance to change could be supplied regarding microforms and computer terminals, but we shall allow the reader to supply his own examples from the immediate past.

ASSOCIATIONS

We intend the term "associations" to refer to those organizations of persons or agencies that band together for the improvement of library service and the status and salaries of the profession's practitioners.

The origin of our profession's associations may be traced to two attempts within the United States, the first a false start in 1853 and the second a successful attempt in 1876. Timing was the critical factor both in the failure of the 1853 Librarians' Convention in New York to stimulate subsequent meetings, and in the success of the 1876 meeting of the American Library Association (ALA) in Philadelphia.

The establishment of the ALA stimulated further associations, for example, an association in England. One year following the founding of the ALA, the British established in 1877 their association, which they modestly called *The* Library Association.

Various categories of associations function within our profession at various levels: (1) international, (2) regional, (3) national, (4) intranational, and (5) specialized associations. An international body was founded in 1927. Originally called the International Federation of Library Associations (IFLA), it is now known as the International Federation of LibraryAssociations and Institutions, its new name more accurately describing the scope of its membership. An example of the regional category is the Scandinavian Federation of Research Libraries (NVBF). Established in 1947, the NVBF aids in the development of communication and cooperation among Scandinavian and Icelandic scientific libraries and librarians.

The ALA (of the United States) and the LA (of the United Kingdom) are two outstanding examples of national associations; however, both associations may be criticized for their total preoccupation with the improvement of library service to the total neglect of attention to raising of the status and salaries of librarians. The numerous regional and state associations that are to be found in various countries of the world comprise the category we designate as intranational associations, two examples being the Pacific Northwest Library Association, begun in 1909, and the New York Library Association, established in 1890. Lastly, the specialized category may be illustrated through the Association of Research Libraries, organized in 1932.

The variables that interact with the existence of associations are at least: (1) an awareness among practitioners that the ideals that they profess, for example, adequate library service throughout a country, state, region, or society can no longer be met by the activities of individual librarians, regardless of their commitment to the ideal or their zeal in attempting to establish the ideal, and (2) the awareness among practitioners that common ideals of librarians can best be attained through the concerted efforts of groups rather than the isolated efforts of individual librarians. The strength of belief of practitioners in these ideals and their ability to transform then into purposeful action determine the existence or demise of library associations.

EDUCATIONAL AGENCIES

The term "educational agencies" denotes the various schools and programs through which the aspirants to the profession learn its theory and practice. Such agencies may include (1) schools which have college or university affiliation, (2) technical institutes, (3) libraries which provide in-service training, (4) organizations that provide correspondence courses, and (5) regional schools.

The status and prestige that academic affiliation would bring was, undoubtedly, a prime factor in Melvil Dewey's mind when he took his idea for a School of Library Economy to the authorities at Columbia College, in 1887, where it was accepted. Also, as far back as 1923, C. C. Williamson published his study on *Training for Library Services,* in which he advanced the argument that the interdisciplinary character of library science would develop best in an academic atmosphere where additional study in subject fields and opportunities for investigating research problems in the discipline might be provided.

The second school for librarians established in the United States, the training class of the Pratt Institute Free Library, begun in 1890, belonged to the second category, "technical institutes." Similar programs at Drexel Institute, established in 1892, and the Armour Institute, founded in 1893, as well as counterparts in other countries were also begun.

Examples of the third category may be found around the world. Organizations in different parts of the world have offered training in librarianship by correspondence. Within the United States, however, such training is not acceptable for accreditation by the American Library Association.

Regional schools of librarianship exist in South America and Africa. The Escuela Interamericana de Bibliotecologia, of the Universidad de Antioguia, established in 1956, serves as our first example. The University of Dakar's School for Librarians, Archivists, and Documentalists, was established in 1963 to meet the needs of French-speaking countries in Africa.

Aspiration for an international agency for our profession's education has been expressed periodically in the twentieth century. The idea was advanced as early as 1904 by Guido Biagi, writing in the *Library Journal*. The location of the proposed school, the language of instruction, curriculum, recruitment, and payment of the faculty are some of the many problems which have arisen in discussions of the project, and which may continue for a long time to be insurmountable. Meanwhile, a functional intermediate step is the International Graduate Summer School (IGSS), held annually at the College of Librarianship Wales (CLW).

Closely related to the topic of educational agencies is their evaluation. At least three categories of methods are used: (1) accreditation of the training agency by a library association, (2) certification of the practitioner by an examining body, and (3) approval of a training agency by the ministry of education that created it.

LITERATURE

This term, as it is used here, has been defined by Jean Key Gates as the body of writings by or for librarians that concern themselves with (1) the historical bases of the profession, (2) library functions, techniques, and activities, as well as the principles underlying them, and (3) the profession itself. While elaborating on the topic, Gates identifies fourteen categories of library literature, many of which have been found throughout our world study. These categories range from histories to biographies, case studies, intructional materials, statistical compilations and many other categories of reference books, to professional journals.

At least four determinants appear to influence the writing of library literature, namely: (1) adequate educational preparation on the part of librarians and
library educators, enabling them to become knowledgeable in library science, research methodology, and writing skills, (2) existence of publishers committed to
specialized publishing, (3) existence of a market within the language and country
of origin of the library science text, and (4) sufficient time for the above elements to develop.

The emergence of library literature within various countries of the world has
been noted in the foregoing area studies. Although its first appearance usually
coincides with the beginning of formal library education within a country, the
first work in library science may appear before such attempts. One of the first
examples of library literature to appear in various countries has been an explanation of some classification scheme by a scholar who proposed its adoption by
libraries throughout his country. Guided by the misconception that classification is not a difficult skill, the scholar/proponent may have even provided a
do-it-yourself instruction for any would-be catalogers among his readers.

Serious attempts to initiate a library literature within a given country are
usually made in conjunction with the first formal attempt at library education.
After the eager instructor has conducted a thorough literature search through
the country's professional writings, he discovers to his dismay that there is little
or no published material. At this point the instructor resorts to one of two possible alternatives: (1) he decides to instruct through the use of textbooks from
his own country, or (2) he attempts to create textbooks or at least handouts or
exercises that he might use as instructional materials.

While resorting to the expedient use of textbooks from his own country, an
English-speaking instructor, for example, may find himself having to explain
in the language of the host country the concepts that his students have already
read, and only partially understood. Or the instructor may purchase textbooks
from outside the host country, from a country whose language is the same as that
of the host country. Saudi Arabians, for example, have for years been using Arabic library science textboods published in Egypt, while Canadians have been
doing the same with textbooks from either the United States or the United
Kingdom.

Unfortunately, neither of the situations described above is satisfactory because in the first case, that of the library science texts in foreign languages, the
student is compelled to study an unfamiliar subject through an equally unfamiliar language. And even in cases where the language is the same, as in the case with
Saudi Arabia and Egypt, as described above, the underlying assumptions of the
textbooks—their legal systems and social customs—may be quite different. One
of the present writers recalls instances of students from tropical countries in Africa who grumbled about having to waste class and study time in a U.S. course in
library administration on problems of heating when the situation in their African
countries is quite the reverse.

Most library educators familiar with the problem would appear to have concluded that the only satisfactory solution to the problem of using library literature is having it produced locally in the language of the country, and describing situations based on that country's culture.

Practitioners have generally been critical of the quality of our profession's literature. This evaluation results, we believe, from an ignorance of the reality of the professional literature of all other fields. Although as librarians we may marvel at the high quality of the writings of Edith Hamilton in the humanities, Thorstein Veblen in the social sciences, or Albert Einstein in the sciences, we must realistically admit that not all writings in the three fields cited rise to the level of Hamilton, Veblen, or Einstein; furthermore, we hypothesize that if librarians were as intimately acquainted with the output of the chemical, psychological, or medical literature, he or she would not be so critical of the quality of library literature. While our field boasts the writings of individuals like Justus Lipsius, Edward Edwards, Pierce Butler, José Ortega y Gasset, L. N. Malclés, Louis Shores, and Jesse Shera, we need not be overly critical of our professional literature.

SERVICE AGENCIES

The term "service agencies" includes those establishments maintained by the profession's practitioners for the care, lending, and administration of graphic records essential for the provision of information services to the agencies' users. Specifically, such agencies are most commonly called libraries, although variants of the term include "materials centers," "information bureaus," or "documentation centers."

Our study has revealed seven categories of service agencies in various parts of the world: (1) public, (2) school, (3) academic, (4) special, (5) research, (6) national, and (7) the libraries of regional and world organizations.

Of the six types of service agencies, school libraries are the most poorly developed throughout the world. Although they abound in Canada, the United States, and Western Europe, elsewhere school libraries are usually composed of small randomly assembled collections that are to be found in classrooms rather than in an area separate from classrooms. This situation is lamentable because in order for school libraries to realize their maximum potential to children in every part of the world, it is necessary for librarians to convince politicians and officials holding decision-making positions in national departments of education that school libraries are essential agencies that complement the school in educational programs.

Academic, special, and national libraries are, for different reasons, generally the best supported libraries in a country. In the Middle East, for example, where education is a priority item for development, academic libraries are extremely well supported financially. Because special libraries are necessary units of the competitive business and commercial sectors of the economy, special libraries also tend to receive adequate collections and financial support from their parent organizations.

National libraries exist in most countries of the world, with some countries having more than one; for example, Germany and Italy have more than one national library. As students of history know, both countries were once composed of various separate kingdoms, many of which had their own royal libraries. After unification Germany and Italy converted the former royal collections into separate national libraries.

Research libraries are unevenly developed and financially supported throughout the world. This situation may be explained by the many disciplines that research libraries encompass. Generally, it may be stated that research libraries devoted to the natural, applied, and social sciences tend to be better developed and more adequately supported than those in the humanities.

Despite the many differences in service agencies, a discernible pattern of development characterizes them. The sequence tends to be as follows: (1) religious archive, (2) royal archive, (3) religious library, (4) royal library, (5) public library, (6) academic library, (7) research library, (8) special library, (9) school library, (10) regional and world organization libraries.

Regarding the variables that interact with the service agencies of our profession, we can cite at least six in the following categories: (1) social, (2) cultural, (3) economic, (4) scientific, (5) technological, and (6) geographical. Rather than mere interacting variables, each item is a sine qua non of library development.

Libraries require stability rather than mobility. It is no accident that the Mesopotamians, the Egyptians, and the Greeks, who were noted for massive structure—for ziggurats, pyramids, and temples like the Parthenon—were also noted for having great libraries. Cultures like the Vikings and the American Indians are known to have had mobile items like graceful ships and wigwams, but they were never known to have built a library.

As a summary of the conditions that contribute to the prospering of libraries, Jean Key Gates states the following: (1) in societies of political and cultural maturity which recognize the necessity of preserving, transmitting, and enlarging the body of knowledge, (2) during periods of relative peace and tranquility which afford time to play and pursue cultural and intellectual activities, (3) when individuals have both the leisure and the means to "cultivate the finer arts and improve the common stock of knowledge," (4) in periods of intellectual creativity and scholarly activity, when large and varied collections of materials are required for study and research, (5) when there is a large societal emphasis on self-improvement and a well-informed citizenry, (6) during revivals of learning which center around and depend upon accumulations of graphic materials and access to them, (7) when institutional stability and security of tenure offer permanence and continuity, (8) in areas with concentrated population in especially an urban environment which can provide the leadership, the financial means to support libraries, and the cultural and intellectual interest to stimualte their use, (9) when economic prosperity provides sizeable individual and corporate wealth and encourages philanthropic giving, and (10) in times when, as in recent decades, economic growth and national power and status are considered to be dependent upon the wide dissemination and use of information and knowledge which have utilitarian value.[12]

Our research has indicated that types of service agencies are influenced by the determinant of demography and geography. Although the basic type of agency is located within a building, demographic extremes such as low population and density as well as a preponderance of geographical factors, for example, rivers and waterways, influence the service agencies to assume various types; for example, bookmobiles are used extensively in Australia and New Zealand, and helicopters are employed within the Soviet Union because the low population densities in some areas of these countries make the construction of library buildings impractical. Also, the extensive system of waterways in the Scandinavian countries has made bookboats a common type of service agency. In heavily populated areas within the United States, various "store-front" libraries have been created by renting vacant facilities in central cities.

PLANNING

The *A.L.A. Glossary of Library Terms* defines planning as the "formulation of comprehensive integrated plans for library objectives in city, county, region, state, or nation."[13] Library planning is carried out for the purpose of defining goals and objectives for one or a group of libraries with the end of providing the public with improved service.

A British librarian who was the son of an exiled Polish army officer, Louis Stanley Jast (family name, Jastrzebski), was one of the early library planners. After becoming librarian of Croydon and afterwards chief librarian of Manchester during the early part of the twentieth century, Jast conducted extended and serious study of the design of large libraries in England and the United States; consequently, he enunciated four principles of library planning: (1) a properly designed library should not be a building containing books but books in an appropriate setting; (2) there are limits to the value of subject departmentalization; therefore, the stock should be kept as intact as possible; (3) the book stack should be "the central nerve ganglion of the whole building;" and, (4) in the collaboration between librarian and architect, the premier role should be assigned to the librarian.[14]

A definition of planning appropriate for a national scale proceeded from the Ibero-American Seminar on Planning and Documentation Services of 1968. Its definition of planning is as follows:

The planning of library and documentation services is regarded as one aspect of educational, scientific, and cultural planning within the social and economic planning of a country or region, for only within this context can library and documentation planning acquire the foundations of support which it needs if it is to be effective.[15]

At the national level, library planners are involved in either microplanning or macroplanning of library facilities. Planning individual units of service is denoted as microplanning; whereas, macroplanning concerns itself with the simultaneous consideration of the sum total of the needs of a country—educational, economic, and social.

As we view library planning throughout the world, we see that within the developed world, planning is generally at the macrolevel and is concerned with creating and linking library networks. Within developing countries, planning is generally at the microlevel, dedicated to improving units within national librarianship. In each part of the world, planning tends to be more successful in centralized rather than decentralized governments. Success also depends on the commitment of a country's politicians to achieving library objectives.

PHILOSOPHICAL GUIDELINES FOR WORLD LIBRARIANS

It may be proper now to summarize the thinking, implied or expressed, of world librarians concerning the profession's proximate task. Within the developed countries librarians must effect the professional standardization necessary to internationalize the linking of libraries into networks. Within developing countries librarians must concentrate on eradicating illiteracy, promoting the development of national publishing industries, and creating the library units indispensable to the eventual linking of their countries' professional practice into regional and world standards and networks.

The unique role of world librarianship has already been succinctly defined by an outstanding and often eloquent spokesman of the global library community, Louis Shores, who calls upon librarians everywhere to be steadfast in supporting "humanity in its search for truth."[16]

FOUR LAWS OF WORLD LIBRARIANSHIP

Our investigation has revealed to us four laws of world librarianship. They are (1) the Law of Appropriateness, (2) the Law of Interdependence, (3) the Law of Partial Convergence, and (4) the Law of Total Convergence. Further studies involving the hypotheses and theories revealed in *World Librianship* should lead to the formulation of additional laws of this field.

The Law of Appropriateness

Successful aspects of librarianship, for example, legislation, literature, and services, that satisfy national needs, must be planned in accordance with the realities of the country, including the country's historical background, economic conditions, political situations, and cultural context. When planning a new variant of a library aspect, the library planner can control the success of the variant through correct application of the historical, economic, political, and cultural factors to the variant. When adopting a variant to one context from another, the success of that variant can be controlled through modifying the constituents of the variant from one context to the historical, political, economic, and cultural factors of the host context.

The Law of Interdependence

All aspects of librarianship in one context are interdependent. The qualities of one aspect will be reflected in all other aspects; the strength of a context's educational agencies will contribute to the strength of all other aspects; conversely, the weaknesses of a context's library legislation will reflect in all other aspects of the context, especially its bibliographic control. The success of the aspects can be controlled through modifying, strengthening, or weakening the constituent elements of the aspects.

The Law of Partial Convergence

As library aspects cross national boundaries, they require modification of their constituent elements in order to create the standardization of the elements involved. The success of the standardization will be controlled by the preciseness by which the various elements are standardized.

The Law of Total Convergence

Eventually all world variants of librarianship will, through standardization, converge to form a global librarianship. The success of the global librarianship will be controlled by the preciseness by which all elements of world librarianship are standardized.

NOTES

1. Dorothy Anderson, *Universal Bibliographic Control: A Long Term Policy/ A Plan for Action* (Pullach, Munich: Verlag Dokumentation, 1974), p. 11.
2. Frank M. Gardner, *Public Library Legislation: A Comparative Study* (Paris: UNESCO, 1971), p. 18.
3. Ibid.

4. Ibid.
5. Conversation between Fiolina Mills and Richard Krzys.
6. Thomas Landau, ed., *Encyclopedia of Librarianship*, 3rd ed. (New York: Hafner, 1966), pp. 248-249.
7. Jean Key Gates, *Introduction to Librarianship* (New York: McGraw-Hill, [c1968]).
8. Natalia I. Tyulina, "Library Science," *Great Soviet Encyclopedia: A Translation of the Third Edition*, ed. by A. M. Prokhorov, Vol. 3 (New York: Macmillan, 1970), pp. 716-717.
9. Pierce Butler, *An Introduction to Library Science* (Chicago: University of Chicago Press, [c1961], pp. xi-xiv.
10. Jesse H. Shera, "Librarianship, Philosophy of," *ALA World Encyclopedia of Library and Information Services*, ed. by Robert Wedgeworth (Chicago: American Library Association, 1980), pp. 316-317.
11. Sidney L. Jackson, *Libraries and Librarianship in the West: A Brief History* (New York: McGraw-Hill, [c1974]), pp. 400-401.
12. Gates, *Introduction to Librarianship*, pp. 92-93.
13. American Library Association. Editorial Committee. Subcommittee on Library Terminology. *ALA Glossary of Library Terms* (Chicago: American Library Association, 1943), p. 82.
14. James G. Ollé, "Jast, Louis Stanley," *ALA World Encyclopedia of Library and Information Services*, ed. by Robert Wedgeworth (Chicago: American Library Association, 1980), p. 282.
15. Jesse H. Shera, *Introduction to Library Science: Basic Elements of Library Service* (Littleton, Colorado: Libraries Unlimited, 1976), pp. 161-162.
16. Conversation between Louis Shores and Richard Krzys, February 1964.

CONCLUSIONS

8

Our Professional Destiny: A Global Librarianship

Richard Krzys and Gaston Litton

The efforts and tendencies toward international standardization and cooperation presage a global librarianship, which we defined earlier in our study as that
phase of our profession's development to be characterized by its decision-making
to be made in terms of satisfying humanity's bibliographic and information
needs rather than purely regional or national needs. In terms of the aspects of
our profession previously examined, what deeper meaning does this concept
have, and what are its purposes?

NATURE AND PURPOSES OF A GLOBAL LIBRARIANSHIP

With the achievement of a global librarianship various significant changes will
have occurred in the aspects of our profession. Undoubtedly, the most notable
will be the achievement of universal bibliographic control (UBC). Through UBC
all publications of every nation will be accurately, rapidly, and continuously
recorded through a uniform technique. This technique, as useful as it will be, is
merely a means to the end of providing public access, both bibliographic and
physical, to the world's documents.

Within each country certainly, or within a world government possibly, legislation will be enacted and enforced that will assure the realization of the constituent elements of a global librarianship; for example, to realize UBC, legislation relating to copyright and depository will have to be enacted and enforced.
Similar legislation, relating to the realization of all other aspects of our concept,
would also have to be enacted and enforced.

Librarianship will have become a profession throughout the world, and its body of knowledge—library science—will by then be composed of the philosophy and theory adequate to the realization of the profession's problems and goals. Not only knowledge, as just described, but also freedom will characterize the practitioners of a global librarianship. This freedom will be shown through the inner-directed mobility of the librarian of the future. With a global librarianship, no longer will a practitioner feel compelled, through lack of confidence, to work in one city or be ordered by a government official to work in a particular city of a country; rather, the global librarian will through mastery of a professional knowledge, attitudes, skills, and possibly a universal language of English be able to practice librarianship wherever in the world he or she might choose.

Part of this freedom will originate from the practitioner's professional associations which will be dedicated not only to the noble ideal of the betterment of library service, but also to the practical end of advancing the individual practitioner to improved status, salary, and working conditions. This advancement must be based on vital educational systems that not only train librarians adequately for the needs of the times but also *educate* them to respond to the changing human needs of the future. Not only will minimum universal standards have been established for library education, but a global school of library, information, and communication studies will have been established as well, possibly at the United Nations Library in New York in conjunction with the various universities of that city, where research-oriented study at the graduate level may be pursued.

Reflecting the deepened philosophical and theoretical bases required by a global librarianship, our professional literature will contain articles, monographs, etc. that will be available either in the profession's universal language, or in the practitioner's native language, quickly translated by a computer. The seven types of service agencies—public, school, academic, special, research, and national libraries, as well as libraries of regional and world organizations—will abound and through improved techniques of interlibrary loan, resource sharing, and telereprography be able to create true *libraries without walls* for all users. Financial support will be adequate and continuous to achieve objectives that have been arrived at through long-range planning with necessary annual modifications.

Professional utopia? No! These concepts represent merely the realization of the elements of a prototype for a model librarianship that will be realizable within the lifetime of many of us reading this book.

THE FUTURE OF GLOBAL LIBRARIANSHIP

With the achievement of a global librarianship, will our profession have reached its ultimate frontier? An affirmative answer many have seemed appropriate for the sixteenth century when Konrad Gesner attempted unsuccessfully to compile a universal bibliography. Today, however, more exciting challenges loom over our professional horizon.

"That's one small step for a man, one giant leap for mankind."[1] Those famous words uttered on the moon by the U.S. astronaut, Neil Armstrong, may have provided a hint for the future of librarianship, for the thrust of the space-craft's rockets not only lifted Armstrong and his crew into the space-age, but all of mankind as well. In order to continue to function as a service profession, librarianship will also have to satisfy the needs of a space-age.

EXTRATERRESTRIAL LIBRARIANSHIP

Because of Armstrong's achievement, we who profess and practice librarianship must now begin to think in terms of an *extraterrestrial librarianship*. If we accept the assumption that information represents a basic human need, then we can reason that wherever man explores outer space—on space platforms, satellites, or other celestial bodies—he will need data and libraries as their reposi-tories. If we accept that line of reasoning, we can prophesy that librarians of the future will create libraries in space—if they do not already exist there, created by an extraterrestrial intelligence. The speculation of the Princeton physicist, Gerard O'Neill, may have some implications for the direction that library planning of the future may take; he speculates that "setting up . . . a space community is economically feasible, within the limits of the technology of this decade. Initially it would support 10,000 people. . . ."[2] O'Neill foresees . . . "colonies of perhaps a million people, possibly within 30 years from now."[3]

How will such advances in our professional development occur? By con-sidering the pattern of man's past achievements and extrapolating to the future, we may have a clue. The renowned British humanist, Kenneth Clark, speculated, ". . . nearly all the steps upward in civilization have been made in periods of internationalism."[4] When tested in the light of library development, Clark's hypothesis is validated; consider the cultural confrontations that produced the Alexandrian Library, Charlemagne's Court library, the library developed by Gabriel Naudé, Sir Anthony Panizzi's achievements at the British Museum, and the accomplishments of IFLA.

Although librarians presently are involved in world librarianship, and global librarianship still represents an ideal, we believe that another step forward in civilization will be made during the space-age. Recently Isaac Asimov, the most acclaimed popularizer of science, revealed his carefully calculated conclusion: "We are not alone in the universe."[5] If extraterrestrial contact is ever made—and is it not a logical extension of Clark's cultural confrontation hypothesis?—a quantum leap in civilization will be made, unless, of course, the confrontation is a hostile one. The future of civilization, including librarianship, we believe, lies in outer space.

NOTES

1. Fred Hoyle and Chandra Wickramasinghe, *Lifecloud: The Origin of Life in the Universe* (New York: Harper & Row, 1978), p. 135.
2. Gerard O'Neill is quoted in Ian Ridpath, *Worlds Beyond: A Report on the Search for Life in Space* (New York: Harper & Row, [c1975]), p. 58.
3. Ibid.
4. Kenneth Clark, *Civilisation: A Personal View* (New York: Harper & Row, [c1969]), p. 160.
5. Isaac Asimov, *Extraterrestrial Civilizations* (New York: Crown, 1979), p. 174.

Appendix

The International Library Information Center
of the University of Pittsburgh*

The International Library Information Center (ILIC) was established in 1964 at the Graduate School of Library and Information Sciences of the University of Pittsburgh for the purpose of serving information, training, and research functions in international and comparative librarianship. In conformity with the customary developmental pattern of agencies, ILIC's establishment may be attributed to an unanswered need, in this case the necessity for library-related data created by the increased bibliographic activity which occurred in various areas of the globe during the twentieth century. Owing to its position as a world leader in librarianship, the United States sent vast numbers of its librarians to serve professionally in foreign countries; between the years 1900 and 1964, several hundred librarians from the United States had gone abroad as consultants to all types of libraries in various countries, aided their programs of library education, or worked professionally in specific institutions.[1]

Although one could not doubt the considerable international involvement with libraries of professionals from the United States in the 1960s (it was then estimated that 200 librarians and 300 experts in related fields, such as education, literacy, community development, agriculture, and health, left the United States annually on professional assignments involving library development),[2] serious doubts were raised by these professionals and their sponsoring agencies with regard to the actual accomplishments resulting from their efforts. In cases

*This article originally appeared in the *Encyclopiedia of Library and Information Science.*

where professionals from the United States had been unsuccessful working abroad, their failure was attributed to the following factors: (1) lack of appropriate educational background in international and comparative librarianship; (2) lack of current information on the library situation in the country to be visited; and (3) inadequate understanding of the historical, political, economic, and social factors operating in the country to be visited and their relationship to national library development.

This need for data about the international library scene which existed among librarians and other professionals from the United States represented the smaller part of the information need; far greater was the corresponding need among foreign librarians who visited the United States. As the result of the considerable influence of the library consultants and practitioners from the United States, who were looked at by foreign librarians as models of mature professionalism, the United States had a magnetic attraction for librarians throughout the world; consequently, an estimated 1000 foreign librarians annually came to the United States during the 1960s under the sponsorship of various governmental, international, philanthropic, and professional organizations in order to observe the country's library achievements.[3] In the true spirit of comparative librarianship, they also came in search of and to share solutions to professional problems.

Keenly aware of these information needs and the leadership role which the United States exercised in international librarianship, Dr. Nasser Sharify, then assistant professor in the Graduate School of Library Science, proposed the creation of the International Library Information Center to Dr. Harold Lancour, then the school's dean. Dean Lancour enthusiastically supported the proposal and empowered Dr. Sharify to establish ILIC in January 1964 and to serve as the center's first director. This position has always been a part-time appointment which has been filled by a faculty member of the university's Graduate School of Library and Information Sciences. The International Library Information Center was to serve two major functions: (1) to act as a clearinghouse of data on library development, documentation, and book production and distribution, with regard to both U.S. and overseas resources; and (2) to serve as a training and research center in the field of international librarianship. These functions may be described as follows: The information function is concerned with the systematic gathering of information relating to three principal topics: (1) technical assistance to developing countries, (2) U.S. resources in the library, documentation, and book production fields, and (3) overseas resources in the library, documentation, book production, and distribution fields. Included in the training and research function are four major activities: (1) conducting courses in librarianship and documentation on an international and comparative level; (2) developing a curriculum devoted to the international aspects of librarianship; (3) conducting seminars and institutes to discuss various problems such as those relating to the development of libraries and documentation centers in developing countries, and the education of foreign librarians and documentalists both in the United States and their home countries; and (4) conducting studies and research in the area of comparative librarianship.[4]

Financial support for the center has come from three sources—institutional funds, philanthropic organizations, and private contributions. Dr. Lancour obtained the initial support of ILIC from the University of Pittsburgh; subsequently, Dr. Sharify obtained a grant from the A. W. Mellon Educational and Charitable Trust for $18,000, and at the request of Dr. William V. Jackson, ILIC's second director, the Ford Foundation approved the transfer of $10,600 from a grant which the foundation had made previously to the University of Pittsburgh. In addition, one individual made a contribution to ILIC's support. These sources have all been combined to support ILIC which has no separate budget.

In order to enable ILIC to realize its formation, training, and research functions, the center has maintained a professional staff of a director and librarian, who have been assisted by various part-time employees.

Dr. William Vernon Jackson, the second director of ILIC, was responsible for the organization and growth of the center's collection. Composed mainly of primary source materials useful for international and comparative study in librarianship, and emphasizing library development in countries other than the United States, the collection numbers approximately 22,000 items in 33 languages.[5] It is strongest in materials from Australia, Canada, Great Britain, Pakistan, East and West Germany, and Latin America, reflecting Dr. Jackson's broad interests in the Latin American countries where he travels extensively as a consultant, educator, and researcher. Of major importance are the center's reports and studies, representing the experiences of librarians, educators, and scholars throughout the world. Libraries in 142 countries have generously supplied such primary source material as annual reports and in-house publications; and librarians from the United States, as well as those from other countries, have contributed their reports and surveys. Data on library standards, statistics, and legislation have been furnished by library associations and government agencies. In addition, the collection includes newspaper and journal articles, papers and proceedings of library and documentation conferences, dissertations and reports concerning library and information science abroad, and the publications of libraries and library-related institutions and associations, many from newly established library schools in Africa, Asia, and Latin America. The center holds comprehensive studies in library education, especially from Colombia, France, Great Britain, and Southeast Asia. Holdings are strong in the area of library development and planning and include plans for national library services in many developing countries. Data relating to overseas book and library activities of the U.S. government, such as the Franklin Book Programs and the U.S. Book Exchange, as well as philanthropic and international agencies are acquired. The international scope of its holdings makes ILIC unique.

Bibliographic access of ILIC's collection is facilitated through its card catalog where a unit card is provided for each item in the collection. Physical access is allowed through placement of all items in pamphlet files in two categories: (1) broad topics related to international library development, for example, education, area studies, book production, literacy, congresses, geographical areas of the world, and foundation reports; and (2) countries of the world, arranged alphabetically from Aden to Zambia. Subject access to materials from individual countries is permitted by a classification scheme which divides countries according to sixteen classes and five subclasses. Material from each country may be classed as follows: (1) background, (2) general, (3) periodicals, (4) publishing and communication, (5) education, (6) library legislation, (7) national libraries, (8) university libraries, (9) public libraries, (10) school libraries, (11) special libraries, (12) USIS libraries, (13) library education, (14) library associations, (15) library meetings, (16) special topics. Where necessary, classes may be subdivided as follows: (1) selection and acquisition, (2) technical services, (3) reader services, (4) administration, (5) systems analysis; for example, reader services in national libraries would be designated as 7.3.

Since ILIC's establishment in 1964, its users have come from countries the world over. The location of the center's collection on the premises of the School of Library and Information Science of the University of Pittsburgh affords its students and faculty a unique opportunity to delve deeply into primary source documents recording the activities of international librarianship and information science. Users with similar interests have come from various areas of the United States. In addition, requests for information come from sectors of the United States having overseas interests related to library development, for example, governmental agencies such as AID and the Peace Corps. Private sectors of the U.S. community who have used ILIC are foundations, programs of international education of universities and other institutions, and special information centers outside of librarianship. But requests for ILIC's data and materials have also originated from points outside the United States; librarians, professionals in related fields, and various types of agencies abroad have benefitted from the center's collection, services, and activities.

The center's activities may be categorized into four main areas: (1) information, (2) briefing, (3) publication, and (4) education. Its information activities involve answering inquiries from anywhere in the world about developments in international librarianship. Through its briefing sessions the center has assisted librarians and information scientists to carry the torch of U.S. expertise to various countries, including Ecuador, Greece, Guatemala, the Crown Colony of Hong Kong, Iran, Israel, Lebanon, Malaysia, Nigeria, Pakistan, the Philippines, South Africa, Taiwan, Thailand, Turkey, and Vietnam.[6] These briefings included not only information on the history of library development and the current conditions of library service in the country to be visited, but also the factors —political, economic, social, and cultural—relevant to national library development. Functioning on the philosophy that comparative librarianship is a two-way process, ILIC has assisted various governmental, intergovernmental, and private agencies in the preparation of study plans and itineraries for visiting librarians from Australia, Czechoslovakia, Egypt, England, Ghana, India, Indonesia, Israel, Kenya, New Zealand, the Philippines, Venezuela, and Yugoslavia.[7] One publication of the center is the *Foreign Service Directory of American Librarians*, edited by Janet C. Phillips and sponsored jointly by the International Relations Round Table of the American Library Association and the International Library Information Center. This directory lists 1009 individuals from the United States who have undertaken library missions in other countries. ILIC's educational activities have included planning and teaching of courses and conducting an institute related to international and comparative study in librarianship. As faculty members of the Graduate School of Library and Information Sciences of the University of Pittsburgh, the center's directors have taught courses in international library services and resources and Latin American bibliography as well as a seminar in comparative study in librarianship. Upon request from other educational institutions, ILIC has assisted in the planning of courses in these fields by supplying course syllabi. On June 13-16, 1965, in commemoration of the United Nations' International Cooperation Year, and in collaboration with the Office of Cultural and Educational Exchange of the University of Pittsburgh and Regional Council for International Education, the center conducted an institute in international and comparative librarianship with the theme of "The Increasing Responsibility of American College and University Libraries in International Activities." Summarizing the institute, Dr. Nasser Sharify, then ILIC's director, and Mr. Roland Piggford stated the following:

> The First Institute on International Comparative Librarianship had as its purpose the examination of the increasing responsibility of the American college and university library in international activities, both at home and abroad: that is, the increase in acquisition activity with regard to overseas material, particularly material in the so-called "exotic" languages, necessary to support expanding language and area study programs at both graduate and undergraduate levels; and the growing involvement of college and university library personnel in the planning, staffing, and executing of technical assistance to libraries in developing countries.
>
> Thirty-three participants represented thirteen academic and research libraries and three large public library systems. Representatives were present from five foreign countries: Brazil, India, Iran, Liberia, and the United Arab Republic.[8]

Dr. Nasser Sharify, then assistant professor in library science and education and director of ILIC, directed the institute. Various speakers participated in the sessions of the institute, including Dr. Harold Lancour, dean of the Graduate School of Library and Information Sciences; Dr. A. C. Van Dusen, vice-chancellor for the professions at the University of Pittsburgh; Dr. Walter Stone, director of libraries at the University of Pittsburgh; Dr. Andrew D. Osborn, professor of library science, University of Pittsburgh; Dr. Nasser Sharify; Mr. Norman Horrocks of the University of Pittsburgh; Mr. Frank McGowan, librarian of the Graduate School of Public and International Affairs, University of Pittsburgh; Dr. Jay E. Daily, then consulting librarian for the Franklin Book Programs, assistant director for technical services, University of Pittsburgh; and Mr. J. Clement Harrison, assistant dean of the Graduate School of Library and Information Sciences of the University of Pittsburgh.[9]

During the initial phases of existence of the International Library Information Center, its staff, collection, and activities have served students, researchers, educators, and consultants involved in the international and comparative aspects of librarianship, information science, and communication. The center's future plans, guided by Dr. Richard Krzys, ILIC's director since 1971, include continuing these activities, as well as adding services which are designed to increase ILIC's informational and educational value to its world community.

NOTES

1. *International Library Information Center*. (Pittsburgh: University of Pittsburgh, Graduate School of Library and Information Sciences, 1964), p. 1.
2. Nasser Sharify and Harold Lancour, *A Proposal for the Expansion of the Activities of the International Library Information Center (I.L.I.C.)* (Pittsburgh: University of Pittsburgh, 1965), p. 1.
3. Note 1, p. 2.
4. Note 2, pp. 3-7.
5. This figure represents the most recent estimate of ILIC's holdings (1982).
6. Nasser Sharify and Roland R. Piggford, "First Institute on International Comparative Librarianship," *Pennsylvania Library Association Bulletin* 21 (2) (November 1965), p. 73.
7. Ibid., p. 73.
8. Ibid., p. 74.
9. Ibid., pp. 74-76.

Bibliography

CHAPTER 1

Bereday, George Z. F. *Comparative Method in Education*. New York: Holt, Rinehart and Winston, [c1964].

Butler, Pierce. *An Introduction to Library Science*. Chicago: American Library Association, [c1933].

Conference of Librarians. *Proceedings*. London: 1877.

Dane, Chase. "The Benefits of Comparative Librarianship." *The Australian Library Journal* 3 (July 1954): 89-91.

Danton, J. Periam. *The Dimensions of Comparative Librarianship*. Chicago: American Library Association, 1973.

Foskett, D. J. *Introduction to Comparative Librarianship*. Bangalore: Sarada Ranganathan Endowment for Library Science, 1979.

Hessel, Alfred. *A History of Libraries*. Translated, with supplementary material, by Reuben Peiss. New Brunswick, New Jersey: Scarecrow Press, 1955.

Johnson, Elmer. *A History of Libraries in the Western World*. New York: Scarecrow Press, 1965.

Munthe, Wilhelm. *American Librarianship from a European Angle*. Chicago: American Library Association, 1936.

Naudé, Gabriel. *Advice on Establishing a Library*. Berkeley, California: University of California Press, 1950.

Platthy, Jenö. *Sources on the Earliest Greek Libraries with the Testimonia*. Chicago: Argonaut, Inc., 1969.

Shores, Louis. "Comparative Librarianship: A Theoretical Approach." In *Comparative and International Librarianship: Essays on Themes and Problems*. Edited by Miles M. Jackson. Westport, Conn.: 1970.

Utley, George Burwell. *The Librarians' Conference of 1853*. Chicago: American Library Association, 1951.

Vann, Sarah. *Training for Librarianship Before 1923: Education for Librarianship Prior to the Publication of Williamson's Report on Training for Library Service*. Chicago: American Library Association, 1961.

Winger, Howard W. "Aspects of Librarianship: A Trace Work of History." In *Seven Questions about the Profession of Librarianship*. Edited by Philip H. Ennis and Howard W. Winger. Chicago: University of Chicago Press, [c1962].

Winsor, Justin. "A Word to Starters of Libraries." *Library Journal* 1 (September 1876): 1.

CHAPTER 2

Bereday, George Z. F. *Comparative Method in Education*. New York: Holt, Rinehart and Winston, 1964.

Blondel, Jean. *An Introduction to Comparative Government*. New York: Praeger, 1969.

Butler, Pierce. *An Introduction to Library Science*. Chicago: University of Chicago Press, 1933.

Collings, Dorothy G. "Comparative Librarianship." In *Encyclopedia of Library and Information Science*, vol. 5, pp. 492-502. Edited by A. Kent and H. Lancour. New York: Marcel Dekker, 1971.

Dewey, John. *How We Think*. New York: Heath, 1933.

Goldhor, Herbert. *An Introduction to Scientific Research in Librarianship*. Champaign, Illinois: Illini Union Bookstore, 1969.

Heckscher, Gunnar. *The Study of Comparative Government and Politics*. London: Allen and Unwin, 1957.

Loucks, William N., and Whitney, William G. *Comparative Economic Systems*. New York: Harper & Row, 1969.

Mill, John S. *A System of Logic*. New York: Harper, 1846.

Munthe, Wilhelm. *American Librarianship from a European Angle*. Chicago: American Library Association, 1939.

Northop, Filmer Stuart Cuckow. *The Logic of the Sciences and Humanities*. New York: Macmillan, 1947.

Qureshi, Naimuddin. "Library Education in Pakistan and the Philippines: A Comparative Study." Unpublished Seminar Paper, University of Pittsburgh, 1971.

Schermerhorn, R. A. *Comparative Ethnic Relations: A Framework for Theory and Research*. New York: Random House, 1970.

Simsova, S., and Mackee, M. *A Handbook of Comparative Librarianship*. London: Bingley, 1970.

Simsova, S. *A Primer of Comparative Librarianship*. London: Bingley, 1982.

Van Dalen, Deobold. *Understanding Educational Research*. New York: McGraw-Hill, 1966.

CHAPTER 3

Andreozzi, M. R. del V. "Towards a Methodology for Librarianship: Report on an International Course held in Denmark." *UNESCO Bulletin for Libraries* 23 (1969): 178-182.

Barnes, Fred B. *Research for the Practitioner in Education*. Washington, D.C.: National Education Society, Department of Elementary School Principals, 1967.

Bereday, George Z. F. *Comparative Method in Education*. New York: Holt, Rinehart and Winston, 1964.

Bereday, George Z. F. "Reflections on Comparative Methodology in Education 1964-1966." *Comparative Education* 3 (1967): 169-187.

Best, John W. *Research in Education*. 2nd ed. Englewood Cliffs, New Jersey: Prentice-Hall, 1970.

Blondel, J. *An Introduction to Comparative Government*. London: Weidenfeld, 1969.

Carroll, F. L. "Internationalism in Education for Librarianship." *International Library Review* 4 (1972): 103-126.

Cirigliano, G. F. J. "Stages of Analysis in Comparative Education." *Comparative Education Review* 10 (1966): 18-20.

Collings, D. G. "Comparative Librarianship." In *Encyclopedia of Library and Information Science*, vol. 5, pp. 492-502. Edited by A. Kent and H. Lancour. New York: Marcel Dekker, 1971.

Dane, C. "The Benefits of Comparative Librarianship." *Australian Library Journal* 3 (1954): 89-91.

Dane, C. "Comparative Librarianship." *Librarian* 43 (1954): 141-144.

Danton, J. P. *The Dimensions of Comparative Librarianship*. Chicago: American Library Association, 1973.

Foskett, D. J. "Comparative Librarianship." *Library World* 66 (1965): 295-298.

Fox, David. *The Research Process in Education*. New York: Holt, Rinehart and Winston, 1969.

Gates, Jean Key. *Introduction to Librarianship*. New York: McGraw-Hill, 1968.

Goode, W. J., and Hatt, P. K. *Methods in Social Research*. New York: McGraw-Hill, 1952.

Harrod, L. M. *The Librarians' Glossary of Terms Used in Librarianship and the Book Crafts*. 3rd rev. ed. London: Andre Deutsch; New York: Seminar Press, 1971.

Harvey, John F., ed. *Comparative and International Library Science*. Metuchen, New Jersey: Scarecrow Press, 1977.

Hillway, Tyrus. *Introduction to Research*. 2nd ed. Boston: Houghton Mifflin, 1964.

Hoadley, Irene Broden, and Clark, Alice S., eds. *Quantitative Methods in Librarianship: Standards, Research, Management*. [Proceedings and Papers of an Institute held at the Ohio State University, August 3-16, 1969.] Westport, Connecticut: Greenwood Press, 1972.

Idenburg, P. J. "Statistics in the Service of Comparative Education." *International Review of Education* 11 (1965): 434-450.

Johnson, Elmer. *A History of Libraries in the Western World*. New York: Scarecrow Press, 1965.

Koehl, R. L. "Methods and Evidence in Comparative Studies." In *Assistance to Libraries in Developing Nations: Comparative Studies*, pp. 5-14. Edited by W. L. Williamson. Madison: University of Wisconsin Library School, 1971.

Kottak, C. P. "Towards a Comparative Science of Society." *Comparative Studies in Society and History* 12 (1970): 92-109.

Krzys, Richard. "Library Historiography." In *Encyclopedia of Library and Information Science*, vol. 15, pp. 294-330. Ed. by A. Kent, H. Lancour, and J. E. Daily. New York: Marcel Dekker, 1975.

Landau, T. *Encyclopedia of Librarianship*. 3rd ed. New York: Hafner Press; Lexington Park, Maryland: Bowes Books, 1966.

McNiff, P. J. "Foreign Area Studies and Their Effect on Library Development." *College and Research Libraries* 24 (1963): 304-305.

Sable, M. D., and Deya, L. "Outline of an Introductory Course in International and Comparative Librarianship." *International Library Review* 2 (1970): 187-192.

Scarrow, H. A. *Comparative Political Analysis: An Introduction*. New York: Harper, 1969.

Shera, Jesse. *The Foundations of Education for Librarianship*. New York: Becker and Hayes, [c1972].

Shores, Louis. *Around the Library World in 76 Days: An Essay in Comparative Librarianship*. Berkeley, California: Peacock Press, 1967.

Shores, Louis. "Comparative Librarianship: A Theoretical Approach." In *Comparative and International Librarianship*, pp. 3-24. Compiled by M. M. Jackson, Jr. Westport, Connecticut: Greenwood Press, 1970.

Tuckman, Bruce W. *Conducting Educational Research*. New York: Harcourt Brace Jovanovich, c1972.

Wach, J. *The Comparative Study of Religions*. New York: Columbia University Press, 1958.

CHAPTER 4

Anderson, D. P. "International Seminar, Moscow-Tashkent April 1972: The Public Library and its Readers, a Comparison of the Aims and Objectives of the Public Libraries in Developed and Developing Countries." *International Library Review* 4 (1972): 433-442.

Arntz, H. "The Role of Documentation in Developing Countries." *UNESCO Bulletin for Libraries* 25 (1971): 12-17.

Asheim, L. "University Libraries in Developing Countries." *American Library Association Bulletin* 59 (1965): 795-802.

Asheim, L. *Librarianship in the Developing Countries.* Urbana, Illinois: University of Illinois Press, 1966.

Bramley, G. A. *A History of Library Education.* London: Clive Bingley; Hamden, Connecticut: Linnet Books, 1969.

Brewster, Beverly J. *American Overseas: Library Technical Assistance, 1940-1970.* Metuchen, New Jersey: Scarecrow Press, 1976.

Campbell, H. C. *Metropolitan Public Library Planning throughout the World.* Oxford: Pergamon Press, 1967.

Campbell, H. C. *Public Libraries in the Urban Metropolitan Setting.* London: Clive Bingley; Hamden, Connecticut: Linnet Books, 1973.

Chandler, G. *International Librarianship; Surveys of recent Developments in Developing Countries and in Advanced Librarianship.* [Submitted to the 1971 IFLA pre-session Seminar for Developing Countries sponsored by UNESCO, Liverpool City Libraries, August 24-September 1, 1971.] London: Library Association, 1972.

Clapp, Verner W. *The Future of the Research Library.* Urbana, Illinois: University of Illinois Press, 1964.

Clarke, D. A., ed. *Acquisitions from the Third World.* [Papers of the Lique des Bibliothèsques Européennes de Recherche, Seminar 17-19 September, 1973.] England: Mansell, 1975.

Clark, Jack A. *Gabriel Naudé 1600-1653.* Hamden, Connecticut: Archon Books, 1970.

Dale, D. G. *The United Nations Library: Its Origin and Development.* Chicago: American Library Association, 1970.

Estabrook, Leigh, ed. *Libraries in Post Industrial Society.* Phoenix, Arizona: Orynx Press, 1977.

Fang, Josephine Riss, and Songe, Alice H. *International Guide to Library, Archival, and Information Science Associations.* New York: R. R. Bowker Company, 1976.

Foskett, D. J., ed. *Reader in Comparative Librarianship.* Englewood, Colorado: Information Handling Services, 1976.

Francis, Frank. *Many Cultures: One World.* [Isabel Nichol Lecture, Graduate School of Librarianship, University of Denver, April 28, 1970.] Denver, Colorado: University of Denver Press, 1970.

Garde, P. K. *The United Nations Family of Libraries.* Ranganathan Series in Library Science, 22. New York: Asia Publishing House, 1970.

Gardner, Frank M. *Public Library Legislation, a Comparative Study.* Paris: United Nations Press, 1971.

Gelfand, M. A. *University Libraries for Developing Countries.* Paris: UNESCO, 1968.

Hessel, Alfred. *A History of Libraries.* Translated by Reuben Peiss. New Brunswick, New Jersey: Scarecrow Press, 1955.

Houghton, Bernard, ed. *Standardization for Documentation.* Hamden, Connecticut: Archon Books & Clive Bingley, 1969.

International Federation for Documentation, Committee for Developing Countries [FID/DC], Harald Schütz, Director. *Function and Organization of a National Documentation Centre in a Developing Country.* Paris: UNESCO, 1975.

International Federation of Library Associations. International Organization for Standardization. *The International Standardisation of Library Statistics. A Progress Report.* London: International Federation of Library Associations, 1968.

Irmler, J. "Rural Libraries: A Comparative International Study." *International Library Review* 2 (1970): 49-55.

Jackson, Sidney L. *Libraries and Librarianship in the West.* New York: McGraw-Hill, 1974.

Jain, T. C. *Professional Associations and Development of Librarianship: Case Studies of the Library Association and the American Library Association.* Delhi, India: Metropolitan Book Co. (PVT), Ltd., 1971.

Johnson, Elmer D. *Communication: An Introduction to the History of Writing, Printing, Books and Libraries.* 3rd ed. New York: Scarecrow Press, 1966.

Johnson, Elmer D. *History of Libraries in the Western World.* 2nd ed. Metuchen, New Jersey: Scarecrow Press, 1970.

Kanevsky, B. P. "International Exchange of Publications and the Free Flow of Books." *UNESCO Bulletin for Libraries* 26 (1972): 141-149.

Kent, Allen, ed. *Library Planning for Automation.* [Based on the Proceedings of a Conference Held at the University of Pittsburgh, June 2-3, 1964.] Washington, D.C.: Spartan Books, 1965.

Krishan, K. *Research Libraries in Developing Countries.* New Delhi, India: Vikas Publishing House, 1973.

Licklider, J. C. R. *Libraries of the Future.* Cambridge, Massachusetts: M.I.T. Press, 1965.

Lowrie, Jean E., ed. *School Libraries: International Development.* Metuchen, New Jersey: Scarecrow Press, 1972.

Malclès, Louise Noëlle. *Bibliography*. Translated by Theodore Christian Hines. New York: Scarecrow Press, 1961.

Malek, R. "On the Origin of the International Organization of Librarians (IFLA)." *Libri; International Library Review* 20 (1970): 222-224.

Penna, Carlos Victor. "Seminar on Planning of National Scientific and Technical Information Structures, Madrid, 28-28 November, 1970." *UNESCO Bulletin for Libraries* 25 (1971): 186-190.

Ranganathan, S. R. *The Five Laws of Library Science*. Bombay, India: Asia Publishing House, 1963.

Schick, F. L. "The International Standardization of Library Statistics." *UNESCO Bulletin for Libraries* 25 (1971): 2-11.

Shera, Jesse H. *Libraries and the Organization of Knowledge*. Edited by D. J. Foskett. Hamden, Connecticut: Archon Books, 1965.

Shera, Jesse H. *Knowing Books and Men; Knowing Computers, too*. Littleton, Colorado: Libraries Unlimited, 1973.

Smith, Josephine Metcalfe. *A Chronology of Librarianship*. Metuchen, New Jersey: Scarecrow Press, 1968.

Steele, Colin. *Major Libraries of the World: A Selective Guide*. New York: R. R. Bowker Company, 1976.

Taubert, S., ed. *Book Trade of the World*. Vol. 1: *Europe and International Section*. Hamburg, Germany: Verlag für Buchmarkt-Forschung; London: Andre Deutsch; New York: R. R. Bowker Company, 1972.

UNESCO. *World Survey of Education. Handbook of Educational Organizations and Statistics*. Paris: UNESCO, 1959.

UNESCO. *World Guide to Library Schools and Training Courses in Documentation*. Paris: UNESCO; London: Clive Bingley, 1972.

Wales, A. P. *International Library Directory: A World Directory of Libraries*. 3rd ed. London: Wales, 1968.

Whatley, H. A. "Comparative Study of Education for Librarianship in Twenty Five Countries." M.A. thesis, Strathclyde University, 1968.

White, Carl M., ed. *Bases of Librarianship: A Study of Library Theory and Practice in Britain, Denmark, the Federal Republic of Germany and the United States*. New York: Macmillan, 1967.

World of Learning. London: Europa Publications, 1947-

CHAPTER 5

Aman, Mohammed M. "Middle East." [Area Study prepared to provide data for *World Librarianship: A Comparative Study*.]

Anuar, Hedwig. "Central, South, East, and Southeast Asia." [Area Study prepared to provide data for *World Librarianship: A Comparative Study*.]

Borchardt, Dietrich H. "Australia, New Zealand, and Oceania." [Area Study prepared to provide data for *World Librarianship: A Comparative Study.*]

Borchardt, Dietrich H. "Library Services in Underdeveloped Areas; A Critique of Some Basic Issues." *Journal of Education for Librarianship* 9, no. 2 (Fall 1968): 123-137.

Campbell, H. C. "United States-Canada." [Area Study prepared to provide data for *World Librarianship: A Comparative Study.*]

Clavel, Jean-Pierre. "Western Europe." [Area Study prepared to provide data for *World Librarianship: A Comparative Study.*]

Coleman, R. "Library Service to the Urban Aboriginal." *Australian Library Journal* 22, no. 10 (November 1973): 391-400.

Collings, Dorothy G. "Library Development in Africa." In the article, "Library," in *The Encyclopedia Americana*, vol. 17, pp. 320-321. New York: Americana Corporation, 1977.

Ifidon, Sam. "Special Problems Facing African Librarians: The West African Experience." *Libri* 24, no. 4 (1974): 311.

Kanevsky, B. P. "Soviet Union." [Area Study prepared to provide data for *World Librarianship: A Comparative Study.*]

Kaser, David. "Library Development in Asia." In the article, "Library," in *The Encyclopedia Americana*, vol. 17, p. 324. New York: Americana Corporation, 1977.

Kibirige, Harry. "Africa." [Area Study prepared to provide data for *World Librarianship: A Comparative Study.*]

Krzys, Richard, and Litton, Gaston. "Latin American Librarianship." In *Encyclopedia of Library and Information Science*, pp. 294-330. New York: Marcel Dekker, 1975.

Litton, Gaston, and Krzys, Richard. "Latin America." [Area Study prepared to provide data for *World Librarianship: A Comparative Study.*]

Montes de Oca, Antonio. "Mexico." In *Lands and Peoples*, vol. 5, pp. 317-360. Edited by Jay Bennett et al. n.p.: Lexicon Publications, c1977.

Nabatova, M. B. "European Socialist Republics." [Area Study prepared to provide data for *World Librarianship: A Comparative Study.*]

Piñeiro, Miguel Angel. "UNESCO and Library Services in Latin America." *UNESCO Bulletin for Libraries* 20, no. 5 (September-October 1966): 245-251.

U. S. Department of Commerce. Bureau of the Census. *Current Population Report*. Washington, D.C.: Government Printing Office, 1976.

U.S. Department of Health, Education, and Welfare. Office of Education. *Digest of Educational Statistics*. Washington, D.C.: Government Printing Office, 1975.

CHAPTER 6

Clavel, Jean-Pierre. "Western Europe." [Area Study prepared to provide data for *World Librarianship: A Comparative Study*.]

CHAPTER 7

American Library Association. Editorial Committee. Subcommittee on Library Terminology. *ALA Glossary of Library Terms*. Chicago: American Library Association, 1943.

Anderson, Dorothy. *Universal Bibliographic Control: A Long Term Policy/A Plan for Action*. Pullach, Munich: Verlag Dokumentation, 1974.

Butler, Pierce. *An Introduction to Library Science*. Chicago: University of Chicago Press, [c1961].

Gardner, Frank M. *Public Library Legislation: A Comparative Study*. Paris: UNESCO, 1971.

Gates, Jean Key. *Introduction to Librarianship*. New York: McGraw-Hill, [c1968].

Jackson, Sidney. *Libraries and Librarianship in the West: A Brief History*. New York: McGraw-Hill, [c1974].

Landau, Thomas, ed. *Encyclopedia of Librarianship*. 3rd ed. New York: Hafner, 1966.

Ollé, James G. "Jast, Louis Stnaley." In *ALA World Encyclopedia of Library and Information Services*. Edited by Robert Wedgeworth. Chicago: American Library Association, 1980.

Shera, Jesse. *Introduction to Library Science: Basic Elements of Library Service*. Littleton, Colorado: Libraries Unlimited, 1976.

Tyulina, Natalia. "Library Science." In *Great Soviet Encyclopedia: A Translation of the Third Edition*, vol. 3. Edited by A. M. Prokhorov. New York: Macmillan, 1970.

CHAPTER 8

Asimov, Isaac. *Extraterrestrial Civilizations*. New York: Crown, 1979.

Clark, Kenneth. *Civilisation: A Personal View*. New York: Harper & Row, [c1969].

Coblans, Herbert. *Librarianship and Documentation: An International Perspective*. Edited by Evelyn F. A. Evans. London: Andre Deutsch (A Grafton Book), 1974.

Collyns, Robin. *Did Spacemen Colonize the Earth?* Chicago: Henry Regnery Company, 1976.

Hoyle, Fred, and Wickramasinghe, Chandra. *Lifecloud: The Origin of Life in the Universe.* New York: Harper & Row, 1978.

International Standardization of Library Statistics. Final Report. Paris: UNESCO, 1969.

O'Neill, Gerald K. *The High Frontier: Human Colonies in Space.* New York: Bantam Books, 1978.

Ridpath, Ian. *Worlds Beyond: A Report on the Search for Life in Space.* New York: Harper & Row, 1975.

Withers, F. N. *Standards for Library Service.* Paris: UNESCO, 1970.

APPENDIX

International Library Information Center. Pittsburgh: University of Pittsburgh, Graduate School of Library and Information Sciences, 1964.

Sharify, Nasser, and Lancour, Harold. *A Proposal for the Expansion of the Activities of the International Information Center (I.L.I.C.).* Pittsburgh: University of Pittsburgh, 1965.

Sharify, Nasser, and Piggford, Roland R. "First Institute on International Comparative Librarianship." *Pennsylvania Library Association Bulletin* 21 (2) (November 1965): 73-80.

Index

Academic libraries, 67,193,194
Academy of Sciences (Russia), 73
Accessibility principle, 68
Accession number, arrangement by, 68
Achimoto (Ghana), 67
Administrative College in Port Moresby (Australia), 98,100
Advice on Establishing a Library (Naudé), 13,68
African bibliographic services, 116
African depository laws, 116
African library associations, 116
African library development, characteristics, 116,118
African library legislation, 116
Alexander III (The great), 60
Alexandrian Library, 60,116,203
Alfonso (King of Aragon), 14
All-Union Library Census (USSR), 75
Alphabet, Cyrillic, 73
  Glagolithic, 73
  Korean, 65
  modern Russian, 73
Altamira, Spain, 58
American Librarianship from a European Angle (Munthe), 21,23
American Library Association, 84,89
  Board of Education for Librarianship, 20
  Conferences of (1876), 17,189
American Library Journal, 17,19,89
Anderson, Colonel James, 93
Appropriateness, law of, 197

Arab script, 66
Arabian literature, 66
Archives, 62,63,65
  man's need for, 57
  religious, 194
  unclear distinction between libraries and, 57
Area concept of librarianship, rationale underlying the, 48,49
Area knowledge, need for, 30
Area studies, 27
Armenia, 72,74
Armstrong, Neil, 203
Artemon of Cassandreia, 7
Ashurbanipal, 7,59
Ashurbanipal's library, lines of connection between Alexandrian Library, 9
Asia Foundation, 176
Asian (Central, South, East, and Southeast) library development, characteristics, 107,108
Asimov, Isaac, 203
Aspects of librarianship, 28
  analysis of, 51
Aspects of Librarianship in Latin America (Jackson), 23
Association of Research Libraries, 190
Associations, definition of, 48
  development of, 69,70,95
  juxtaposition of area characteristics, 173
  theory of, 189,190

Augustus, 14
Australasian Library Association, 95
Australian Advisory Council on Bib-
    liographical Services (AACOBS),
    177
Australian, New Zealand, and Ocean-
    ian library development, charac-
    teristics, 163,164
Australian Subscription Library, *see*
    Free Public Library of Sydney
Australian UNESCO Seminar on the
    Role of Libraries in Secondary
    Education, 100
Authority, 27
    central government, 71
Avila Camacho, Manuel, 84
Avis pour Dresser une Bibliothèque
    (Naudé), *see Advice on Estab-
    lishing a Library* (Naudé)
Azerbaijan, 74

Bacon, Francis, 12
Baghdad, 60,61
Basra, 60
Belgian Congo (Zaire), 67
Belgium, 72
Belgrade, 79
Belon, Pierre, 12,13
Bereday, George Z. F., 28,30,31,37,
    41
Bernard, Charles, 65
Bernard Free Library, 65
Biagi, Guido, 191
Biases, control of, 30
Bibliographic control, analyzing, 52,
    180,181
    definition of, 47
    juxtaposition of area characteristics,
        167,168
    theory of, 167,168
Bibliographic techniques, 27
*Bibliographical Services throughout
    the World, 1960-1964* (Avi-
    cenne), 23
Bibliographies, 70
Bibliography, 73,83

Biblioteca Benjamin Franklin, 84
Biblioteca Luis-Angel Arango, 85
Biblioteca Nacional of Madrid, 71
Biblioteca Pública Piloto de Medellín,
    see Pilot Public Library of
    Medellín
Bibliotekar, 74,75
Bibliotheca Bogoriensis, 63
    Nazionale of Florence, 71
    Universalis (Gesner), 68
Bibliothecal Museum, 19
Bibliothèque Cantonale et Univer-
    sitaire de Lausanne, 71
Bibliothèque Nationale de Paris, 71
Bibliothèque Royale de Bruxelles, 71
Bibliothèque Universitaire de Gre-
    noble, 70,71
Bibliothèque Universitaire d'Utrecht,
    71
Binational center libraries, 84
Block printing, 63
Blondel, Jean, 37
Boccaccio, Giovanni, 11
Bogor, Indonesia, 63
Bolsheviks, 74
Book of the Apostles (Fyodorov), 73
Book, perception of, 105
Book publishing (seventeenth cen-
    tury), 73
    (sixteenth century Russia), 73
Bookmobile services, 93
Books, destruction of, 63
Boston Public Library, 18,88
Bowker, R. R., 89
Brezhnev, Leonid, I., 132
British Council, 176
British Library, 70
British Museum, 16
Brno Congress of Czech and Slovak-
    ian libraries, 79
Brussels Convention for the Interna-
    tional Exchange of Official Docu-
    ments and Library Publications,
    83
Bucharest, 133
Buddhism, 65

Buddhist libraries, 64,65
Budé, G., 68
Budgets, 68
Bulgaria, oldest collections in, 77
Burma, 62,64
  Literacy rate (eighteenth century),
  64
  Royal Library of, 64
Butler, Pierce, 20,21,24,186,193
Byrd, William, 86

Cairo, 60
Callimachus, (of Cyrene), 187
Campbell, Henry C., 23
Capitulum in Gnezno (oldest Polish
  collection), 77
Card catalogs, 69
Carnegie, Andrew, 92,93
Carnegie Corporation, 20,21,67,101
Carnegie libraries, Study of (Johnson-
  1915), 20
Carnegie Library of Pittsburgh, 91
Carnegie public libraries, 92,93
Casanova, Giovanni Giacomo, 188
Case method, 29,32
Case studies, 27,28
Cassiodorus, Flavius Magnus Aurelius,
  11,188
Cataloging, Ninety-one rules for
  (Panizzi), 16
Cataloging practices, 69
Cave paintings, 58
Centralized libraries, 63
Centralized processing services, 100,
  101
Certification of librarians, 69
Ceylon, 62
Chair in librarianship, first, 69
Charlemagne, 14
Charlemagne's court library, 203
Charles III (Spain), 82
Checklist for research topics, 33,34
Chemical Abstracts, 91
Chernigov (Russia), 73
Chiang Kai-Shek, 106
Chicago Public Library, 88,91

Chicago University, Graduate Library
  School, 20,22
Chi'ing Dynasty (1644-1912), 63
China, 62,64
Chou Dynasty (1122?-256 B.C.), 63
Cincinnati Public Library, 88
Clark, Kenneth, 203
Clark's (Kenneth) cultural confronta-
  tion hypothesis, 203
Classification schemes, 67,68,90
  Nineteenth century, 68
  Renaissance, 12
Clavel, Jean-Pierre, 168,170
Clay tablets, 57,59
Clement, Nicholas, 188
Climate and library development, 122
"Clues" of sleuthing, 51
Codification of cataloging rules, 67
Coleman, R., 159
Collection development, 107
College of Librarianship (Wales), 191
College Library (North America), first
  in North America, 87
Collings, Dorothy G., 118
Colombo Plan, 176
Colonial Sugar Refining Company
  (Fiji), 97
Colonization (of Africa), 67
Columbia College, School of Library
  Economy, *see* School of Library
  Economy (Columbia College)
Columbus, Christopher, 79
COMECON, *see* Council for Mutual
  Economic Assistance
Comfort, principle, 68
Commonwealth Scientific and Re-
  search Organization (Australia),
  97
Communication and library develop-
  ment, 58,124-126,146,161
Comparative anatomy, 13,36
  anthropology, 36
  attitude, 7,13,16,17
  economics, 36
  education, 15,31
  government, 36

[Comparative]
  librarianship, 5,22,24,58
  library education, 37
  library science, 6,21,22,24
  literature, 36,37
  method 30,32,36-41,42
Comparative method in Education
  (Bereday), 30
Comparative method, limitations of,
  42
Comparative methodology, 24-30,36-
  41,42
  pedagogy, 15
  politics, 36
  principle (and librarianship), appli-
    cation of, 6-8
  psychology, 36-37
  religion, 36
  study in librarianship, 6,13,28,36,
    41
Comparative study in librarianship,
  elements useful to, 13
Comparison, 41
Composite method, 30,32
Comprehensive collections, concept
  of, 11-12,68
Conference of Librarians of all na-
  tions (London-1877), 18
Confucianism, 65
Constantinople, 60
Control (as a goal of science), 29
Convention of Librarians (Librarians'
  Conference of 1853-New York),
  16
Cooperation, 71,133
Cooperative cataloging, 17
Cooperative indexing, 17
Copyright law, 181
Copyright (U.S.), 17
Correspondence schools for library
  education, 191
Corvininiana, 77
Corvinus (Corwin), Matthias,14,77
Cotton des Houssayes, Jean Baptiste
  (Abbé), 15

Council of the British National Biblio-
  graphy in London, 71
Council for Mutual Economic Assist-
  ance (COMECON), 71
Courses for the training of librarians,
  69
CPSU Central Committee Directive
  on Librarianship in the Soviet
  Union, 76
Cradle of librarianship, 54
Crestadoro, Andreas, 18
Criterion of comparability, 40
Cro-Magnon, 58
Crystal Palace, 16
CSIRO, see Commonwealth Scientific
  and Research Organization
  (Australia)
Cuban Revolution, 85
Cultural borrowing, 8
Culture and library development,
  123-124,144
Culture shock, 31
Cutter, Charles Ammi, 18,19,90,91,
  92
Czech readers' societies, 78
Czechia, 77-78

Daily, Jay E., 210
Damascus, 60
Dana, John Cotton, 91,92
Dane, Chase, 22
Darío, Rubén, 84
Deductive reasoning, 27,49
Delisle, Leopold, 69
Demetrius of Phalerum, 9,187
Democracy in America (Tocqueville),
  23
Department of Scientific and Indus-
  trial Research (New Zealand), 97
Depository law, 182
  British, 16
  French, 16
Derick Technical Institute of Suva, 99
Description, 37-38
Deutsche Bibliothek of Frankfort, 71

Dewey Decimal Classification, 90
Dewey, Melvil, 18,19,31,32,89,90,91,
92,172,187,190
Dictatorships and library develop-
ment, 120
Doctoral dissertation, 30
Dordogne, France, 58
Doyle, Arthur Conan, 125
Drexel Institute, 191
DSIR, *see* Department of Scientific
and Industrial Research (New
Zealand)
Dubois, Felix, 66
Dury, John, 15
Dziatzko, Karl, 69

Economic studies, role of, 71
Economy and library development,
122,124,139,146-147
Economy, "one crop," 107
Edmands, John, 91
Education and library development,
122-123,143-144,160-161
Educational agencies, definition of,
48
Educational agencies, juxtaposition
of area characteristics, 173-176
Educational agencies (of librarian-
ship), theory of, 190-191
Edwards, Edward, 15,16,193
1876 (year), 86
Einstein, Albert, 193
Enlightenment, 68
Escuela Interamericana de Bibliotec-
ología de Medellín, *see* Inter-
American Library School
Ethiopia, 66
Etymologiarum Sive Originum (Isi-
dore of Seville), 8
European (Eastern) library develop-
ment, characteristics, 134-135
European (Western) librarianship,
origin of, 118
library development, character-
istics, 126
Ewart, William, 16

Experience of Russian Bibliography
(Sopikov), 74
Experimental method, 30,32
Explanation (as a goal of science), 29
Extraterrestrial librarianship, 203
life, contact with, 203

Fabinyi, Andrew, 100
Federation International de Docu-
mentation (FID), 125
Fiji, 96-97
School of Medicine, 99
Financial support, definition of, 47
juxtaposition of area characteristics,
169-171
for libraries, theory of,
182-184
Fiscal accountability of the librarian,
182
Ford Foundation, 176
Foreign language, need for, 30
Foreign residence, need for, 30,32
Foskett, D. J., 24
France, 72
Francis I., 68
Franklin, Benjamin, 84,87
The Free Public Library of Sydney,
95,96
Free Town Libraries . . . (Edwards),
16
French Indochina, 62
French, Jaime, Duarte, 85
French Revolution, 68
Fukuzawa, Yukichi, 65
Fyodorov, I., 73

Gandhi, Mohandes, K. 106
Gardner, Frank M., 181
Gasset, José Ortega y, 193
Gates, Jean Key, 48,185,191,194
General Assembly Library (New
Zealand), 97
Generalization of findings, need for,
29
Gennadi, G. I., 74
Geography of librarianship, 47

Geography and library development, 141

Georgia (USSR), 72,74

Germany, 72

Gesner, Johann, 68

Gesner, Konrad von, 202

Gestures, 58

Global librarianship, definition of, 45
    future, 202-203
    nature, 201
    purposes, 201-202

Global school of library, information, and communication studies, 191,202

Göttingen system, 70
    University, 68,69

Götze, Bernt, 10

Government and library development, 145-146

Great Britain, 72

Great Exhibition of 1852 (London), 16

Great October Socialist Revolution of 1917, *see* Russian Revolution

Green, Samuel Sweet, 18

Gutenberg, Johann, 77,189

Hamilton, Edith, 193

A Handbook of Comparative Librarianship (Simsova), 22

Harrison, J. Clement, 210

Harrod, Leonard Montague, 48

Harun-al-Raschid, 62, 105

Harvey, John, 24

Hecksher, Gunnar, 37

Heian Period (A.D. 794-1185), 65

Herder, Johann Gottfried, 15

Herodotus, 7

Hessel, Alfred, 9,11,60

L'Histoire de la Nature des Oyseaux (Belon), *see* The History of the Nature of Birds (Belon)

Historical method, 29-32

History and library development, 140

The History of the Nature of Birds (Belon), 12

Hitler, Adolf, 76

Holmes, Sherlock, 49,50,51

Horrocks, Norman, 210

How We Think (Dewey), 31

Hungary, National Library, 78

Hypothesis, 40,41

Hypothesizing, 49

Ibadan (Nigeria), 67

Ibero-American Seminar on Planning and Documentation Services, 195-196

Ifidon, Sam, 116

IFLA, *see* International Federation of Library Associations

Iguiniz, Juan, 81

Illiteracy (Latin America), 137

Imperial Library (of Japan), 66
    see also Shojakukan

Imperial Public Library (St. Petersburg), *see* Saltykov-Shchedrin State Public Library of Leningrad, 73

Index Medicus, 91

India, 62

Inductive reasoning, 27

Information services, 27

Instauratio Magna (Bacon), 12

Inter-American Library School, 83-84,191

Interdependence, law of, 197

INTERMARC, 71

INTERMARCS, 71

Institutions Divinarum et Saecularium Litterarum (Cassiodorus), 11

International and comparative library science, 42

International Federation of Library Associations, 69,72,125,190

International Federation of Library Associations and Institutions, 190

International Graduate Summer
  School, 190
International Library Information
  Center (ILIC) University of
  Pittsburgh, 22,205-210
International Standard Bibliographic
  Description (ISBD), 86
International Standard Book Number
  (ISBN), 72,181
International study, research in, 27
Internationalism, 22,203
Interpretation, 38-39
Intranational comparative librarian-
  ship, 19
Introduction to Library Science
  (Butler), 20
ISBD, *see* International Standard
  Bibliographic Description
Isidore of Seville, 8
Islam, 60,66
Islamic empire, 60

Jackson, Sidney L., 188
Jackson, William V., 207
Jakarta, 62
Japan, 62
Japan, earliest libraries in, 65
Japan Library Association, 65
Jast (Jastrzebski) Louis Stanley, 195
Jefferson, Thomas, 86
Jesuit Mission in Canada, 87
Jesuits, expulsion of in Latin Amer-
  ica, 82
Jewett, Charles Coffin, 16,88
Johnson, Alvin S., 20,186
Johnson, Alvin, study of public li-
  braries, *see* Carnegie Libraries,
  Study of (Johnson-1915)
Johnson, Elmer, 6,7,59,60
Joseph (King of Portugal), 82
Journal Meiner Reise im Jahre 1769
  (Herder), 15
Jullien de Paris, Marc-Antoine, 15
Juxtaposition, 39-41

Kalingas, 64

Kaser, David, 108
Kenya Colony, 67
Keppel, F. P., 21
Khan, Genghis, 61
Khan, Halagu, 61
Khavkina, L. G., 74
Kilwa, 66
Kirkwood, James, 15
Knizhnaya Letopis, 74
Koran, 59,105
Korea, 62
  first library in, 65
  first royal library in, 65
Korean librarianship, Chinese in-
  fluence on, 65
  influence of Japanese rule, 65
  Western influence on, 65
Korean Library Association, 65
Korean Library Law (1963), 65
  War (1950-1953), 65
Krzys, Richard, 210
Kufa, 60
Kuwait, 61

Lancour, Harold, 206,207,209
Landau, Thomas, 184
Languages and library development,
  71,107,132,138
Lascaux, France, 58
Latin American librarianship, United
  States influence on, 84
Latin American library development,
  characteristics, 140
Latin countries of Europe, 72
Laws of world librarianship, 196-197
League of European Research Li-
  braries (LIBER), 69,72
Leakey, Louis, 66
Legislation, juxtaposition of area
  characteristics, 168-169
Leibniz, Gottfried Wilhelm von, 15,
  68,188
Lenin, Vladimir, I., 74,130,132,135,
  185
Lenin's decree on libraries, 75
Lenin State Library, 74,75

Leopoldville (Kinshasa), 67
Lessons of world librarianship, 181,
    182-184,186-187,188-189,190,
    191-193,194-195,196
LIBER, see League of European Re-
    search Libraries
Liber de Scriptoribus Ecclesiasticis
    (Tritheim), 68
Librarians, basic function of, 3
    characteristics of, 6,187-189
Librarians' Conference of 1853 (New
    York), 16,189
Librarians, first scholar, 68
    Soviet, 131
Librarianship
    African, 66-67
    areas of, 47
    Asian, 62-66
    aspects of 33-34,47
    Australian, New Zealand, and
        Oceania, 94-101
    European Socialist, 77-79
    factors relevant to the development
        of, 39
    interdisciplinary nature of, 37
    in the Developing Countries
        (Asheim), 23
    Latin American, 79-86
    Middle Eastern, 59-62
    national, 24
    nature of, 180
    philosophy of, 24,68
    problems of, solutions to, 27
    Soviet, 72-77
    United States and Canada, 86-94
    Western European, 67-72
Libraries of ancient Greece, physical
    layout of, 9
    of ancient Rome, physical layout
        of, 10
    (of the czars), 73
    of the Middle Ages, 11
    personal, 86-87
    (Russia), number of, 74
    (Soviet Union), numbers of, 75-76
Libraries Association of New Zealand,
    95

[Libraries]
Libraries and Bibliographical Centres
    in the Soviet Union (Horecky),
    23
Libraries, church in Russia, 73
    conditions contributing to develop-
        ment, 194
    monastic of Byzantium, 11
    monastic in Russia, 73
    in Scandanavia (Harrison), 23
Library of the Academy of Sciences
    of Leningrad, 73
Library Association of Australia, 101
    of the United Kingdom, 69,190
    of the United Kingdom (1877), see
        Conference of Libraries of all na-
        tions (London-1877)
Library Association Record, 69
Library Bureau, 92
Library catalogs, 27,68
    reasons for collecting and studying,
    14
Library of Congress (United States),
    92
Library Congress (Soviet Union-
    RSFSR), first, 75
Library Development, 49
    economy, 17
    education, core curriculum of, 24
    first library in Russia, 73
Library Journal, 89
Library (Latin America), first in,
    81
Library legislation, 201
    (Bulgaria), first in, 79
    definition of, 47
    theory of, 181-182
Library literature, sources for search-
    ing, 35
Library networks, 15,79
Library periodicals, 69
Library philosophy and theory, 24,
    185,196-197
Library Quarterly, 20
Library relations, among Socialist
    countries of Europe, 71

[Library relations]
among Western European librarians and Socialist librarians, 71
Library school (Soviet Union), first, 75
Library schools, 17,19,84
Library science, 25
development of, 3
nature of, 180
theory of, 24
Library service, prerequisites of, 67
to children, 92
Lipsius, Justus, 193
Literacy (Czarist Russia), 74
(Kirghizia), 74
(Russia), 73
(Soviet Union), 131
(Tajikistan), 74
(Uzbekistan), 74
Literature, definition of, 48
necessity for immersing oneself in, 32
(of librarianship), theory of, 191-193
search, 32-36,52
Lithuania, 74
Lomonosov, Mikhail V., 73
Los Angeles Public Library, 89,91
Loucks, William N., 37
Lucullus, 14
Luis-Angel Arango Library, *see* Biblioteca Luis-Angel Arango
Luxembourg (Benelux), 72
Lvov (Russia-formerly in Poland), 73
Lydenberg, Harry M., 84

Machine Readable Cataloging project, 86
MacKee, M., 22,24
Mcgowan, Frank, 210
Mcgrath, L. H., 100
Mcluhan, Marshal, 146
Mainz, Germany, 77
Makere (Uganda), 67
Malaysia, 62
Malclés, Louis, 193

The Mali Empire (14th century West Africa), 66
Malindi, 66
Manchester, Public Free Libraries, 18
Manchu Dynasty, 106
Manchus, 63
Manuscripts, comparing variants of, 7,8
Mao Tse-Tung, 106
MARC, *see* Machine Readable Cataloging project
Marc II, 70
Master's thesis, 30
Mather, Cotton, 86
Mather, Increase, 86
Mecca, 60
Mechanics institutes, 88, 95
Medici, Cosimo de, 11-12
Medina, 60
Meiji Restoration of 1867, 65
Melbourne Public Library, 95
Mercantile libraries, 88
Mesme, Abbé de, 14
Henri de, 13
Metalibrarianship, definition of, 3
tentative elements, 179-197
Metropolitan Public Library Planning throughout the World (Campbell), 23
Mezhov, V. I., 74
Middle Eastern library development, characteristics, 105-106
Mill, John Stuart, 29
Ming dynasty, (1368-1644), 63
Mise en Ordinateur de Notices Catalographiques de Livres (MONOCLE), 70
Mnemonic devices, 58
Mohammed (prophet), 60
Moldavia, 74
Mombasa, 66
Monastery libraries, 68
Monastic libraries (Latin America), first in, 81-82
Mongols, 61
MONOCLE, see Mise en Ordinateur

[MONOCLE]
  de Notices Catalographiques de
  Livres
Moscow, 73
  University of, 73
Mouly, George J., 30
Munn, Ralph, 101
Munn, Robert, 66
Munthe, Wilhelm, 21,22,23,24
Museums, 62

Nalanda, 64
Napoleonic compaigns, 119
Narratives of experiences, 29
National bibliographies, 68
*National Bibliography of the Nether-
  lands*, 71
National Commission on Libraries
  and Information Science, 94
National Diet Library, 66
National libraries, 63,134,193-194
National library, concept of, 59
  of Australia, 96
Natural and social sciences, areas of
  common agreement to, 29
Nature, principle of uniformity of, 29
Naudé, Gabriel, 13,14,15,68,185,203
Nazi Germany, 76
Nepal, 62
Netherlands, 72
  East Indies, 62
New France, number of books in, 87
Newspaper, first Russian printed, 73
New York Library Association, 190
New Zealand Library Association, 99
The New Zealand Library Association
  (McEldowney), 95-96
The New Zealand Library School, 101
Niccoli, Niccolo, 11,12
Ninety-one rules for cataloging (Pan-
  izzi), 16,69
Nineveh, 59
Nordic countries of Europe, 72
*Nordisk Tidskrift für bol-och Biblio-
  theksvasen*, 69
North American librarianship, char-
  acteristics of, 94

Norton's Library Gazette, 17
Novgorod (Russia), 73
NVBF, *see* Scandinavian Federation
  of Research Libraries

OAS, *see* Organization of American
  States
OCLC, *see* Ohio College Library
  Center
Oil reserves, 61
OECD, *see* Organization for Eco-
  nomic Cooperation and Develop-
  ment
Ohio College Library Center, 86
On Collecting Books (Artemon of
  Cassandreia), 7
O'Neill, Gerard, 203
On-site visiting, 36
On the Use of Books (Artemon of
  Cassandreia), 7-8
Open stack system, 92
Organization of American states, 84,
  117
Organization for Economic Coopera-
  tion and Development (OECD),
  71,72
Osborn, Andrew D., 209
Ottoman empire, 61
Ottoman Turks, 61

Pacific Northwest Library Associa-
  tion, 190
Panizzi, Anthony, 15,16,69,92,203
Panizzi, Anthony, comparative study
  of foreign libraries by, 16
Pankhurst, Rita, 66
Paper, invention of, 57,63
Papermaking (Korea), 65
Papua, New Guinea, 97
Papua New Guinea University of
  Technology, 98
Papyrus, 57,59
Partial convergence, law of, 197
Peisistratus, 8
People's libraries (Germany), first, 78
  (Poland), first, 78
Pergamon library, 9

Pericles, 7
Personal experience, 27
Peter I (the Great, Emperor of Russia), 73
Petrarch (Petrarca, Francesco), 11,12
Philadelphia Public Library, 92
Phillips, Janet C., 209
Philosophy of librarianship, Soviet, 186
Pictographic writing, 59
Piggford, Roland, 209
Piñeiro, Miguel Angel, 138
Planning for the future, definition of, 48
Planning, juxtaposition of area characteristics, 176-177
Planning, principles of, 195
theory of, 195-196
Plumbe, Wilfred J., 66,67
Plummer, Mary Wright, 188
Political structures, 71
Politics and library development, 139-140
Poole, William F., 18,88,91
Poole's Index to Periodical Literature, 91
Population and library development, 120,141-143,158-160
Port Nicholson, Australia, 95
Portuguese, 64
Practitioners, definition of, 48
Practitioners, juxtaposition of area characteristics, 173
Practitioners, theory of, 187-189
Pratt Institute Free Library, 191
Pre-Columbian libraries (Latin America), 79-81
Prediction, 52
(as a goal of science), 29
Prefectural libraries, 65
Preussische Instruktionen (Dziatzko and Delisle), 69
Printing
(Japan), 65
(Korea), 65
Printing from movable type, 57,67-68,77,119

Printing press (Latin America), first in, 81
Private book collections, Renaissance, 11
Private libraries, 62,63,65,82
Profession, advancement of the, 49
definition of, 48
(of librarianship), juxtaposition of area characteristics, 171-172
The Profession (of librarianship), theory of, 184-187
Proprietary libraries, 62
Psychological processes, principle of reliability of, 29
Ptolemy (Soter), 9
Public librarian, Japanese, 65
Public libraries, 62,68,83,194
Public Libraries Act of 1850 (England), 16
Public Libraries Act of 1869 (Australia), 96
Public libraries (Australia), first in, 94
Public libraries, Korean, 65
Public libraries, Renaissance, 11
Public libraries (Russia), first, 73
Public Libraries in the United States of America (U.S. Bureau of Education), 90
Public library of Athens (established by Peisistratus (605-527 B.C.), 8
Public library (Eastern Europe), first, 78
Public Library Law of 1950 (Japan), 66
Public library networks, 79
Public Library of New South Wales, 96
Public library (New Zealand), first in, 95
Public library (North America, first in, 88
Public library training classes, 91-92
Public Library of Victoria, 96
Public reading room (Serbia), first, 78
Public taxation for library support, 92
Publishing, 107

Putnam, Herbert, 92

Qualitative judgment, 37
Quantitative judgment, 37
Qureshi, Naimuddin, 40

Radio, television, and library development, 125,161
Reader services, 27
Reader's Guide to Periodical Literature, 91
"Reading houses" (Bulgaria), 78
Reading (Soviet Union), 132
Reasoning analytically, 50,51
  backwards, 50
Reference service, 92
Regional and world organization libraries, 194
Religion and library development, 122
Remington Rand Company, 92
Research libraries, 194
Research, preliminaries to initiating, 30-34
Research methods, 29-30
  report, 30,41
  study, elements of, 32
  topic, selecting, 30-34
  topic, suggestions for selecting, 30
Revista delle Bibliotheche, 69
Revue des Bibliothèques, 69
Rhodesia, 67
Rockefeller Foundation, 84
Roe, Ernest, 100
Rouss, J. D., 68
Rovira, Carmen, 85
Royal libraries, 194
Royal Library in Copenhagen (Denmark), 71
Rubakin, N. A., 74
Rules for a Dictionary Catalog (Cutter), 90
Rumania, oldest collections in, 77
Rumyantsev-Museum, Library of, see Lenin State Library
Russian Revolution, 75

Sabor, Josefa, 82
Saltykov-Shchedrin State Public Library of Leningrad, 73
Sankore, 66,116
Sanskrit, 64
Sanz, María Teresa, 82
Sarmiento, Domingo Faustino, 83
Saudi Arabia, 61
Scandinavian Federation of Research Libraries (NVBK), 190
School libraries, 63,100,101,193-194
School of Library Economy (Columbia College), 17,19,91,190
The School Library Service (New Zealand), 100
Schools, first book collections in, 68
Schools, secular schools in Russia, 73
Schrettinger, Martin, 24
Science, goals of, 29
Scientific method, 27,28-29
  steps in, 28-29
  validity for natural and social sciences, 28
Serapeum (Anzeiger für Literatur des Bibliothekswissenschaft), 69
Service agencies, definition of, 48
  juxtaposition of area characteristics, 175
  theory of, 193-195
Services, definition of, 48
  juxtaposition of area characteristics, 175-176
Sexes, separation of, 107
Shaman artists, 58
Shang Dynasty (1765?-1123?), 63
Shanghai (North China), 62
Sharify, Nasser, 206,207,209,210
Shera, Jesse H., 52,59,193
Shera's theory of library development, 52
Shih Huang-ti, 63
Shogunate, 65
Shojakukan (Imperial Library of Japan), 65
Shores, Louis, 23,24,193,196
Sibiu (Rumania), 78

Sigismund I, 77
Simenon, Georges, 125
Simsova, S., 22,24,32-36
Sitzman, Glenn, 118
Slavery (in Africa), 67
Sleuthing, 49
Smithsonian Institution, 16
Sobolshchikov, V. I., 74
Socialism and library development, 120
Socialist librarianship, distinguishing features of, 75-76
Society of Library Science (Russia), 74
Soter, Ptolemy, (see Ptolemy), (Soter)
South Pacific Commission, 98
Soviet Libraries and Librarianship (Ruggles and Swank), 23
Soviet library development, characteristics, 132
Special libraries, 63,68,97,193-194
Sri Lanka, 62,64
Standardization of library procedures, 71,92,197
"State library" (Australia), 96
Statistical method, 29,32
Stone, Walter, 209
Strickland, John, 67
A Study of History (Toynbee), 23
"A Study in Scarlet" (Doyle), 49
Study problem, example of, 49
Subscription libraries, 62,64,87
Sun Yat-sen, 106
Survey method, 29,32
Switzerland, 72,180-181
Sydney, Australia, 94
Sydney University, 99

Tang Dynasty (618-907), 63
Tax on bibliographic records, 182
Tax on reading, 72
Taxila, 64
Technical institutes, 191
Technical services, 27
Temple libraries, 65
Tenochtitlan, 81

Texcoco, 81
Textbook, first secular (in Russia), 73
Thailand, 62
Thematic study, 28
Themes of librarianship, 28
"A Theoretical Framework for Comparative Librarianship" (Shores), 23
Theorizing, 52-53
Theory of library development, 52
Thinking, reflective, 31
Third world, 70
Thirty Years' War, 119
Timbuctu, 66
Tocqueville, (Charles) Alexis de, 23
Tokugawa Shogunate, 65
Topical study, 28
Topics of librarianship, 28
Total analyses, 27,28
Total convergence, law of, 197
Toynbee, Arnold, 23
Toyo Bunko, 66
Trade union libraries (Eastern Europe), 78-79
Tradition, role of in library development, 105
Training for Library Services (Williamson), 190
Transport and library development, 124,125
Travellers' tales, see Narratives of experience
Tritheim, J., 68
Turkmenia, 74
Tyulina, Natalia, I., 185
Tzetzes, 8

UBC, see Universal bibliographic control
UNESCO, 85,116,176,177
Union of South Africa, 67
UNISIST, see World Scientific Information System
United Nations, 22

United Nations Educational Scientific
    Cultural Organization, *see*
    UNESCO
United States and Canadian library
    development, characteristics,
    147-148
Universal bibliographic control
    (UBC), 181,201
Université Lovanium, 67
University (Latin America), first in,
    81
University of Guam Library, 99
University libraries, 68
University of New South Wales, 101
The University of the South Pacific
    (Fiji), 98
Urbanization and library develop-
    ment, 119-120
Utley, George Burwell, 17

Van Dalen, Deobold B., 31
Van Dusen, A. C., 209
Van Praet, Joseph, 15
Vann, Sarah, 18
Variables, 37
Veblen, Thorstein, 193
Vivarium monastery, 11
Vladimir (Russia), 73

Waples, Douglas, 32
Warsaw, University of, 78
Watson, John H., 49,50,51
Western European library policy, 70
White House Conference on Library
    and Information Services, 177
Whitney, William G., 37
Wilhelm, Friedrich, 77
Williamson, C. C., 20,186,190
Williamson Report (1919), 20
Wilson, H. W., 91
Winger, Howard W., 17
Winsor, Justin, 18,88,91
Women in librarianship, 91
World librarianship, 24

World librarianship, definition of, 3
    philosophy and theory of, 3
    (Krzys and Litton), 52
    research in, 179-180
    suggestions to researchers, 180
World Scientific Information System
    (UNISIST), 70
World study in librarianship, defini-
    tion of, 3
World study in librarianship, develop-
    ment phases of, 5,5-23; phase I:
    Application of the comparative
    principle to librarianship, 5-8;
    phase 2: Borrowing of library
    practices or concepts, 8-12; phase
    3: Appearance of a comparative
    attitude in a treatise on librarian-
    ship, 12-15; phase 4: Publication
    of a monograph comparing as-
    pects of librarianship, 15-20;
    phase 5: Search for an identity,
    20-22; phase 6: Publication of a
    manual outlining the research
    methodology of world study in
    librarianship, 22-23; Phase 7:
    Appearance of a magnum opus
    in the field, 23; Phase 8: full de-
    velopment of world study in li-
    brarianship, 23; Phase 9: dissolu-
    tion of the discipline into its
    principal areas, 23
    development of, 5-23,42,58
World study in librarianship, distinc-
    tion between library science re-
    search, and 4-5
    ends of, 4,24
    fundamental problems of, 49
    nature of its reasoning process, 49
    objectives of, 45-46,52
    relationship to crime detection, 51
    requirements for research in, 30,32
    research in, 27
    research methods for, 29-30
    social science nature of, 24

[World study in librarianship]
   sources to identify problems in, 32
   suggestions for, 51
World War I, 119
World War II, 22,119
Writing, 58-66
Writing materials, man's first, 57,62,
   63-64
Writings (in Russia), 73

Xerxes, 8,14

Yale University, 91
Yaroslav the Wise, 73
Yuan dynasty (1260-1368), 63

Zalusski Brothers, 78
Zamora, Rosa, 80,81
Zenodotus (of Ephesus), 187
Zentralblatt für Bibliothekswesen, 69

About the Area Research Associates

Mohammed Aman, coauthor with Richard Krzys of the Middle Eastern analysis of this comparative study, is dean and professor of the School of Library Science at the University of Wisconsin, Milwaukee. He received the B.A. from Cairo University (Egypt), the M.S. from the School of Library Service of Colombia University, and the Ph.D. in library science from the School of Library and Information Science of the University of Pittsburgh. Dr. Aman is an active consultant in the Middle East as well as a frequent contributor to professional literature about that area. Dean Aman's consulting has included academic as well as library development, and his writing has been devoted to research on cataloging and classification of non-Western library material as well as various aspect studies of Middle Eastern librarianship. A recent publication of Dean Aman is: Huq, A. A. Abdul, and Aman, Mohammed M., *Librarianship and the Third World: An Annotated Bibliography of Selected Literature on Developing Nations, 1960-1975.* New York: Garland, 1977.

Hedwig Anuar, author of the history of Central, South, East, and Southeast Asia, is director of the National Library of Singapore and is well known for her contributions to Asian library development. She graduated from the University of Malaya in 1951 with first-class honors and attended the Northwestern Polytechnic in London, earning the Associateship of the Library Association (U.K.) in 1956 and the Fellowship two years later. Mrs. Anuar returned to the University of Malaya Library in Kuala Lumpur, was assigned to the National Library of Singapore, and became its director in 1965. To conduct a survey of Malaysian libraries for the Library Association of Malaysia in 1968, she travelled throughout the country. Mrs. Anuar has been actively involved in the Library Association of Singapore and became its president. Her research and writing include contributions to books, encyclopedias, and professional journals.

Dietrich H. Borchardt, author of the analysis of the librarianship of Australia, New Zealand, and Oceania, is the chief librarian of La Trobe University, Bundoora, Victoria, Australia. He received the H. C. L. Anderson Award of the Library Association of Australia. Mr. Borchardt is the author of *Australian Bibliography.* 3d ed. Rushcutters Bay, N. S. W., Pergamon Press (Australia), 1976; *Librarianship* *in Australia*, *New Zealand and Oceania* with John I. Horacek. Rushcutters Bay, N. S. W., Pergamon Press (Australia), 1975; *The Spread of Printing*: *Australia*. Amsterdam, Vangendt, 1969.

H. C. Campbell, author of the analysis of the librarianship of United States-Canada, is director of the Urban Libraries Study Project, Toronto, Ontario. He earned the B.A. degree from the University of British Columbia, the M.A. from the University of Toronto, and the B.L.S. from Columbia University. Mr. Campbell was librarian of the National Film Board; assistant, United Nations Archives; head, Bibliographical Development Section, Libraries Division, UNESCO, Paris; head, Clearing House for Libraries, Libraries Division, UNESCO, Paris; and chief librarian of the Toronto Public Library. Mr. Campbell is the author of *Metropolitan Library Planning throughout the World*. Oxford: Pergamon Press, 1967 as well as numerous articles in library literature.

Jean-Pierre Clavel, author of the analysis of Western European librarianship, is head librarian of the Canton and University Library of Lausanne. He received the A.M. in theology and the A.M. in philology from the University of Lausanne. Mr. Clavel was the first president of the Ligue des Bibliothèques europeenes de recherche (LIBER), a consultant in UNESCO, consultant for the Pahlavi National Library from 1974 to 1978, and treasurer for the International Federation of Library Associations and Institutions (IFLA). Mr. Clavel has also contributed articles to the professional literature.

Ann Hewitt, bibliographer of *World Librarianship*, is director of the Long Branch Public Library in New Jersey. She earned the B.A. degree from C. W. Post College of Long Island University and the M.L.S. from Dalhousie University in Halifax, Nova Scotia (Canada). In 1978 she received an award for distinguished service to senior citizens from the City of Long Branch. Presently Ann Hewitt is doing postgraduate study at Brookdale Community College.

B. P. Kanevsky, author of the analysis of the librarianship of the Soviet Union, is chief of the Department of Foreign Acquisitions at the Lenin State Library, Moscow, USSR. He is a frequent contributor to the literature of librarianship through books, encyclopedias, and journal articles.

Harry Kibirige, the contributor of the African analysis of librarianship, is a librarian and library educator/administrator from Uganda. He received his Ph.D. in library science from the University of Pittsburgh, after having received the M.A. from the University of Wales, College of Librarianship, Wales Aberystwyth, the A.L.A. (postgraduate) from Liverpool Polytechnic (U.K.), and the B.A. from the University of East Africa, Makerere University College. Dr. Kibirige's doctoral dissertation was entitled "The Information Market: A Statistical Methodological Study of the Issues Associated with Fees and the Uses of Information." His awards have included the University of Pittsburgh Honors List, the Harold Lancour Award, UNESCO Scholar, and British Council Scholar, Liverpool, Polytechnic, U.K.

Clayton Kie, the collaborator with Ann Hewitt on the bibliography of *World Librarianship*, received his M.L.S. from the University of Pittsburgh. He is now a reference librarian at the Toledo-Lucas County (Ohio) Public Library.

M. B. Nabatova, contributor of the analysis of the librarianship of European Socialist Countries, is the deputy-chief of the Library Science Research Department of the Lenin State Library of the USSR, and has also contributed to library literature through writings in books and journals.

Natalia I. Tyulina, author of the Foreword, is the former director of the Dag Hammarskjold Library of the Headquarters of the United Nations in New York. In 1945 she graduated from Moscow State University, and in 1954 she received her Doctor's degree in philology. Upon graduation, Dr. Tyulina worked in the Lenin State Library in Moscow, beginning as bibliographer and becoming subsequently chief of the Department of Bibliographical and Information Service, scientific secretary of the Library (equivalent to the U.S. assistant librarian), chief of the Department of Foreign Librarianship, chief of the Department of Library Science and Research, and lastly deputy librarian of the Lenin State Library, the national library of the Soviet Union. In addition, from 1959 to 1970 she was chief editor of the Russian journal *Bibliotekovedenie i Bibliografia za Rubezom* ("Librarianship and Bibliography Abroad"). Dr. Tyulina's research and writing deal with the present and future development of national libraries as one of the main types of contemporary library systems, methodological and organizational aspects of library science, as well as various problems of library practice of the United Kingdom and United States.